KUNDALINI

EMPOWERING
HUMAN EVOLUTION

OMEGA BOOKS

The OMEGA BOOKS series from Paragon House is dedicated to classic and contemporary works about human development and the nature of ultimate reality, encompassing the fields of mysticism and spirituality, psychic research and paranormal phenomena, the evolution of consciousness, and the human potential for self-directed growth in body, mind and spirit.

John White, M.A.T., Series Editor of OMEGA BOOKS, is an internationally known author, editor, and educator in the fields of consciousness research and higher human development.

OTHER TITLES IN THE OMEGA BOOKS SERIES

KUNDALINI EVOLUTION AND ENLIGHTENMENT
Edited by John White

LIFECYCLES
Reincarnation and the Web of Life
Christopher M. Bache

THE MEANING OF SCIENCE AND SPIRIT
Guidelines for a New Age
John White

WHAT IS ENLIGHTENMENT?
Exploring the Goal of the Spiritual Path
Edited by John White

THE RADIANCE OF BEING
Complexity, Chaos and the Evolution of Consciousness
Allan Combs

BEYOND THE HUMAN SPECIES
The Life and Work of Sri Aurobindo and The Mother
Georges Van Vrekhem

KUNDALINI

EMPOWERING HUMAN EVOLUTION

SELECTED WRITINGS OF GOPI KRISHNA

EDITED BY

GENE KIEFFER

PARAGON HOUSE
St. Paul, Minnesota

First revised edition, 1996

Published in the United States by

Paragon House
2700 University Avenue West
St. Paul, MN 55114

Copyright © by Gene Kieffer

All rights reserved. No part of this book may be reproduced, in any form, without the written permission from the publishers, unless by a reviewer who wishes to quote brief passages.

Printed in Canada

Library of Congress Cataloging-in-Publication Data

Gopi Krishna, 1903-
    Kundalini, empowering human evolution : selected writings of Gopi krishna / edited by Gene Kieffer.
    p. cm.
    Rev. ed. of: Kundalini for the new age. 1988.
    1. Kundalini. I. Kieffer, Gene. II. Gopi Krishna, 1903–
    Kundalini for the new age. III. Title.
BL1238.56.K86G66   1995
294.5'4--dc20   95-21768
                                                                       CIP

10 9 8 7 6 5 4 3

www.paragonhouse.com

CONTENTS

Introduction 1

CHAPTER I   Kundalini, the Guardian of Human Evolution 25
Distorted evolution and evolutionary theories could be catastrophic for the race, and our cooperation is essential for the healthy functioning of the processes.

CHAPTER II   About My Way of Writing 49
I saw myself floating in a lustrous world of being in which the material world had lost its tangibility, only pure consciousness persisted everywhere.

CHAPTER III   Professor Weizsacker's Introduction to the Biological Basis of Religion and Genius 63
Internationally reknowned scientist-philosopher presents an analysis of Gopi Krishna's thought and contributions toward understanding the nature and spirit of evolution and its ultimate goals.

CHAPTER IV The Biological Basis of Religion and Genius 87
From the shortfall of religion and the error of science to the evolutionary mechanism and the divine possibilities in man.

CHAPTER V   Beyond the Higher States of Consciousness 109
A turning point in our present concepts about the universe as a whole will occur when the biological relationship between expanded consciousness and the brain is understood.

CHAPTER VI Is Meditation always Beneficial? 115
Only when there is a flow of psychic energy to
the brain can the mind slip its tether of the body
and observe its transformation into an oceanic
entity.

**CHAPTER VII A Paradoxical Episode
in the Life of Gandhi** 131
He firmly believed that the sublimation of his
sexual energies would give him the moral and
spiritual power to accomplish his mission in life.

CHAPTER VIII Accelerating Brain Evolution 139
Civilizations, families, and individuals rose and
fell because of the ignorance of the cosmic law
ruling the life of man.

**CHAPTER IX About Psychic Phenomena,
Psychology, Prana, and Freud** 155
Let a Team of open-minded scientists, in the
service of knowledge, call by means of wide
publicity for personal histories of those who have
had or are having Kundalini experiences.

CHAPTER X The Splendorous Eden in Which I Live ...175
I see my whole body and surroundings permeated
by this luster, a living radiance which fills all the
space within and outside me.

CHAPTER XI On Meditation 189
In all these disciplines, we are trying to seek
audience with the Lord of the universe.

CHAPTER XII The Case of Alan Watts 195
It is not difficult to see that he was one of those
intellectuals in whom the evolutionary
metamorphosis was almost complete.

CHAPTER XIII Writing for the Future Generations 205
Intellect and moral evolution involves a constant
process of purification and regeneration of the
nervous system and brain.

CHAPTER XIV The Scientific Investigation 225
There are devices that will come into operation at
the time of a seemingly annihilative nuclear war
to save the race from extinction.

**CHAPTER XV Professor Von Weizsacker
as a Thinker of the Future** 245
He comes nearest to the picture of one who
presents a happy blend of the scientist, the
philosopher and the mystic in his personality.

CHAPTER XVI Supernatural Powers and Physiology ...265
Death and Fear then lose their hold, for what can
harm the ocean of everlasting life beyond the
farthest reach of any material influence?

CHAPTER XVII Life is Everlasting 281
The riddle of consciousness is a mystery so
profound that human intelligence will not be able
to unravel it in the coming tens of thousands of
years. But it is the great mystery that man is born
to solve.

The Ointment of Sweet Savour

It is recorded that when Clement asked Peter the meaning of Messiah's name, Peter replied that in the beginning the Creator set up an ideal type for every species of thing created; an ideal angel for the angels, a fish for the fishes, a bird for the birds, and a man for the men; that ideal man is Christ Jesus. He has the right to the name of Messiah because the Jews call their kings the Christ, the Persians call theirs Arsaces, the Romans Caesar, and the Egyptians Pharaoh.

The cause of this denomination is this: because he was the ideal son of God, the beginning of all things, and became the ideal man. The father first anointed him with the oil which he had taken from the tree of life, and because of this ointment he is called the Christ.*

It is said by Esdras of these who are to be saved "They shall have the tree of life for an ointment of sweet savour."** And Celsus affirms that, in answer to a certain question, the initiate in the Christian mysteries said: "I have been anointed with white ointment from the tree of life."† This ointment is called spiritual when the doctrine is abstractly applied, but there is also a physical basis for it. As shown herein, the manipulation of the biological counterpart of this ointment was at the core of all the esoteric teachings of antiquity designed to achieve Christ Consciousness or Enlightenment, the mark of the ideal man or woman.

---

* *Recognitions* i, 45.
** Book of Esdras, ii, 12.
† Origen, *Cont. Celsum.*

INTRODUCTION

Gopi Krishna said more than once that Kundalini was the most jealously guarded secret in history. Millions may know of the most recent breakthroughs in physics, astronomy, medicine, chemistry, and other branches of science, but hardly anybody is familiar with a far more important development—the discovery of an almost unbelievable potential, lying dormant in their own brain. This potential could be said to originate from a "power center" in the body, known to the sages of India by the name Kundalini, and to adepts in other parts of the world by other terms, such as "chi," the "sun behind the sun," and the "philosophers' stone." Although a definite physical organ, this power center is of such subtle design and construction that verifying its existence scientifically may take decades or even centuries.

Why Kundalini was kept secret for thousands of years is not an easy question to answer, but it is fascinating just to contemplate the reasons for such secrecy. For instance, there is no mention of

Kundalini in the standard reference works, such as the *Encyclopedia Britannica* or *Oxford English Dictionary*. Gopi Krishna's autobiography, *Kundalini: The Evolutionary Energy in Man*, does bring the secret to light, but even today, two decades after its publication, the word "Kundalini" is still rarely seen in the media.

Fortunately, one can get an almost instant understanding of what Kundalini is, short of having the experience, by reading Gopi Krishna's description of his own state of consciousness. He had unwittingly roused to activity what he described as "the most wonderful and stern power in man." It was also a key to the most-guarded secret of the ancients. "Thenceforth for a long time," he said, "I had to live suspended by a thread, swinging between life on the one hand and death on the other, between sanity and insanity, between light and darkness, between heaven and earth."

The cause behind this extremely frightful condition, lasting a full twelve years, cannot be found in the popular books on yoga. And though Gopi Krishna would never say so, he, remarkably, came as close to understanding Kundalini as perhaps anyone in history. Many factors were involved, ranging from an improper diet and lack of knowledge, to heredity and the absence of a teacher to guide him. Without a reliable teacher, a healthy and entirely successful transition from human to transhuman consciousness is much more difficult than for an ordinary man or woman of 60, without training, to win an Olympic Gold Medal.

During recent times, there have hardly been any instances of individuals in whom Kundalini was fully active from the day of the awakening until the last. For Gopi Krishna, it was akin to living on a razor's edge, what with the energy circulating throughout his brain and nervous system day and night. Even the slightest mistake on his part could, and most likely would, spell death.

His daughter Ragina remembers that when she was about 7 years of age she would see her father suffering intensely from the immense heat generated in his body by the Kundalini force, which had awakened abnormally and was at that time only flowing through the solar nerve (*pingala nadi*). "His cheeks glowed like charcoal," she said, "and his parched lips appeared to be as brittle as burned wood."

When I first met Gopi Krishna he was 70 and as healthy and vigorous as a man of 50, and he remained so up until just a few months before his death at the age of 82. Though robust and strong, he was always on the alert for any signal that he might somehow have disturbed the delicate balance of his super sensitive nervous system. He was very careful about his diet, for example, often adding to or subtracting from it in minute amounts. And he would never skip a meal nor, if possible, permit himself to slip past its normal time. His family would see to that, knowing well the consequences to his health if that should happen.

He enjoyed conversation and could easily lose track of time if it were not for his wife, Bhabi, who watched over him with the utmost solicitude and care. When he began making his visits to Europe and America, although infrequent, he was always attended to by Margaret Kobelt, a musician and lifetime student of religion, who lived in a small apartment building, which she owned in Zurich, Switzerland. Without her concern and unstinting care, none of his trips to the West would have been possible, for his wife had no desire to travel outside of India. In fact, as late as 1983, she had never been in an airplane and had no intention of ever flying in one. Even though the comparatively short distance from Srinagar, in Kashmir, to New Delhi, took less than an hour by jet, she always took the crowded bus, which lacked heat or air-conditioning. As far as she was concerned, the long, bone-jarring ride over the Himalayan Mountains was far preferable to risking her life in a jet. This was told to me by her family when I flew from New Delhi to Dehra Dun, where the author and Bhabi were living in 1983. She had been visiting her two sons, Jagdish and Nirmal, and their families in New Delhi, and for some reason agreed to return to Dehra Dun with me by air, making that Bhabi's first flight ever. To my knowledge, she hasn't flown since.

It was Ms. Kobelt's generosity and assistance, then, that made it possible for Gopi Krishna to come to the West. Without a personal secretary to schedule appointments, prepare meals, provide the necessities, arrange an itinerary, and drive a car for him on various occasions, he would have been confined to a small area in and around New Delhi and Srinagar. The two first met in 1967 in Stuttgart, Germany, where he had been invited by Ursula von Mangoldt, the editor and publisher who later translated his autobiography into German for Otto Wilhelm Barth Verlag.

Ms. Kobelt accompanied the author on the three visits he made to Canada and the United States in 1978, 1979, and in 1983. The last visit was at the invitation of a group of Native American elders, who had asked him to speak to some six hundred of their people meeting at the United Nations that October. According to them, the gathering was the fulfillment of an ancient Hopi prophecy.

My first meeting with the author was in November 1970 at Ms. Kobelt's home. We had been corresponding for two or three months. He had given a talk in Florence, Italy, just two weeks before, and I had received an advance copy of it in order to have it set in type for a booklet to be called, *The Biological Basis of Religion and Genius*. To me, the speech seemed as revolutionary as Galileo's "Dialogue of the Two Chief World Systems," which had first been made public in Florence in 1632. In 1972, Dr. Ruth Nanda Anshen, editor of two prestigious imprints—Religious Perspectives and World Perspectives—had it published by Harper & Row, New York.

This publication represented a real breakthrough for me, considering Dr. Anshen's almost legendary reputation. At an early age, she had been a protege of Dr. Alfred North Whitehead, had lectured widely in Europe and Asia, and over the years counted as friends such luminaries as Albert Einstein, Werner Heisenberg, Pope Pius XII, Hans Kung, Mircea Eliade, Jonas Salk, Karl Barth, Erich Fromm, Paul Tillich, and many others of comparable stature. As a Fellow of the Royal Society of Arts of London and an editor and author long concerned with the interaction of science, philosophy, and culture, Anshen's eagerness to publish *The Biological Basis of Religion and Genius* meant that it would be given the best possible publicity.

The Introduction to the book, written by Professor Carl Friederich F. von Weizsacker was, of course, both extraordinary and unprecedented. In Germany, the von Weizsacker name was held in the same high regard as the Huxley name in England.

Von Weizsacker had been a student and longtime friend of Heisenberg's and, like the Nobel Prize physicist, he too had his own Max Planck Institute for Life Sciences just outside of Munich. To risk an illustrious reputation, by introducing Gopi Krishna's ideas to the West, was an act of professional courage rarely if ever seen in academic circles.

Although interest in human evolution has grown considerably since Professor von Weizsacker's Introduction and now, twenty-five years later, is taken for granted by the vast majority of scholars, there are still some eminent scientists who are persuaded to accept a contrary view. "It may even be that we are near the end of our evolutionary road, that we have got as close to Utopia as we ever will," writes J. S. Jones, head of the genetics department at University

College, London.* "If we can be sure about anything it is that humanity will not become superhuman."

What Gopi Krishna was saying, that human beings *will* become superhuman, was one thing; but of much greater importance was the fact that he was prepared and eager to prove it. He believed he had pinpointed the actual biological mechanism that would make such an evolutionary leap possible. Verification, if and when it came, would be science's greatest triumph—the ultimate prize to be won. Instead of worrying about the dangers of genetic engineering, and other risky experiments—as great as they might be—it would be much more advantageous if science were to investigate the physiological process of evolution as it is occurring now. This would place science in a position to counter potential catastrophes.

According to the author, Kundalini is the evolutionary mechanism dormant in every human being, a psycho-physiological phenomenon resting on a hitherto unsuspected activity of the cerebrospinal system. We empower evolution to the extent that we fix our attention on it. A traditional method of effecting the arousal of Kundalini is to concentrate the mind on it—as Divinity—with or without form.

The fact that Gopi Krishna recorded both his subjective and objective observations for almost half a century is of tremendous importance to the understanding of our own potential development and the future of humanity. It is one thing to speculate on whether we are making use of only one tenth of the brain's capacity, as is often stated, and quite another to assert that it is possible to empirically demonstrate its full potential in a manner acceptable to science. We should not allow ourselves to be burdened by what we have previously believed were limitations to mental achievement. Paths to the summit have been worn into the mountains once thought impossible to climb until some indomitable spirit showed the way. The history of the Olympic Games is one of records that fell to that same all-conquering spirit. Gopi Krishna was not the first to become Illuminated or Enlightened, but he was the first in modern times to put down in writing what it was like to go through the entire transformative process. He was also the first to describe

---

* Article on Op-Ed Page of the *New York Times,* Sunday, September 22, 1992, adapted from the *Cambridge Encyclopedia of Human Evolution*, edited by Professor J. S. Jones, R. D. Martin and David Pilbeam.

what this knowledge could mean to every human being, now, not at some vague time in the distant future. Widespread knowledge of Kundalini alone is enough to rapidly change the course of history.

"This is the civilization of the computer, the satellite and Internet," say futurists Alvin and Heidi Toffler.* They may be right, but neither they, nor anyone else, has the slightest notion whether computers will have been to the long-term benefit of the race or to its detriment. Neither they, nor any other futurist writing today, factors evolution into their thinking. Consider the Toffler's speculations on virtual reality. They write: "Virtual reality points to a boundless capacity for deception, not simply by governments or corporations, but by hostile individuals acting on each other. We can do this today, but we are increasing the sophistication of deception faster than the technology of verification."

Could *virtual reality* deceive the race anymore than it is already being deceived by its own faulty thinking? Kundalini, on the other hand, makes it possible for certain individuals to see into the future, an ability essential for survival in the Nuclear Age. Kundalini enables humanity to steer clear of the pitfalls that can spell catastrophe.

Hardly a week goes by that we don't learn about yet another grave crisis caused by the mistakes made by political leaders. Though they try to consider all factors and weigh the consequences of every alternative, ensuing events prove their judgment was often wrong. This is because it is only the inner light that can guide the world safely through the minefields of the twenty-first century. But that lesson has yet to be learned, however painful it might be. Kundalini is the channel, aligned by nature, through which the individual consciousness can merge with the super intelligence of Universal Consciousness. When the channel is unobstructed, life-or-death decisions can be made with full awareness of the consequences, even though they may still be years in the future.

This channel, however, is not meant to be used for predicting the rise or fall of the stock markets or for other mundane reasons. For such prognostications, a well-honed intellect and a powerful intuition are better suited. Rather, Kundalini is intended for the guidance of the race. That is why, in these times, those who have awakened the Power in a healthy way almost immediately become more concerned about the welfare of humanity than about their personal desires and problems.

---

* The *New York Times Magazine*, June 11, 1955. Page 48.

We have to wonder what it would be like to be in such a state of awareness. The few who have been there agree that it is beyond description. For the ordinary person, to even begin to fathom the mind of a genius would be an impossibility, not to mention the mind of an Enlightened man or woman.

"It is impossible to describe the overwhelming state of astonishment that fills the soul when, with the inflow of the new psychic currents into the brain, the area of individual consciousness begins to widen until, like an ocean, it spreads everywhere as far as the mind can reach," Gopi Krishna wrote.

Throughout his life, his perceptions continued to change. This amazing change in the perceptive faculties of the individual is the crux of the entire mystery of Kundalini."* The perceptual powers of the human mind are taken to a new dimension, Gopi Krishna says, where the objective world presents a new appearance to the observer.

The ecstatic experience did not happen to the author only once or just a few times; it continued, hour after hour, day after day, year after year, until the moment of his death. In all that time—a full half-century—he never ceased to be amazed, thrilled, and humbled, by what was occurring in his interior. The experience of being immersed in a sea of light persisted even in his sleep. A diligent search of the world's literature on the subject would probably fail to produce anything comparable to the descriptions provided in Gopi Krishna's voluminous writings.

Since it is believed that all mystical and psychic phenomena owe their origin to the activity of the hidden power center the author has named, the information imparted here and in his other writings signifies the rediscovery of one of the greatest secrets of nature known to man. The question as to when and how the original discovery came about has never been answered. There is no mention of it in the ancient texts. All that we know for certain is that nature did not leave it up to mere chance. The biological mechanism was already in place, albeit dormant, from "the beginning."

When it is suggested, or even asserted, that Kundalini represents humankind's only chance to avert a catastrophe, the usual response is that even though we all have the potential to awaken the Power in ourselves, it would take thousands of years before everyone became enlightened, and therefore would have no effect on the present course of events; that by the end of the century, or not too

---

* *Living With Kundalini,* Shambhala, Boston, 1993.

long thereafter, the catastrophe would have already struck. So deeply is the idea of an Apocalypse impressed on the consciousness of the race, its inevitability is almost universally accepted.

But Gopi Krishna, taking a longer view, and considering factors that would probably not enter the mind of most thinkers, saw the future differently. He was both optimistic and pessimistic. In the widest sense, Kundalini was for him the key to a heaven on earth. While only a tiny number would reach Enlightenment, those few would provide the rest of the world with new knowledge undreamed of by traditional futurists.

If, as the author believes, the blueprint of evolution is indelibly stamped on the brain, we need only learn how to read it in order to design our institutions and lifestyles to conform to the demands of evolution. When scholars and scientists begin to consider the possibility that the human race *is* evolving, and that evolution is progressing toward a specific goal, they will overwhelm the media with their new insights and conjectures. The light at the end of the tunnel will then become so alluring that funds to either prove or disprove the theory will flood their institutes and laboratories.

Just as being on the Internet cannot approximate Being, neither can virtual reality ever be the same as *the Reality*. The intellect may argue to the contrary, that we *can* come to know the Reality, and probably with impunity, but like so many other long-held assumptions, this may be tested by events not too far off.

Although more than a dozen of the Gopi Krishna's books have been published, several thousand pages of his writings have not, and of these a large number were written prior to 1968, when the autobiographical account of his awakening was published in England. In that same year, he had a small book privately printed in Srinagar, entitled, *The Shape of Events to Come*, to convey his great concern for the future. It was this concern that brought him to the West, where he hoped to meet scientists who would take an interest in his theories and help promote the idea of a Kundalini research project. But he knew it could not be undertaken without first laying a foundation based on documentary evidence or information gathered from sacred texts scattered throughout the world. Such an exciting undertaking, he thought, would be picked up by the media and would fuel the public's interest. With sufficient funds, an experiment involving a hundred or more candidates could furnish the proof necessary for universal acceptance of his ideas. The evidence would come in the form of two or three individuals in whom Kundalini would be aroused to full activity by means of certain mental disciplines.

In those few, the physiological changes attending the awakening would be easily observed and measured, while the psychological effects would manifest as extraordinary productions in literature, science, mathematics, art, music, etc. The implications for the race, if that were to happen, would pile be to up one on top of the other until hardly a single institution would survive unaltered. A bridge would be thrown over the chasm separating the two great theories of this century—Evolution and Creation.

Darwin's ideas, which first came to public attention with the publication of *The Origin of Species* in 1859, quickly spread over most of the world at a time when there were no electronic media. Newspapers, magazines, and word of mouth were sufficient to start a controversy that has not been settled to this day. But the debate, Gopi Krishna believed, would dissolve the moment scientists observed and measured the physiological changes brought about by an active Kundalini. These, he thought, would be seen as evolutionary changes that would otherwise take perhaps twenty to thirty thousand years to occur. The promises held out by the kind of research he wanted to do exceed those of even the most enthusiastic physicists, who dreamed of discovering the spark of creation in a super-conducting super collider.

That a rapidly growing number of problems, seemingly beyond the power of science to solve, threaten our existence is not disputed. Deadly new viruses that behave as though guided by an intelligence greater than our own resist the most sophisticated drugs. An exploding population, like a raging forest fire, is consuming the earth's resources and polluting the environment at such a tremendous speed that we feel powerless to do anything about it. In a nutshell, we are lost in a labyrinth of our own design, caught in a trap of our own making.

It must have seemed the same to our distant ancestors when they had reached a certain point in evolution beyond which they could not proceed except by undergoing a tremendous change. For what else could be the meaning of Atlantis, and so many other Deluge legends, in which only a handful survived? Civilization reached a stage at which the old concepts had to be updated so that evolution could proceed unobstructed and in a healthy way. That these mental upheavals seem to have coincided with the commencement of a new age makes it even more urgent that we act without delay.

According to the concept of the Kundalini, the outer world is a projection of the inner. The majority of the population is being overwhelmed by the magnitude and rapidity of the changes occurring around them. Bewilderment is everywhere to be seen. Without a corresponding change within, the people—or a person—cannot cope with the changes occurring without. For many educated individuals, the old-time religion has lost its validity.

Although the Information Superhighway and the Worldwide Web of Cyberspace may provide an abundance of facts and shopping galore, we still have no way of acquiring wisdom except by combining knowledge with experience. We have matured sufficiently to know that playing with fire is a danger to be avoided. But we have yet to learn that throwing a challenge in the face of the Almighty by stockpiling nuclear missiles, nerve gas, new viruses, and other doomsday weapons, is more dangerous than anything yet experienced by humanity.

In the last two letters he wrote to me from Srinagar, one dated June 19, 1984, and the other a month later, July 19, 1984, Gopi Krishna made some extraordinary observations about the future. Because he had been extremely ill, due in part to the extreme heat in New Delhi where he had been staying for several weeks prior to going to Kashmir, and the lack of effective air-conditioning in his home there, the letters were relatively brief. The June 19 letter reads as follows:

> The one or two small letters which I wrote to you during the period of my illness [in New Delhi] were dictated with great difficulty. From the period I had a relapse in Delhi to but a few days ago, that is a span of more than a month, I was completely incapable of doing any mental work and part of the time I was even oblivious to what was happening around me. It is only during the last 5 or 6 days that I have started to take interest in the affairs of the family and feel myself in touch with the world. I am now able to move about in the small compound of our building and I prefer to sit there during the day in the open air, rather than in the closed atmosphere of a room. I also feel an inclination to write, though in a very restrained form at present.

There has occurred a remarkable change about which I am not sure yet, but may gain more understanding of it in the course of the next two or three weeks. My last volume, entitled, "The Way To Self-Knowledge," to which I attach the greatest importance, appears to me [now, only weeks later] to have been written in a dream from which I have awakened. I know that this work is of paramount importance and all that is revealed in it will come to pass. I know that it is obligatory to publish this work in as many languages as possible—I place the figure at fifty. But if someone were to ask me to quote even a single verse of this wonderful creation, I would not be able to do so.

This last statement was disturbing to me because Gopi Krishna had a remarkable memory and frequently quoted lengthy passsages both from his own writings and those of others. His second letter, dated July 19, reached me about a day or two prior to my receiving a phone call from Ms. Kobelt, telling me that he had died. It read as follows:

Many thanks for your letter dated July 10, which I received today. Since writing my last letter, I had to pass through another crisis for a few days, due to my still partial knowledge of the extraordinary process now at work in my body. It is, as it were, that I am now being introduced to a new aspect of the Kundalini Power out of the infinite forms in which it will manifest itself in the ages to come. I am still not in a position to write a book. But the state might soon be reached. My first book will be exactly what you wish it to be—a description of this extraordinary experience and the visions I had during this period.

I am sure some of the experiences I have passed through during this period of serious illness will sound like a fairy tale until the accounts of the illuminated ones in the future will corroborate, almost to a word, what I shall present to mankind at this time.

As regards poetic faults in some of the verses in the "Way to Self-Knowledge," you can gladly send me a list of them. The better course would be to send a copy of it to a known poet for his comments. Judged from this point of view, even great poets, including Shakespeare, have been guilty of the same fault. One has to remember that the work professes to be a prophetic record for the next thousand years. To understand this fact comprehensively, one should compare a masterpiece written today with a book on the same subject written 1,200 years ago. This poor human creature often believes that what he knows is the last word on the subject. For most people, this book will continue to be a mystery until the prophecies made come true. If you cast a look at the political changes that have occurred, since this book was written, in most countries of the world, you will find that the prophecy has already started to come true. In another six months, I am sure, the world conditions will make the people realize the importance of the work. Can we call it a coincidence or destiny that on the very next day, when I had intimated the last correction,[*] I was taken ill and became incapable of adding or changing a single line of this extraordinary work.

But death holds no fear for the Enlightened. Gopi Krishna was fully alert, seated, and with his wife, Bhabi, who held him in her arms during his final moments. After taking a few labored breaths, he expired. The cause of death was a lung infection. With him at the time of his passing were, besides his wife, two young volunteers who had been helping him with his work. The following is an edited version of their account of his last days:

> On Saturday, July 28, Gopi Krishna had a heavy day of meetings with groups and individuals. That night his sleep was disturbed until 2:00 a.m. due to intermittent pains. He attributed these to a chronic weakness in his gallbladder and liver, which he thought had flared up due to irregular timings in his diet as a result of the meetings the day before.
> On the morning of Sunday, July 29, he took a familiar antibiotic, which he used from time to time for this difficulty. He rested most of the day as he felt dull, and his head was aching. Still, in his kindness, he could not refuse to see three American visitors, who came to meet him before noon, for about half an hour.
> By 4:00 in the afternoon, he developed a fever, which

often accompanied the chronic gallbladder attacks.

By early morning of Monday, July 30, the continuing high pulse and pain made it clear that this was not a normal gallbladder attack and liver pain. Pandit Ji's elder son, Jagdish, in New Delhi, arranged that the family doctor in Srinagar should make an exception and pay a house call immediately. When he arrived he stated it might not be a case of gallbladder at all but, perhaps, a lung infection. Tests and x-rays confirmed that it was pneumonia in the right lung. The prescribed doses of medicine were administered by evening. We thought it good fortune that he was prescribed a drug which he had experimented with and already found suitable. The doctor said that he would be well within a week.

But Pandit Ji found that the drug had a disturbing effect on his [Gopi Krishna's] mind. He [Gopi Krishna] thought it was because his system had grown more sensitive during his convalescence in Srinagar. In spite of the side effects, he continued the doses throughout the night, experimenting with frequency and quantities to see if he could tolerate the medicine that would fight the infection. Later, we remembered his explanation some weeks prior that in the enlightened man, the nervous system is organized in a different way. Whereas in the normal person there is a set of nerves feeding the life-energy to each organ independently, in the case of an enlightened individual, the energy runs through the whole body, interconnecting all the organs, including the brain. Hence any drug has a strong and immediate effect on the brain and consciousness of one who is awakened.

During the night of the 30th, his breathing became more and more labored. He could only lie down for ten to fifteen minutes at a time before he had to sit up due to breathing difficulties and pain. The doctor advised that he be hospitalized immediately. An ambulance was brought and a stretcher laid out beside his bed within 15 minutes of the doctor's visit. In spite of our pleadings, and the gentle urgings of his dear wife, he remained firm in his resolve not to leave his house, refused any further medicine or injections and urged our kindness not to force him to go, as he felt he would pass away en route.

His movements and simple communications during this entire period gave proof that his mental faculties were fully intact. The obvious clarity of his mind did not allow us to overrule his decision.

Looking back, we realize that all these things indicated that he was keenly aware that this would be his last day. Some days after his death, his wife shared with the family that in the early morning he quietly went to the sink and, according to custom, sprinkled water on himself for the last sacred bath. Since Srinagar was curfew-bound and air flights were canceled, it became apparent that his sons and daughter would not be present at his passing to give him the last drink of water. To prepare his wife for this disappointment, he explained that for one who is filled with the Divine Nectar, bestowed by Kundalini, the symbolic act of offering nectar in the last drink of water is not necessary. Likewise there is no need to weep for an enlightened *sanyasi,* for it benefits neither the mourner nor the departed Soul.

As the morning of the last day progressed, each breath was taken with great pain in a quiet and calm manner so as not to alarm his wife. There were no dramatic scenes, no final advice, no fond farewells to wrench the hearts of those around him and break their courage. He could no longer draw a breath when lying down, so a chair and cushions were placed before him as he sat at the side of his bed. This enabled him to lean his weight forward and take rest. After the first sleep of about ten minutes, he awoke, clearly refreshed for the first time after the long struggle of the night before. Soon after, he lay forward again for a second rest. After about ten minutes he drew two muffled breaths. His wife was called and he was lowered into her arms. Several moments later, there were two more attempts to draw breath. This marked the end. The time was 12:02 in the afternoon of Tuesday, July 31, 1984. His face was serene.[*]

As his letter of July 19 intimated, Gopi Krishna had a great deal more to write about and, his wife said, in those last days that was of great concern to him. From this, one could infer that being Enlightened doesn't mean one ceases to be human; also that what-

---

[*] This account, somewhat shortened by the editor, was written on August 11, 1984.

ever he had planned to reveal about the transcendental realms was apparently not meant to be made known to the world at the present stage of evolution. Gopi Krishna's longtime friend, Dr. Karan Singh, the former Maharaja of Kashmir and Ambassador from India to the United States, officiated at the traditional cremation rites.

Among the fifteen published books Gopi Krishna referred to in the aforementioned letter were four written in verse, *The Way to Self-Knowledge* being the last.* To give the reader a sample of the style in which the book was written, these few stanzas will serve as well as any of the more than 770.

> Empiricists lack, as a class,
> In knowledge of religious lore,
> And have no inkling what a mass
> Of data there exists to explore.
>
> Which bears out that the ancients knew
> How to manipulate the brain,
> And that, known only to a few,
> The Secret has since buried lain.
>
> They still have no idea how
> Essential is this Secret for
> The safety of the race right now,
> For it alone can outlaw war.

Regardless of the form and meter, verse was often the author's favorite mode of expression. In 1972, after Dr. Anshen had sent a copy of *The Biological Basis of Religion and Genius* to Sir Julian Huxley, the famous biologist replied on March 1, 1972, to the effect that to him the book was just so much idle speculation, that in fact there was no purpose whatsoever behind evolution. Gopi Krishna, who was in Zurich at the time, replied in just a few days with a letter of some two thousand lines entirely in verse. It was not because he believed it necessary to carry the issue to such Herculean lengths; rather, Huxley's comments served to trigger a natural process spoken of in the ancient texts as *Vaikhari,* "the spontaneous flow of words, whether in poetry or prose, full of wisdom and worth."* In

---

* The other three books in verse were *The Riddle of Consciousness,* 1974; *The Shape of Things to Come,* 1978; and *The Present Crisis,* 1981.

the Tenth Book of the Rig Veda, the oldest and most important of the Vedic texts, dating back some thirty-five hundred years, Kundalini is addressed as Vak, the deity of speech. And in some of the Tantras, also of great antiquity, the Power is called Vegashwari, the Goddess of Speech.

Here, it is important to make a distinction between "the spontaneous flow of wisdom," one of the first symptoms of genuine Kundalini awakening, and glossolalia, which is primarily a Christian phenomenon and means the utterance of speech or language-like words unknown to the speaker. In the former, the subject knows exactly what he or she is saying.

About a week after writing to Julian Huxley, Gopi Krishna, still in Zurich, received a letter from Captain Edgar D. Mitchell, the Apollo XIV, astronaut, telling him about his plans to establish the Institute of Noetic Sciences, and asking him what he thought about them. The reply, dated March 15, 1972, consisted of approximately eighteen hundred lines in verse. Time alone can be the judge as to how much wisdom the letter in poetry contained, but its purpose was to point out what would be involved if he and his colleagues were to effectively begin exploring some of the more baffling aspects of consciousness. There are psychological devices, Gopi Krishna said, "that will prevent the whole global body of science from penetrating into the mystery of the super-physical forces hidden from them."

Gopi Krishna thought it unlikely that science would ever succeed in solving the mystery of consciousness, because mind itself is beyond the probe of sensory observation, which is the main channel of study for empiricists.

He believed that mankind must first ascend another step on the ladder of evolution before this could become possible. It is necessary for the progress of an intelligent species like the human race to nurture lofty ideals about Creation, the Author of Creation, the sanctity of human life, and the sublime nature of the goal. His response to Mitchell's letter began with the following lines:

> Dear Captain Mitchell, Thanks for your letter
> May God bless your fine efforts for a cause
> Which, at the moment, is and always was
> The Most important project one could take

---

* Appendix to *The Secret of Yoga*, Harper & Row, New York, 1972.

In hand, with all his heart and soul, to slake
The burning thirst to peer behind the scenes
Of this Creation to know what it means,
To find out of what stuff our soul is made:
A lasting substance or a fleeting shade,
To explore the mystery of life and death,
And know what happens after the last breath.
Does any fragment of our conscious being
Survive the end, still knowing, feeling, seeing,
And in what form or to what planes ascends
This deathless essence when life's drama ends?

Some scientists persist in the notion, however mistaken, that with the recent advances made in physics they now are in the position to tackle what were formerly purely religious questions. Sensory examination, and the exercise of the intellect, can reveal facts about the body and the visible universe, but for the mind—and the world of life to which it belongs—inward study and reflection are necessary. Science has become lopsided because it has paid less attention to consciousness and, even in the exploration of the mind, it still uses methods that depend solely on the intellect. The intelligent forces of life, which fashion the body and the brain, are far superior to the product they create.

This realization was accepted by the sages of ancient times, but much of the knowledge they had acquired, over thousands of years, has been lost. What survives, however, can still be found in hundreds of volumes in libraries all over the world, and especially in India. They would be of great value to any research on consciousness undertaken in the future. "We are at the still dim dawn of a new age," Gopi Krishna said. "Both in its wonder and its utility, spiritual science will completely dwarf the material science of our day."

So, the time has come when the knowledge of Kundalini needs to become the common property of all mankind in order to counterbalance the unlimited power science has gained over the material forces of nature. But, Gopi Krishna said, the two components of human personality—the body and the mind—need two different ways of approach for their study and exploration.

Throughout the ages, man has sought for the Elixir of Life, the Holy Grail, the Tree of Life, the Fountain of Youth, the Alchemical

Dross Turned into Gold, the Third Eye, the Magician's Wand, Cosmic Consciousness, Enlightenment, Illumination, and in every case, the purpose of the search was the same. Whether the aspirant was aware of exactly what it was he or she was striving for, the hoped-for prize required the awakening of Kundalini.

Without Enlightened leaders, the world cannot survive in the nuclear age. Gopi Krishna hoped that his writings would encourage scholars to imbibe in the Perennial Wisdom by turning their attention toward the neglected and forgotten esoteric literature of the past, believing that the moment this occurred, Kundalini would become "the most hotly discussed topic of the day."

Throughout history, India was regarded as a center of spiritual knowledge. The oldest scriptures, the Vedas, had been transmitted orally from one generation to the next with such care that hardly a single syllable was lost.

But even before the Vedas, Kundalini was known to the sages of the Indus Valley civilization. And there is evidence to show that in Egypt, too, the disciplines employed to awaken the power were practiced by the high priests and royal families. But the earliest known evidences of Kundalini appear on a number of seals found in the Indus Valley excavations, dating from about 2500 B.C. Describing some of the figures engraved thereon, Joseph Campbell writes:

> Two attendant serpents elevate their giant forms behind a pair of worshippers kneeling at either hand of an enthroned figure seated in what appears to be a posture of yoga. And the fact that the elevation of the so-called Serpent Power is one of the leading motifs of yogic symbolism suggests that we may have here an explicit pictorial reference not only to the legend of some prehistoric yogi, but also to the unfoldment through yoga of this subtle spiritual force.[*]

Although Gopi Krishna had no credentials as scholar or scientist, it was his life's mission to make the secret of Kundalini widely known. He, himself, was tremendously interested in learning whatever had already been written on the subject. On his first visit to America, he came across a copy of a strange work published in Paris three hundred years ago by the Abbe N. de Montfaugon de villars. Entitled *Comte de Gabalis*, it was a surprise to him for what it had

---

[*] *The Mythic Image*, Princeton University Press, Princeton, N.J., 1974.

to say about Kundalini, while referring to Indian sources only in passing. Almost all of the references were from the Old and New Testaments, the Koran, Plato and other Greek writers, as well as numerous Western legends and myths, going back hundreds and thousands of years. The book had been published by "The Brothers," and printed in London at The Old Bourne Press, under the supervision of W. H. Broome.

Scores of relevant and revealing passages could be cited from this little volume, now available in many bookstores, but the following is enough to show that much was concealed in our own classical literature:

> In the early Christian Church the word Christ was used as a synonym for the solar principle in man. 'But as Christ is in you, though your body must die because of sin, yet your spirit has life because of righteousness.' Romans 8:10. [Solar principle signifies Kundalini.]
>
> The day has come when we should seek to unlock the treasure of this ancient volume with a key fashioned from the Philosophers' Stone.
>
> The allegory of Eve and the Serpent: The primordial electricity or solar force, semi-latent with the aura of every human being, was known to the Greeks as the *Speirema*, the serpent coil; and in the Upanishads, the sacred writings of India, it is said to lie coiled up like a slumbering serpent. In the third chapter of the Book of Genesis it is symbolized as the serpent, 'more subtle than any beast of the field that the Lord God had made.' Eve, when this force stirred within her, was tempted to its misapplication. Directed downward through the lower physical centers for generation, unhallowed by a consciousness of responsibility to God and the incoming soul, the serpent force or Fire brought knowledge of evil; directed upward toward the brain for regeneration, the formation of the deathless solar body, it brought knowledge of good. Hence the dual operation of the solar force is symbolized as the tree of the knowledge of good and evil.

Cabalists used the term "Philosophers' Stone" to denote the supreme wisdom, the union of the divine consciousness or omniscient solar principle in man with the lower consciousness or personality in all ages. This mystical union has been the goal of initiates in all ages. "Through knowledge of the law governing the solar force man shall gain power to awaken those ganglia corresponding to the planets, and thereby controlling the planetary forces manifesting in him shall unfold the immortality of his own being and become master of his destiny."*

There are thousands of books on religion, mysticism, and magic that could be read with new understanding once the Rosetta stone of Kundalini is applied to what so far has remained obscure. Whether Masonic, Hermetic, Rosicrucian, Qabbalistic, or Alchemical, all such philosophies would then glow with a fresh, new light. It would become apparent that Kundalini is the golden thread that runs through all the world's sacred writings, providing the only safe channel for the scientific exploration of the mind. It is, as Gopi Krishna has intimated, the only road aligned by nature to reach the territory of consciousness.

Dr. Frederic Spiegelberg, Professor Emeritus of Comparative Religion and Indology at Stanford University, writes:

> Being exposed to [his] experiences is like meeting a space traveler who seemingly for no purpose has landed on a strange and unknown star without the standard equipment of the professional astronaut, and who simply reports about the bewildering landscape around him, colorfully [and] truthfully. [He] is an extremely honest reporter, to the point of humbleness.**

Humility is an unmistakable sign of any individual who has successfully aroused Kundalini. It makes one more compassionate, more sensitive, and more perceptive of the plight of others. Through the arousal of Kundalini, one can reach a state of cosmic awareness in which the highest secrets of life and existence can be learned intuitively. Gopi Krishna was a living demonstration of the radical transformation this psychosomatic power-reservoir of psychic energy can produce. He himself lived in a shining world in which "every scene and every object glowed with luster against a marvelously luminous

---

* Comte de Gabilis.
** His Introduction to *Kundalini, the Evolutionary Energy in Man,* Shambhala, Berkeley, 1970.

background, the whole presenting a picture of such resplendence and sublime beauty that without implying the least exaggeration, I actually felt as if every night during slumber I roamed in enchanting empyrean regions of heavenly life."

Gopi Krishna was born in 1903 in the small village of Gairoo, about twenty miles from Srinagar, the capital of Kashmir. After failing in his college examinations, he left school, married, and devoted himself to a personal discipline of yoga and meditation while employed as a minor civil servant. In 1937, at the age of 34, he experienced the sudden awakening of Kundalini, but because the energy was aroused in a negative form, it resulted in severe ill health for some twelve years, during which time he was often in great pain. At the same time, and partly because of the suffering, he was destined to witness his own evolutionary transformation. The final state of cosmic consciousness did not appear all at once but marked the culmination of a continuous process of biological reconstruction, covering approximately fifteen years. Even after he had reached the age of 81, the process was still proceeding apace, as was apparent from his correspondence.

What makes Gopi Krishna's writings of such importance today is that they are the product of his own direct observations, just as much as though they were the findings of a competent scientist who has faithfully recorded the results of a series of carefully conducted experiments:

> With the awakening of Kundalini an amazing activity commences in the whole nervous system, from the crown of the head to the toes. The body is now transformed into a miniature laboratory, working at high speed day and night. The nerves, whose existence is never felt by the normal consciousness, are now forced by some invisible power to a new type of activity, which either immediately or gradually becomes perceptible to the subject.
>
> Through all their innumerable endings, they begin to extract a nectar-like essence from the surrounding tissues, which, traveling in two distinct forms, one as radiation and the other as a subtle essence, streams into the spinal cord.... The radiation, appearing as a luminous cloud in the head, streams into the brain.*

---

* *Living with Kundalini*, Shambhala, Boston, 1993.

Along with the stream of radiation came the contents of one book after another. From an ordinary man with little formal education, Gopi Krishna had become a sage and prophet, just as the ancient manuals promised the sincere aspirant. Awakening Kundalini is not meant merely to procure peace of mind, the vision of God, and psychic gifts, it is also meant to raise one to the stature of an intellectual prodigy. For the author, it brought the dream of an emancipated humanity through the convergence of religion and science. "Knowledge of the spirit must become as precise and universal as the knowledge of the physical world," he wrote in a letter to a Bombay newspaper editor. "In this lies the safety and survival of the race."

It is the intention of the present work to help transform that dream into reality. Although a revolution in the study of the brain is already well under way, we are still deplorably deficient in knowledge about our own selves. The widely held opinion that man is merely a machine is gaining more acceptance year by year.

"There is not the slightest reason to doubt that brains are anything other than machines with enormous numbers of parts that work in perfect accord with physical laws," writes M.I.T. computer scientist Marvin Minsky in *The Society of Mind*. "As far as anyone can tell, our minds are merely complex processes."

No matter how much we learn about the mechanical parts of the brain, we must still find a way to illuminate it from within. Otherwise, the invisible planes of creation, to which our mind and spirit belong, can never be brought into sight. To say that every human thought, hope, fear, passion, yearning, and insight results from chemical interactions between the brain's transmitters and receptors simply reveals a failure to understand the actual position. It is also highly dangerous; for if we are only complex computers, then those who say, "God is a myth that nature programmed us to believe," are right and the greater bulk of mankind is wrong. But, "the Intelligence behind the human brain surpasses our understanding a million times more than we surpass the understanding of a mole," says the author.

Most everyone today agrees that world events are in the process of forming a critical mass and that only a drastic change in thinking can save the day. But what is seldom if ever discussed is how this change in thinking can be safely and quickly brought about. The author of *Comte de Gabalis* points the way. If we will concentrate upon the highest that we can evoke from within, says de Montfaugon de villars, "that solar force and power directed upward will awaken and revitalize those ganglia or organs of perception hitherto withheld from our use."

This concentration can be greatly intensified through the publication and publicizing of the works of those men and women who have written about the illuminative state from their own direct experience. Short of actually having the mystical vision, reading their words of wisdom can be a profound experience in itself. Certainly it is one of the most effective ways of transforming one's own consciousness.

The present work contains a wide spectrum of Gopi Krishna's thinking, spanning the two decades—1965 to 1984—in which he wrote. His vision is new, original, and consistent. No other philosopher or mystic of the past has given the same interpretation to mystical experience. He places the whole of religion and mystical ecstasy on the footing of a regular science, demonstrable with empirical methods, of which the laboratory is the human body.

If just a tiny fraction of the billions of dollars that are willingly spent on atom smashers, space telescopes, and other costly instruments—important but intended primarily to satisfy man's curiosity—were made available to develop a science of the soul, who can say what miracles might ensue? Just as a gyrocompass makes it possible for a pilot to fly safely through the clouds, so knowledge of Kundalini can exert a stabilizing influence on the mind and a stimulating effect on the brain.

Gene Kieffer
July 7, 1995

CHAPTER ONE

In 1977, Gopi Krishna embarked on an ambitious undertaking, the publication of a quarterly magazine of "international: spiritual and scientific progress." Called *Spiritual India and Kundalini,* its aim was to demonstrate the empirical basis of religion as well as the spiritual implications of science. His contribution to the first issue, published that October, was an editorial entitled "Kundalini: The Guardian of Human Evolution."

The last issue, published in 1984, contained the text of a speech Gopi Krishna had delivered some months before at a conference of the International Transpersonal Association, held in Davos, Switzerland. The message was the same: Distorted evolution could be catastrophic for the race, and our willing cooperation is essential for the healthy functioning of the process.

If we fail to cooperate, he said, or act in the reverse direction, as is happening today, the process can malfunction and lead to disastrous consequences.

KUNDALINI, THE GUARDIAN OF HUMAN EVOLUTION

The world of today presents a spectacle that is not at all reassuring. There is such a clash of views, such a conflict of opinions, and such a welter of speculations about the nature of man and the purpose of his life that it is almost impossible for a seeker after truth to find his bearings and to anchor his mind in the storm-swept sea of modern thought.

Let us take a few examples. Looking at politics, we find mankind divided into conflicting ideologies and divergent systems of government. Some are democratic, some dictatorial, some monarchical, some autocratic, some oligarchic, and so on. There are powers and superpowers, bristling with armaments, eying each other with supreme suspicion and even hate.

Billions of human beings who now inhabit the earth accept the anomalous position and the hanging threat of instant annihilation on the outbreak of a nuclear war as an inevitable result of human behavior and progress and submit tamely to what is, to say the least, a monstrous situation completely incongruent with the conduct of an intelligent species. All forms of life, with healthy survival instincts, react sharply to a hostile environment. But the elite of the most advanced segments of our race, far from reacting, are creating a most deadly and highly poisonous milieu today, deliberately with their own hands, as the result of blunted sensibility caused by immoderate lust for power or wealth.

Looking at religion, we find the major faiths battling hard with the agnostic and atheistic forces of our day, considerably shattered and shaken in the process. We also see a welter of recently grown cults, creeds, spiritual and meditative systems, divergent schools of mental discipline, and occult practices, each claiming the place of precedence over all the rest.

How far this revolt against the major religions, and their proliferation into innumerable creeds and cults, has benefited the race can be assessed from the orgies of crime, violence, wars, and massacres that have marked the current century, winning for it the unenviable position of the bloodiest in history. The crowning evil of this fateful century might still be lying in wait to pounce in a nuclear holocaust that can spell the doom of humanity or, at least, death and ghastly suffering for a large segment of it.

A Scientific Age Riven with Dissension

Looking at the economic position, one cannot fail to notice awful imbalances. We find about 90 percent of the earth's wealth concentrated in the hands of less than one third of the world's population, while the remaining 10 percent is shared by more than seventy countries, supporting about two thirds of the race. Billions of dollars are spent to explore conditions existing on the moon and planets, with hardly any relevance to the problems of mankind, while millions of children grow blind, consumptive, or afflicted with incurable ailments through lack of proper nourishment. Millions, too, die slow deaths by starvation, or fall victims to diseases without the means to purchase the medicine to cure them, while other millions live in slums under the most unhygienic conditions, or in dirty open spaces with only heaven's starlit canopy over their heads.

Looking at science, we find the confusion even more confounded. There is no doubt that scientific discoveries and inventions have transformed our lives and brought within the reach of every individual amenities and comforts that could not be dreamed of even by kings of the past. But at the same time, science has brought in its wake hedonistic ideas and weapons of mass destruction that threaten the very existence of the race.

The scientific thinking of our age is so riven with dissension that it is hard to find unanimity in any branch of empirical knowledge. For some, evolution is planned, for others it is random. For the newly born sociobiologists, everything is determined by genes. Children are deceitful and hate their parents because it is coded in their genetic structures, a point of view, that can, with more widespread awareness of this pernicious doctrine, and with more knowledge of contraceptives, prevent parents from begetting children, leading to the diminution or even extinction of the groups and nations that believe in it.

There are some scientists who vehemently oppose further expansion of industry and the machine—in the present unplanned form—to avoid pollution and the extravagant waste of our natural resources, which, once exhausted, would be hard to replenish. There are others who are equally vehement in their denunciation of this point of view and believe that further advances in science will also lead to the discovery of methods to overcome these problems.

There are some who are extremely apprehensive of the uncontrolled growth of the population, while there are others who, like (the late) Herman Kahn, entertain the fantastic notion that the planet can sustain a population many times more than the present number. It is obvious that theoretical academicians of this category, residing in opulent countries, have never tasted the awful anguish of life lived below the poverty line in overpopulated lands, with exhausted soil and resources insufficient to meet rapidly increasing demand.

As the situation exists, there appears to be no way out of the present chaos and confusion. There is no political leader, even among the most powerful nations, who can bring peace and harmony to the politically fragmented world. There is no thinker who can show the way to a better understanding of human problems to the scholars; no religious teacher who can bring concord and agreement between the different faiths; and no scientist who can provide a solution to the controversial issues that now rack the brains of biologists, psychologists, astronomers, psychiatrists, sociologists, and the like.

Specialization has created insurmountable barriers between one branch of science and the other, with the result that no one can speak with authority about the numerous knotty problems that confront mankind. And there is every indication to show that this confusion and clash of views would increase with the further growth of knowledge, and specialization would become more proliferated and watertight.

The result would be that the masses, like a rudderless boat in a storm-swept sea, would toss from one line of thought to an other, with no anchor on which to fix the mind or no goal of life on which to concentrate.

To What Purpose?

Can anyone suggest a solution to these problems? Is there any way to bring about unity and harmony to the nations? Is there any way to stop the feverish armament race or to destroy the existing stock of nuclear weapons? Is there any way to restrict the world population at its already excessive limit, or to stop pollution of the environment or extravagant use of our natural resources?

If you feel that these problems are unsolvable, ask yourself to what purpose are billions of our fellow human beings toiling and sweating; to what purpose are the rulers strutting and dancing in front of reporters and their cameras and video recorders; and to what purpose are leaders of thought turning out volume after volume, on every branch of knowledge, when a volcano is rumbling under our feet, ready to erupt and spread its fiery vapor all over the earth?

The issue arises, why, in spite of full awareness of the possibility of a global catastrophe, does the intelligentsia show such a lack of response to the danger and are carrying on as if there were no danger at all? Why is the human population drifting helplessly toward a possible disaster without raising a finger to avert it? If we cannot answer this question, the conclusion is inevitable that there has occurred a blunting of the survival instinct of the race, combined with a disorientation of the intellect, which attaches more importance to wealth, possession, or power than to life itself. This is the malady that has ripped the mind as the result of an unnatural and hedonistic mode of life, and the award of nature for violation of eternal laws.

Disorientation of the intellect is never perceptible to those who fall victim to it. When in the grip of decadence, the once ascendant nations of the past could never correctly analyze their behavior or take instant notice of their fallacies. The Roman nobles and ladies feasted and made merry while gladiators pounded each other to death. Confronted by such a spectacle, many sensitive modern women would turn pale with horror and faint.

It does not matter if the nations that are stockpiling nuclear weapons are rich in intellectual talent or foremost in wealth and military power. Any penetrating intellect can have a stain of abnormality and be totally unaware of it. Intellectuals affected by mental kinks cannot easily be made cognizant of their abnormality.

With irrefutable logic, they justify them to their own satisfaction. But for others, the faults are blatantly clear to see.

No amount of logic can make the foremost nations see the glaring fault in their thinking when they frantically press forward in the armaments' race. But their exhausted descendants will clearly mark the twist in the intellect when the bombast is over, and calm again settles upon the frenzied scene.

Victims of Degeneration and Decay

The incredible nature of what I expound might make it seem highly fanciful and imaginative, or even the product of a deluded mind. But impartial history is a standing witness to the constantly observed phenomenon, that with hardly any exception, all rich kingdoms, all victorious empires, all ruling dynasties, kings, aristocracies, and all very wealthy and affluent families, only in the course of a few generations, have slithered down the height they had once attained and fell victim to degeneration and decay.

Why the sway of an empire, or vast possessions, or excessive wealth should have a deleterious effect on the blood—and even the seed of the families involved—is still a mystery. But the mystery is solved when we realize that the human brain is still in the process of evolution toward a more perfect state in which a still-superior pattern of consciousness is possible. A natural, frugal, healthy life, content only with the basic needs of the body and the mind, free of ego, immoderate ambition, lust and greed for wealth—more ready to serve than to rule, altruistic and compassionate—is the only life concordant with the principles of evolution.

Digression from the righteous life prescribed in all revealed scriptures, in other words, from the principles of evolution, is the surest path to hell, to mental aberration, abnormality, obsolescence and decay. It does not alter the position if the digressers are individuals or whole societies, the result is the same.

It does not change the position if, with only some exceptions, journalists, scholars, scientists, philosophers, politicians, and glittering luminaries adorn a nation guilty of digression from spiritual law. They surrounded Hitler and other inhuman heads of states, also. But it is they who made the gas chambers and other horrors possible; and it is they who will share the responsibility for the future slaughters.

The kingdom, empire, or nation falls because the mind becomes corrupt and the intellect clouded. The Light descending from Heaven that guides the steps of humanity is obstructed. When this happens, wrong values become right and right values wrong.

It is safe to presume that the tense situation of the world cannot endure for ever. A state of saturation must come about, sooner or later, beyond which it would not be possible to proceed further. The steadily diminishing resources of countries must one day impose a limit beyond which it is impossible to advance. In this way, defeated in attempts to outmatch each other in the destructive power of their weapons, the only alternative left would either be to continue living in a state of tension and suspicion indefinitely, while spending all available resources in maintaining their defensive or offensive strength at the permissible peak, or resort to war to settle the long-standing issues between them.

We can also safely infer that if a solution is found, it would either be provided by a combination of circumstances that would alter the world situation, as for instance a natural catastrophe of global dimensions, or the discovery of a new, more lethal instrument of destruction than the missile that can make resistance and retaliation impossible. Alternatively, the solution can also be provided by the genius and tireless efforts of an individual or a band of gifted individuals.

A Safe-to-Carry Nuclear Bomb

In this age of advanced technology, it would be erroneous to suppose that the nuclear bomb marks the limit to which weaponry can go. There might be other and more deadly arms in fabrication at this moment. Alternatively, it might become possible to produce a miniature nuclear bomb that can be easily prepared and smuggled into a country in numbers sufficient to inflict a terrible loss of life in a matter of hours.

The daring exploits of terrorist hijackers during the last few years carry a lesson that no one can disregard. A technological breakthrough, making it possible to produce a small, safe-to-carry nuclear bomb, or any other new type of mass-destructive weapon, can alter the whole strategy of war and provide a weak, aggrieved country with a chance to hit back at the giants who rely on their nuclear arsenals to dominate the world.

The moment a safe-to-handle and easy-to-transport miniature nuclear bomb, or an equally lethal bacterial or chemical weapon, becomes possible, the field of operation of the terrorists will shift to the capture of cities, holding millions ransom and forcing the government to submit to their demands. Of what avail then will be the nuclear arsenals of the super powers when a hundred determined terrorists can paralyze main cities and compel their inhabitants to do as they like?

Armed with weapons of this kind, international gangsters can terrorize the whole world.

Nor is it necessary that they should belong to a foreign land.

Disgruntled and aggrieved nationals can play the desperate role with the same devastating effect. This would introduce a new, highly dangerous factor in the already very delicately balanced political arena of the world, a factor, which being unpredictable, can prove of disastrous consequences for the race.

Just as to pass off a lie, a dozen other lies are needed to prevent detection. In the same way terror and violence are needed to safeguard excessive wealth, possession, or dominance, growing ever greater to meet the threat of larger adverse forces. The rapidly growing armament industry blatantly points to this fact. What frightful situations will arise out of this transgression, and what awful price humanity will have to pay in the decades to come for this insurgence of a clouded rebel intellect, only the future will show.

Failure to Grasp the Lessons of History

It would be ridiculous to suppose that the twenty-first century would be a replica of the twentieth. The dominant empires of today, which now loom invincible, must likewise witness a fall to conform to the cycle of ascendancy and decline that has characterized the career of all great nations of the past.

The intellect that fails to grasp the lessons of history and lives exclusively in the present is pitiably superficial and has no title to be classed as wise. From the dawn of history, superficial and sycophantic intellects surrounded the high and mighty who, smelling of corruption, were heading toward a fall. Had they tried to be accurate and fair in the assessment of the conditions prevailing and given honest expression to their views, disasters might have been averted and historical debacles prevented.

The armies of conceited intellects that now act as guiding lights and fail to read the lesson of history, writ large across the sky, are guilty of the same dissimulation and suffer from the same warp in their judgment as their counterparts of the past.

They simply cannot look beyond the narrow horizon of their own time.

The human personality is not the result of a mysterious biochemical activity of the brain but the product of an intelligent energy, designated as *Prana* by adepts since the time of the Vedas. It is the basis of life just as physical energy is the basis of the multilateral material universe. *Prana* pervades all the cells of the human organism, as also of other forms of life.

There is a spectrum of *Prana* for every form of life and for every individual in each species. This spectrum is formed by a combination of the subtle biochemical components of an organism that makes it peculiar for every individual system. Evolution implies that a gradual transformation of the *pranic* spectrum must conform to the prescribed pattern, or otherwise a lopsided or distorted personality results. Insanity and acute states of delirium, sometimes brought about by serious illness, are instances of a permanent or temporary distortion in the spectrum of *Prana*. The phenomenon of a double or multiple personality is caused by the same factor.

A high-grade intellect, without a corresponding aesthetic or moral sensibility, can result from evolution due to disproportion in the *pranic* spectrum. This disproportion can result from a highly unnatural environment or a faulty mode of life. An example of this kind of disproportion is provided by highly intelligent criminals whose propensity for felonious deeds is irrepressible.

It is not in the brain but in the ill-formed personality behind the brain that the evil propensity resides.

A Highly Developed But Diseased Intellect

Highly intelligent but disproportioned products of evolution and culture can also be disproportionate in their perception. It is intellects of this category that currently lack an accurate perception of the hideous drama being enacted before their eyes as a prelude to the massacre of humanity. Like the color blind who lack in the capacity to distinguish certain hues, these intellects are not able to perceive their own insensibility to what is a most outrageous situation, brought about by a highly developed but diseased intellegence that is dead to the atrocious nature of the milieu it created.

From the earliest times eccentricity and aberration have often been a clearly marked symptom of genius. Likewise, a powerful and highly productive intellect can be attended by varied degrees of aberration without possessing the perceptive power to notice them. This is the tragedy of our age. Not just a few of the presidents, prime ministers, rulers, and commanders are but pitiable dupes of outmoded ideologies that drive them to play leading roles in a monstrous drama, in which millions of intelligent people are acting, to fabricate weapons that can turn the earth into an inferno. These leaders are forced to adopt this suicidal course because they are not able to hit upon a practicable alternative for peaceful coexistence.

The situation is justified in the eyes of those who are responsible because they are not able to notice their own aberration in the same way as one is not able to see a mole in one's eye, or abnormality in one's behavior, when sanity is eclipsed.

A Reconciliation Between Science and Religion

Spiritual discipline is an indispensable prerequisite for healthy evolution of the human brain. This is the reason why the religious impulse is deeply rooted in human nature, and why Revelation came at crucial times to guide the footsteps of humanity toward a goal that is entirely beyond the grasp of the intellect. Without right guidance, man can even evolve towards an intellectual monster, dead to ethical values and impervious to spiritual light.

It is possible that such a species might exist now on some distant planet, or might have existed even on earth, in a vanished civilization of the past, like the fabulous Atlantis, swallowed up in a natural cataclysm without leaving a trace. World mythology abounds in stories of demoniac creatures of this kind.

A spiritual prodigy could have prevented science from becoming so lopsided with materialistic bias, or religion from becoming stagnant with an overgrowth of superstition, dogma, and sectarian belief. An illuminated Einstein, Bertrand Russell, or Jung, with knowledge of both the outer and the inner worlds, could have caused a revolution in thinking and brought about a reconciliation between science and spiritual aspirations. This would have saved the world from assuming the menacing form that it presents today.

But the grace has been denied and, instead, intelligent human monsters were born and came into power in several countries to cause the massacres of innocents in Germany, Russia, Africa, Vietnam, Bangladesh, and other places. This array of morally corrupt, power-hungry psychopaths is nature's forewarning to show what clever but distorted minds may be expected to come to power to cause total devastation, if mankind continues to rely on reason as the sole arbiter of human destiny.

This crop of intelligent mass murderers, who rose to positions of honor by their wit and talent, is the answer of the Divine Power, controlling the evolution of mankind both in the individual and the race, to the intellectual arrogance of the twentieth century.

The world is in a state of turmoil because, like a bolting, mettlesome horse, the human intellect is carrying the cart of humanity, groaning and creaking, in whatever direction it chooses to take. Gasping and panting over rocks, bogs, thorns, hill or dale, highway, or field, the foaming, uncontrollable steed rushes on, dragging the alarmed crowd toward an unknown but predictably disastrous end.

The tragedy is that but few of the leading lights, guiding the race, care to ask themselves to what extent can we adapt a species of life that has led a simple, arboreal, nomadic, or agrarian existence for the last millions of years to the smog-ridden, noisy, mechanized, shrieking, and clanging milieu of a modern industrialized way of life?

Governments Based On Arbitrary Theories

There appears to be a tacit understanding that the victories of science are a guarantee; those who won them are in a safe position to make the best possible use of the knowledge gained. Technology has, therefore, come to be regarded as an Aladdin's lamp that can magically fulfill all the wishes of mankind.

But there are few who seek to know in depth whether the environment created by technology is conducive to the mental and physical health of the species on a long-term basis. Or is this vainglorious display of man's intellectual prowess fraught with the gravest consequences? Except for a discerning few, no one cares to ponder the question whether the social and political systems are in accordance with the psychical and biological needs of human beings. Little attention has so far been given to the fact that there must be a collective instinct governing the social and political behavior of the species, as there is in every other form of gregarious life.

There is no conclusive evidence to show whether man has arrived at a position where he need not concern himself with the problem, and whatever may be the nature of this instinct, he can safely adopt any social organization that suits his own inclination or desire. If it is even remotely conceded that the inherent collective social instinct of human beings cannot be brushed aside with safety, then the issue arises what means has science adopted to ascertain the nature of this instinct and to plan our social life in accordance with it?

The various systems of government current today are all based on arbitrary theories and doctrines, or imitations of ancient models, without any sanction from nature and without any established connection between the instinctual requirement and the pattern in force. Whether it is democracy, dictatorship, monarchy, oligarchy, or any other form of government, it is in no case the outcome of exhaustive study and experimentation on the part of an impartial, wise body of intellectuals. On the contrary, what we now have is a steaming broth of dynastic rule, arbitrary systems, vested interests, individual opinions, doctrines of revolutionaries, and concepts of politicians based entirely on the conclusions of the intellect, without any relevance to the canons of nature or the laws of God.

Of all the sciences, the one that most directly affects the life and happiness of every human being is social science. It has no stronger foundation than that of arbitrary, individual opinion, self-interest, biased calculation, theory, religious belief, or superstition. Nothing can be more tragic than the laws, conventions, and customs, on which depend our security, social life, safety, subsistence, and happiness—the charm and harmony of our homes—resting on insubstantial foundations, e.g., ideas, calculations, and doctrines of frail human beings, without any regard to the collective natural instincts or universal well-being of the race.

Proof is provided by the current politically chaotic situation. Democracies, dictatorships, oligarchies, military rules, etc., are all grappling with each other like a noisy group of wrestlers. Had the various forms of government been in accordance with an instinctual model or a heaven-ordained universal law, the puppet dance of the high and mighty would not then be an unedifying feature of life today.

The insipid drama of forced laughter, sardonic smiles, jack in-the-box appearances before the media, behind-the-back intrigues, and the other embellishments of the black art of diplomacy, which is now an inseparable ingredient of the political structure, would not be there to regale a disenchanted public now satiated with such performances.

Under a Mantle of Closest Secrecy

We all know that even in this self-righteous age most of the nations freely spy on each other. No sane and sober observer can shut his eyes to the reality that in his own government there is a special department maintained to resort to betrayal, treachery, eavesdropping, lies, conspiracy, intrigue, deception, torture, and death in the name of the nation, in this way involving the whole multitude in the game.

In every form of government, the head of state, the ministers, and their confederates—always acting under a shadow of fear from popular opposition, political rivals, a counter-revolutionary movement, or a military coup—can never have the security they need to work soberly and calmly for the trust that the people repose in them. A mantle of closest secrecy hides from sight the ugly scenes too often acted behind the stainless, dignified exterior of government, a position entirely incongruent with the principles of morality and law.

Taking a single department of education, where one would expect models of behavior, these few lines from a recent article by Charles S. Steinberg in the *New York Times* are illuminating:

> Pay no heed to those stories of back-biting on Madison Avenue.
>
> They are a mild broth compared to the witch's brew that professors are capable of stirring up in the deceptively mild environment of the campus. Academy in short can be a jungle more terrifying than the real jungle, where predators kill out of a natural need for food. But academic people on-the-make have an instinct for the jugular that is driven by a deadly combination of ruthless ambition and sheer, malevolent sadistic pleasure . . . . In the desperate need to publish or perish, in the savage struggle for tenure, there is a lethal combination of ambition and malevolence that short-changes the students and demeans the idea of what a university should represent.*

---

* The *New York Times*, December 12, 1977.

Clear-sighted observers have started to take notice of this deterioration in the moral fiber of the arbiters and architects of human society. Here is a sample from one of them, Paul R. Ehrlich.:

> The world is in trouble and we are in trouble with it. One thing is certain, we can't count on our leaders to steer us through the times of crisis. We can only count on them to fumble the ball [if they can ever get their hands on it] and then try to tell us the fumble was a touch-down. Americans have grown accustomed to having their intelligence insulted in this way, and have gradually come to expect lies from politicians.[*]

Commenting on scientific leadership Ehrlich adds:

> Scientific leadership has, if anything, been worse than religious leadership. In theory, at least, scientists ought to know better, but they sent men to the moon when cities on the earth were dissolving and transplanted hearts in preference to tackling the problems of over-population and mass-starvation.
>
> It is no surprise that people have become disenchanted with scientists, and technologists who promised them a good life and gave them smog, pollution, sonic boom, nuclear missiles, biological weapons, poison gas, brainwashing, electronic surveillance and a computer-ridden, dehumanized society. Only the naive still have faith that science can pull some kind of technological rabbit out of the hat at the last minute to save us.[**]

On Whom Does the Responsibility Lie?

The human mind, imbued with the idea that success, high position, ease and comfort, abundance and affluence are the *summum bonum* of life with no higher aim, burrowing like an earthworm deep

---

[**] Paul R. Ehrlich, *The End of Affluence*.
[*] Ibid.

into the soil of ambition, greed, and lust for power. By no means devised by the intellect can a mind set solely on this course be diverted once it becomes possessed with the idea that success and abundance are the only means by which it can win the battle of life.

It is not necessary to dwell more closely on the darker side. Every intelligent person who cursorily glances at the newspaper or watches television can see the deterioration and rot that has set in the world structure, leaving no area immune where one could draw a breath of relief. But on whom does the responsibility lie?

William G. Summer's view that self-made millionaires are the paradigm of the fittest and that they are "a product of natural selection, acting on the whole body of men to pick out those who can meet the requirement" is a striking example of a vacuous product of the intellect. The fate suffered by the wealthy aristocracy in Russia in the Communist revolution, and the success of the penniless, austere Gandhi, completely belie his conclusions.

But the aim is not to sermonize or to contend that modern society is more dissipate and corrupt than it was in the past, or that all men and women of our day should be paragons of virtue as compared to the people of older periods. Nor is it our purpose to show that the individuals in power are any worse than those who ruled in former days. On the contrary, despotism and tyranny, with their long history of cruelty and horror, except at rare intervals, are now a phantom of the past.

There is, however, one significant factor that makes it necessary to make an honest assessment of modern society without fear or favor. This factor was never weighed before with the philosophers and thinkers of the past. Taking but one example, if this single factor had existed in the time of Greece to influence the thought of Plato it would have radically influenced his ideas and his writings would have been entirely different. There is no prophet, sage, or philosopher of antiquity or modern times whose whole thought, and its expression, would not have been drastically altered if he had lived in the shadow of the reality under which we live at present.

Throughout the whole span of human life, to this day the individuals in power never had in their possession an instrument lethal enough to cause total destruction of the human species in a matter of hours. Such a position never existed in the racial memory. That this position exists now, and may even soon rest at the option of terrorist organizations, makes the situation so abnormal and so fraught with danger, that no thinker of the past would have omitted to denounce it with all the force of words at his command.

The fact that, save for a few noteworthy exceptions, modern spiritual teachers, philosophers, thinkers, or scholars do not voice their condemnation of the situation shows that the sensibility of the intellect is blunted and atrophied. This is the direct result of the highly discordant milieu in which humanity lives at present, and on the passive acceptance of the successive massacres that occurred during this century.

Natural Laws Rule Social Behavior

In light of the fact that certain definite, but yet little understood, natural laws rule the instinctive social behavior of gregarious forms of life, it would be irrational to suppose that all human hopes and aspirations for an ideal form of social order are not the outcome of a natural law so comprehensive and elastic, but at the same time so unalterable, that it is difficult to frame a precise picture of it through the intellect. Plato conveys just a glimmer about the way of operation of this Law:

> The ruin of oligarchy is the ruin of democracy; the same disease magnified and intensified by liberty overmasters democracy—the truth being that the excessive increase of anything often causes a reaction in the opposite direction; and this is the case not only in the seasons and vegetables and animal life, but above all in forms of government. The excess of liberty, whether in states or individuals, seems only to pass into excess of slavery. And so tyranny naturally rises out of democracy, and the most aggravated forms of tyranny and slavery out of the most extreme form of liberty.[*]

We can frame a vague picture of the colossal area of operation of this Law when we assume that the vicissitudes of history, the rise

---

[*] Plato. *The Republic*.

and fall of nations, the ascendancy and decline of empires, the periods of unbroken calm and bloody revolutions, have all been in the nature of oscillating movements of a pendulum to bring humanity nearer and nearer to a balanced, healthy form of social order, ideal for the unimpeded working of the evolutionary processes active in the race.

Just as sunset follows the dawn to create the astro-geodic environment essential for the survival of terrestrial life, in the same way the vicissitudes of time that overtake individuals and nations are necessary measures to bring rational beings, liberated from the restrictive fetters of instinct, in the mode of their collective life, closer and closer to the form best suited to the further evolution of the mind. Scholars will only rack their brains in vain attempts to understand human behavior, both at the individual and collective level, as long as they ignore the central pivot around which the whole area of psychology revolves, and that is evolution toward a predetermined mental state. The following passages from Plato express the same idea:

Socrates: It seems that we have found some other things against whose secret entrance into the city of guardians must take every precaution.
What are they? asked Adeimantus.
Socrates: Riches and poverty, for the one produces luxury and idleness and revolution, the other meanness and villainy besides.
Adeimantus: I agree, but Socrates—think about this. How will our city be able to carry on a war if it has no money, especially if it is forced to fight a great and rich city?
Socrates: To me it is obvious that fighting one city will be rather hard, but fighting two will be easier.
Adeimantus: What on earth do you mean?
Socrates: Don't you agree that our men will be soldier-athletes fighting against rich men?
Adeimantus: Yes of course.
Socrates: Well, Adeimantus, don't you think that one perfectly trained boxer is an easy match for two fat wealthy men who can't box?

The inference is clear. Plato refers to a natural law that makes luxury and overabundance a curse, a virus for the mind, the most prolific cause for degeneration and decay recognized and warned against by prophets, sages, and philosophers from a period thousands of years before the birth of Christ.

But why do wealth, abundance, and luxury, or high rank and unrestricted power, have such a deleterious and debilitating effect on the mind? Why should those who command every facility for the finest culture of the mind or the body, with their wealth or position, roll in the dust after only a few generations? Why after a brief interval there should be tottering ruins in place of stately mansions and dissipated profligates in place of robust ancestors who made the fortune, no one has been able to explain in a satisfactory way.

The Deity Who Rules Human Evolution

In Indian wisdom, the deity ruling human evolution is known as the Goddess Kundalini. If souls are immortal there must be a deathless Ocean of Intelligence from which they arise. In that case evolution, too, must be governed by intelligent laws. Indian wisdom has named that Intelligence Kundalini. She is a profound mystery that will always remain beyond the probe of the intellect As the instrument of evolution, her power manifests itself as genius, inspiration, and prophetic revelation to guide the steps of humanity over the serpentine Path.

It is the lack of insight into this Mystery that makes scholars discriminate between religious and secular genius and reject the revelations of the former. They throw blame on one another for the present crisis, but both sides are equally responsible for denying to Revelation its rightful position as a valid authority to be consulted in deciding all social and moral issues of the race.

The question might well be asked: Why should a seeker after spiritual knowledge concern himself with what is happening in the political world? What has a person longing for spiritual unfoldment to do with political or social conditions? Is it not sufficient for him or her to be immersed constantly in the thought of the divine, to be absorbed in reading inspiring spiritual literature, and to live in the company of holy men or those who have the same aspirations and hopes?

These questions are relevant to our issue. If religious striving to gain self-awareness or a vision of the Reality were only a personal concern, based on the individual's own will and choice, uninfluenced by what transpires around him, we would be perfectly right in holding that a person on the path to self-knowledge need not bother himself about the social or political condition of the world. He should only confine himself to his sublime quest, indifferent to the state of society.

As a class, spiritual men seldom occupied themselves with the problems of the world in the past. They had no need to do so. The tacit understanding that those who had entirely dedicated themselves to the quest of the spirit, or the service of God, were a class apart and should be left to work their salvation was prevalent in olden times, when religion had a greater hold on the people. This allowed the seeker a certain immunity from harm and, at the same time, created a friendly feeling in the hearts of others to provide him with what he needed.

During recent times, however, a great change has occurred in the ideas about monasticism, about alms-giving to religious mendicants, and about the philosophy of religious striving as a whole.

The materialistic tendency of the time has invaded the sanctuary of ascetic religious life also. Critics do not hesitate to express their disapproval of a mode of life solely directed to one's own salvation, whatever that might be, without any productive benefit for the society.

An Answer to the Riddle of Existence

This is the age of reason. The very fundamentals of faith have been challenged by science. The empiricists demand an unrebuttable proof for the existence of God. The argument adduced by some spiritual teachers that the existence of God is self-evident and needs no proof is so lame that no sensible person can accept its validity. If the existence of God is so self-evident and needs no proof, why does half the world now deny His existence? Why is it then that great Indian sages, like Kapila and Buddha, did not subscribe to the idea of God?

Whatever might be the reason, the fact remains that anchorite life has lost much of its charm and also a good deal of homage and sympathy of the people. There is no doubt that monastic systems produced and continue to produce outstanding men and women whose contribution to the spiritual life of mankind has been immense.

But the process of change is resistless. Slowly the former inspiring and prestigious image of monastic life is being eroded by the hand of time. Soon it might become necessary to project a new image and a new ideal of the man of God, who has renounced the world to dedicate himself to the service of humankind.

Let us assume that, in a diminished form, monasteries, hermitages, cloisters, and ashrams still exist. It is clear that every individual, tormented by the thirst for spiritual knowledge, would not think of relieving it in a monastic institution. There are legions who would vastly prefer to quench it at their own place and in their own home. But can those myriads, imbued with an irrepressible desire to know more about themselves or to find an answer to the Riddle of Existence, easily find a solution in the present conditions of the world? Can they have the essential tranquility of mind necessary to gain transcendence? With newspapers, radio, and television shrieking themselves hoarse at all hours, how can an ardent aspirant close his eyes and ears to the harsh reality in order to compose his mind and lead it in the direction of God?

It is not only for the spiritual aspirant, but also for the ordinary man and woman, that the world presents a dilemma, which he must resolve as soon as practicable, to live a life of peace and contentment without an overhanging threat of instant disaster. The position created by technology and the armaments race has produced a milieu that is highly antagonistic to the evolution of the brain. Every human being is therefore a helpless victim to a ceaseless inner deterioration on account of the pernicious political and social climate. The world situation has assumed an urgency that no sensible human being can ignore any longer. In concluding their research, the authors of *The Limits to Growth*[*] write:

> The last thought we wish to offer is that man must explore himself—his goals and values—as much as the world he seeks to change. The dedication to both tasks must

---

[*] Published by Potomac Associates with the Club of Rome and MIT research teams.

be unending. The crux of the matter is not only whether the human species will survive, but even more whether it can survive without falling into a state of worthless existence.

But why after the highly optimistic faith reposed in technology has the world situation deteriorated so rapidly as to make even the survival of the species uncertain and doubtful? The terrible loss of life in the global wars fought in this century, the appalling massacres, and the awesome threat of a still greater approaching calamity are sufficient indications to make us wonder what flaw in the thinking and planning of the modern world has been responsible for the disasters suffered and the more frightful ones to come.

The Law Ruling Human Destiny

The aim of spiritual disciplines is not to make one insensitive to the environment or to the pain and suffering of fellow human beings. The one great lesson that the lives of all great spiritual teachers impart is that the greater the degree of illumination the more sensitive does the illuminated mind become to the sorrows of fellow beings and more resolutely does it act to alleviate the condition. The lives of Zoroaster, Buddha, Mahāvîra, Lao-tzu, Moses, Socrates, Christ, Mohammed, Shankaracharya, Guru Nanāk, Saint Teresa of Avila, Rama-Krishna, and Gandhi provide the models for what I say.

Selfish occupation with one's own salvation, when the world is burning, is not a sign of spiritual regeneration. The first effort of one who aspires to the vision of God is to purge his mind from egotistic thought and (as a Karma Yogi) set himself to the task of extinguishing the fire. It is for this reason that I am presenting the world situation in an objective way, to draw attention to the acute problems that need the effort of one and all of us to solve. The warnings that come from the subtler planes of creation are insistent. Mankind has flagrantly digressed from the Path of Evolution or "Dharma" pointed out by every Revealed Scripture. (The *Bhagavad-Gita* is explicit on this issue.)

But even those who believe in God and a spiritual order in the universe do not pay heed to the warning signs. We are all collectively acting against a mighty Law ruling human destiny. If our scholars, God men, thinkers, and social or political leaders have no knowledge about this Law, it does not mean that it does not exist. The great thinkers and potentates of the past had no awareness of the universal Law of Gravity until it was discovered by Newton.

Mankind has still to learn that there is an analogous Cosmic Law governing its behavior, and that is the Law of Kundalini—the Guardian of human existence and evolution. Insensibility to the present grave crisis, even on the part of the learned, is a sign of the mental stasis that has occurred. A state of apathy toward acute problems of life is a prominent symptom of senescence. A mental attitude of this nature among intellectuals is fatal to the balanced and harmonious progress of the race. It is for this reason that the future presents a forbidding and menacing aspect in clairvoyant visionary experiences. The awe-inspiring, dramatic events that shall transpire toward the end of this century will make the Law clearly known to the world.

CHAPTER TWO

The 125th verse of the tenth book of the *Rig Veda*, written some thirty-five hundred years ago, addresses Kundalini as Vak, the deity of speech. This means that from remote antiquity, it has been recognized that the real sign of Kundalini is the talent to write and speak wisely and beautifully from inspiration. In 1952, fifteen years after his awakening, Gopi Krishna published a small book of verse titled *From the Unseen*. It contained poems in several languages, some of which he didn't know at all, including German, French, Italian, and Persian, as well as English and his native Kashmiri.

In the preface he wrote, "All knowledge comes from the unfathomable depths of consciousness—depths unknown and unexplored . . . to find an outlet through the spring of the human mind." Taken largely from *The Shape of Events to Come*, this first chapter describes how words, whole sentences, and finished ideas came to him "like falling snowflakes that, from tiny specks high up, become clear-cut, regularly shaped crystals when nearing the eye."

ABOUT MY WAY OF WRITING

In order to explain how the material contained in my books was written, it is necessary to draw a picture of the present state of my mind. I have tried, as best as language can portray, to describe (in my autobiography)* the expansion in consciousness I experienced on the first day of the awakening of Kundalini in me more than forty years ago, in December 1937.

I still remember the experience vividly, as if it had happened yesterday. The extraordinary nature of the mental transformation undergone had such a powerful impact on my mind that an indelible imprint has been left on my memory. In that supreme moment, I felt myself—or in other words, my awareness—expanding in all directions. I felt as if I had become a vast area of consciousness in which the sensations coming from my senses and my body grew progressively less distinct, giving an impression of incorporeality to the expanded self.

Kundalini: The Evolutionary Energy In Man

Mystical experience is said to be incommunicable, because it is almost impossible to explain to one who has not had it what expansion of consciousness really means.

This now widely used expression, "expansion of consciousness," refers to the target of human evolution and represents the most prominent symptom experienced on the arousal of Kundalini.

My own case makes a strange story. I wonder if there is a parallel example in the world today. I ask this question of myself, because a few parallel cases could provide unchallengeable corroboration for what I state. I do not wish to be accorded any special recognition or credit for the state of cognition that I possess. It is the result of a long chain of transformative processes in my body over which I had no control.

I had started meditating at the age of seventeen, and side by side with meditation, I also began a course of self-discipline that was very necessary, as I had no experience in life as yet. So I somehow felt an urge within me to observe some ideals in my behavior, and I tried my utmost to conform to them. Though I meditated very intensively for the first few years, afterward I continued but not with so much intensity.

It was in my thirty-fourth year, seventeen years after starting the meditation, that I had my first experience of transcendental consciousness. It was in the winter, about the time of Christmas. I was meditating early in the morning when suddenly I found something giving way as if a new aperture had opened, and I felt an energy rising up my spinal cord. At first I was terrified, and my attention went to the sensation caused by the energy. At that moment the vision ceased. Then I again concentrated, and ultimately I managed to keep my attention focused at the crown of my head, while the energy rose upward and upward, through the spinal cord, to the neck and then into my head. I then suddenly found that a stream of silvery light was pouring into my brain.

There was a sound like thunder or like a waterfall in my ear, and it grew louder and louder. At the same time, I began to expand. I cannot describe exactly what I mean by this, but it seemed that my consciousness was now gaining a wider and wider space, and I was leaving my body behind and projecting myself, spreading myself, all around in the universe. My body grew dimmer and dimmer, and I could hardly hear any noises coming from the street. I remained totally engrossed in the vision that was now unfolding before me.

It was the vision of a silvery luster, alive, living, vibrant with life, conscious and spread all around me. The small self that was "I" seemed to become like a point of awareness, watching this great personality that had now developed and seemed to encompass the whole universe. I was like a small cork floating in an ocean of consciousness, aware of the whole surface at every point of the compass. I felt myself expanding more and more, and this expansion was attended by a happiness that is not possible to describe. I was in a state of jubilation, happiness, and elation that I had never experienced in my life before that time. It was an incredible spectacle, and I was completely baffled as to what had happened to me.

What I perceived at the height of the experience was an ocean of consciousness, an infinitely extended area of awareness, which made me feel as if I were spread everywhere, as if my body had been replaced by a bright ethereal mantle of light that accompanied me everywhere. I saw myself floating in a lustrous world of being in which the material world had lost its tangibility. Only pure consciousness persisted everywhere, with an overwhelming sense of rapture impossible to describe.

I continued to sit and to contemplate this vision with all the power of my attention. It was not I. The vision drew me to it. I was fascinated, and my whole attention was attracted to it as an iron filing is attracted to a magnet. I could not withdraw out of it and remained contemplating the vision for some time.

The process of contraction was as distinct as that of expansion. The unbounded ocean of awareness began to shrink, and the volume that my mind had attained began to diminish, until finally this circle of light again grew narrower and narrower. It began to contract, and I, who had now expanded immensely, came nearer and nearer to my original self and the earth, until I felt I was myself again, clearly aware of my body and the impressions coming from the outside world.

But the exquisite memory of the transformation that had taken place, wafting me to a ravishing state of existence I had never experienced before, has continued to be with me ever since. I knew I had been lifted up to another place of being, with all my faculties alert, and then dropped back at the place where I was before the incredible flight.

This extraordinary experience of the first day was repeated only once more before the onset of a long period of suffering and travail, which continued for years. During all that time I could never clearly understand the reason for it. All I knew was that, for some unknown reasons, my system was behaving in an abnormal way. The state of my mind altered between periods of high elation and dark depression, and I continued to vacillate between hope and despair.

It was not my own efforts that saved me from disaster or helped me through the grueling ordeal day in and day out for all those years, but my savior was a mysterious higher self, a superior personality, a divine presence that I could dimly perceive many years later, though even then never clearly make out. It was a personality most intimately connected with my own frail ego consciousness and yet above and beyond it, entirely unaffected by the grief I bore and the torment I endured.

About the end of this period, I felt an irresistible urge to write in verse. This urge culminated in a small booklet of poetry, written in nine languages, of which four were unknown to me. I had never written a line of poetry in my life and in normal conditions was incapable of writing even a few lines in rhyme and meter even if I tried for days. But now I found that finished lines of poetry, whole paragraphs, or even entire poems came to me in a flash, as if emerging from the surrounding emptiness. Sometimes I found it difficult to put them on paper, so rapid was the flow.

The manner in which I write resembles what some poets, philosophers, and even scientists have described as inspiration. They see whole passages, stanzas, poems, chapters of books, finished products of art, etc., flashing across their minds, or as Nietzsche has put it, virtually dropping into their laps. All they do is write down the material arising from the depths of the mind. It would make a very interesting field of study, because many of the great poets, composers, artists, and writers have clearly acknowledged this gratuitous gift and ascribed some of their works to it.

From the day I found myself established in this state of transport I never went back to the chaotic experiences of the past. The new awareness that invested every object and every scene I witnessed with a beauty and a glory I had never perceived before, instead of ceasing after a time, became a more and more stable and lasting feature of my consciousness. Today I live in a veritable paradise in my interior. The colors I see, as for instance the blue of the sky, are so lovely and bathed in a silvery radiance, and the music I hear is at times so melodious that if I did not restrain myself I might swoon with the sheer rapture of it.

I know that what I say might appear incredible, but there is ample material in the Upanishads and in the writings of great mystics, like Abinava Gupta and Shankaracharya and many others, that shows that such a condition of perennial beatitude is possible. Not only this, but soon after my attempts at versifying, I felt an irresistible urge to learn other languages. Unfortunately, utter lack of resources and the unsettled state of my physical health made it impossible for me to satisfy this desire and to engage the services of teachers for this purpose. I did not have even the means to educate my children properly or to provide myself with some of the articles of diet I needed.

This aggravated my health problems, and it was not until I was sixty-four years of age that I could command the means to meet my needs and to settle down to a peaceful and creative life. My first book was published in India in 1967, and since then fifteen more volumes have been printed and about a dozen more unfinished works await publication.

I do not claim that my poetry or my prose possess that excellence that is the hallmark of literary genius, but for one who had never been a poet or a writer all his life, the sudden acquisition of the gifts, at an advanced age, as happened in my case, is not an ordinary occurrence, and I view it in the same way as Newton viewed the fall of an apple as an indication of the universal law of gravity. I am presenting these few facts about my experience not for any personal reasons but on account of the tremendous scientific potential they possess.

When my autobiography was published, I expected trenchant criticism from the skeptics and a barrage of questions from the learned. But although the work has been translated and published in many languages, it has not excited even a fraction of the incredulity I had expected. On the contrary, other books on the subject have been published, a few by scientists, and what is more surprising, even Kundalini clinics have been opened to treat patients with ill effects from the arousal of this power, brought about by the practice of Yoga or other forms of spiritual discipline. The phenomenon has more or less been accepted, perhaps on account of the prevalence of occult traditions concerning this power in many parts of the earth.

Whatever the reason, the phenomenon of Kundalini has become well known. And because of its implications as a major factor in creativity and mental disorder, it stands in urgent need of a thorough scientific investigation, which has not been conducted so far. In order to gain an insight into the phenomenon of creativity, the proper course is to study the lives of the most outstanding examples of the gift, popularly known as geniuses. The study should also include the categories often excluded by the learned, namely concerning those who have evinced extraordinary gifts in the province of psychic phenomena and mystical experience. Why these categories have been omitted so far is because they do not fit in with the present-day conceptions about the mind and consciousness, which treat sentience as the result of biochemical processes of the brain.

Modern psychologists, including Jung, William James, and Maslow, when dealing with the inexplicable phenomenon of mystical experience or psychic faculties, often take refuge in the asylum of the subconscious, overlooking the fact that the subconscious, like the conscious, is a part of the human mind manifested by the brain. If this under-the-surface part of the mind is able to predict the future or to communicate with another mind at a distance, or to look into the past, it means that the mind has potentialities and possibilities that negate some of the fundamental concepts of modern science.

The same is true of inspiration, of poets, writers, and artists or flashes of discovery. It is evident that there is a category of mental phenomena about which, strictly speaking, science is completely in the dark. Instead of bringing these riddles into the open, in order to find a solution, every attempt is made to exclude them from discussion or to ignore them as if they did not exist at all. A striking example of this is provided by Sir Francis Galton. Although an infant prodigy at the age of two, he avoids discussion of this extraordinary gift in children in his work on genius. Even so, there have been many notable examples of it in modern times, as for instance Mozart, Dürer, Pascal, and others.

I have been led to the conclusion that Kundalini is the source of inspiration by comparing the creative process in myself with that reported or narrated by other writers, poets, painters, musicians, and the rest. I often write in full consciousness, weighing every word that flashes across my mind before putting it down on paper. But the material comes effortlessly, sentence after sentence, passage after passage, or line after line of poetry, usually rhymed. It seems as if completed sentences, couplets, or quatrains, already formed, are floating before my mind to be recorded.

Sometimes I am filled with awe at the way in which the creative process works. Whole pages or even chapters flash before my inner eye so rapidly that I am not able to write them down however hard I may try to do so. The gaps left are filled in later. As I have already stated, my whole inner being is now like a brilliantly lighted chamber of immeasurable dimensions. The moment I try to measure its limits, it expands farther and farther until I feel myself floating in a measureless void. In deeper moods, it is from this unbounded emptiness that the words and ideas seem to arise and vanish again after imprinting themselves upon my memory.

Like in other productive minds, my creative moods alternate with infertile periods, which vary in duration mainly according to my state of health. Based on prolonged study of my own amazing state, I can safely assert that during the productive periods, the pranic radiation, streaming into my brain, is purer or at least more in consonance with the creative work to be done. The periods of sterility occur when the radiation in some way falls short of the standard of purity or creativity needed for the purpose. The changes probably correspond to the periodic or cyclical alterations in the purity of the blood and the nerve tissues of my body and the brain. What subtle organic or hormonic ingredients are involved in these changes only prolonged research can determine. It is this variation in the pranic radiation that accounts for alteration in the productive moods of genius and ecstatic states in mystics and visionaries.

During the creative periods, I distinctly perceive that the ideas that flash across my mind and the words I use to express them come from the surrounding emptiness. In the formulation of ideas, the ego is never absent. I know that the idea is mine and that it is I who am the author of it. But both the "I" and the "idea" are not now confined within the narrow periphery of my individual mind but seem to be parts of a vast reservoir of thought encircling me. The ideas and the language for their expression emerge from this reservoir and, soon after, depending on the mood, disappear to sink back into it again.

It is not easy to explain the experience. It means that there is a thought world as there is a world of matter surrounding us. Access to the physical world is gained through the senses, but access to the thought world is won through mind itself. The thought world is as real, at least, as the material universe, and apparently far more extended and profound.

Thoughts have a material of their own. This material is unlike any substance we perceive through our senses or can conceive of with our intellect. Whenever we think, imagine, fancy, or dream we are using this incredible material from the thought world. Every human mind makes use of this ethereal stuff from birth to death without ever discovering the source from which it comes. Thoughts are more indestructible than matter; only because of the limitations imposed by the senses are we unable to perceive this material or to grasp its real nature.

In the normal state, we never perceive the thought world from which we draw the ideas or the mental pictures we evoke at our choice. In the superconscious state, in which entry to the thought world is gained, what is perceived is not an insensible world but an oceanic mind, a stupendous world of thought, a universe of life, a titanic intelligence spread everywhere from which we, too, draw our being.

I have no words to express the staggering nature of the experience. Try to picture a reservoir of mind that every moment supplies the material for the thoughts, fancies, emotions, calculations, and all other mental activity of five billion human beings on earth. Imagine further billions of inhabited planets in space, with countless other species of intelligent life, and you can frame a dim picture of the world to which our soul actually belongs and from which we draw our every breath and every thought.

The realm of creativity does not extend to the rational alone.

It extends into the suprarational also. For instance, there are well-attested cases of artistic, musical, or literary creations of exceptional mediums, done in trance conditions, without the conscious effort of the subject, known as automatism or automatic writing. They are more common than is supposed and much more in numbers than are known or publicized. Then there are the scientific discoveries made or literary compositions revealed in sleep to eminent scientists and writers. Again we have the historically authenticated phenomenon of wonder children or child prodigies who from an early age—say, from eight to twelve—show exceptional proficiency in a subject or art and surpass veterans who had devoted a lifetime to learn it.

For instance, there is no explanation for the riddle presented by Mozart, who was a musical prodigy as a child; Guru Nanak, the founder of Sikhism, who wrote mystical verses at eight; Janeshvar, the famous saint who wrote a monumental commentary on the *Bhagavad Gita* at the age of seventeen; Dürer, the famous German painter; Pascal; and others.

Similarly, there is the category of extraordinary psychic gifts, like the diagnostic skill of Edgar Cayce and the heroic abilities of Joan of Arc, a peasant girl who made herself famous in history by acting on the visions she saw and the voices she heard for which no rational explanation has been possible so far. In the modern treatises on creativity or genius, the cases of extraordinary psychic gifts, even though fully authenticated and proved, are usually omitted; also the cases of wonder children, though they have been a repeated phenomenon of history. Why this is done we have no means to know. It could be due to a prevailing bias against the suprarational and the paranormal that, if the ancient record is to be trusted, have been a constant feature of human experience from the earliest stages of the Egyptian civilization—that is, for a period of nearly seven thousand years, to this day.

Wonder, in the words of Socrates, is the beginning of philosophy. It is indubitably the beginning of science, too. To overlook phenomena that have excited wonder from the earliest stages of history—as, for instance, inspiration and prophetic revelations when discussing the subject of extraordinary ability or genius—is unscientific in the extreme because it tends to ignore a phenomenon that has been responsible for the greatest revolutions in thought for thousands of years.

There has been no other class of men that has influenced the human race or that has been so venerated and followed as the founders of great faiths, namely Moses, Buddha, Christ, Muhammad, and others, and yet they are seldom if ever made the subjects of study in books on genius and creativity. Why this is so no one is able to explain. Perhaps it is because of a prejudice against religion and all that it involves for mankind.

I am convinced that my own compositions in verse (*The Shape of Events to Come* and *The Way to Self-Knowledge* are two examples) come from a superhuman source. From the day I started to write in verse, I have had hints and visions of the awful events to come without interruption. I wish with all my heart and soul that mankind might be saved the horrors of another world war or the dreadful scenes of a natural calamity, but the message unmistakably points in the direction of an oncoming disaster. During these years, world conditions have deteriorated in a manner that is inexplicable. The race for superiority in armaments has so intensified, not only among the superpowers but also among the other nations, that it seems as if a kind of inner compulsion is driving the race toward a course that is disastrous for it.

The message contained in these writings is not a prophecy in the accepted sense of the term. It is an analysis of the present critical situation from the angle of evolution, brought about by our own neglect of spiritual laws. It is also a prognosis of the unhealthy mental conditions resulting from the evils rampant in society, which act as serious blocks in the evolution of the race.

I do not claim finality for the conclusions arrived at in my writings. No one in my position can. The research undertaken, the events to come, and the judgment of the progeny will determine how far I was right. I am giving out exactly what has been revealed to me in a paranormal state of awareness. In this transcendental state, the future, I believe, can be fairly discerned. It is in this state and in this state alone that revelation is possible, and hence has been a feature of certain specially gifted minds throughout the course of history. It is they who have been known as prophets, sages, and seers from remote periods of time.

The need for these specially endowed individuals has not ended now. On the contrary, it has become greater and more urgent to guide mankind to safety in a critical age. The guidance cannot come from unaided intellect. Human nature is so complex, the thoughts, acts, and aptitudes of people are so varied, and the interactions between natural forces are so incomputable that even the combined efforts of all the leading intellects of the earth cannot forecast the march of events even for a decade. But in the case of a gifted mind, one instantaneous flash of precognition can reveal events of the future, even a hundred years away.

Einstein could not reconcile himself to the uncertainty principle of Heisenberg or bring it into accord with his own theories. His view was, "God does not play with dice." But the uncertainty principle, based on quantum theory, is a part of the accepted thinking of the physicists of our day. At the root levels of creation, in terms of this principle, we live in a universe of high probabilities but not of absolute certainty.

The almighty Creator of the universe cannot be a machine in the same way as intelligent human beings are not machines. They have their individual will and choice, which they exercise every moment of their life. Where does this will, choice, and all the thinking of people come from? Not from the cortical matter, which is but the receptor of a transmission entirely beyond the range of our thought. This will, choice, and thinking come from the cosmic fount of mind. Since mind, like matter, is an element of creation, it follows that every thought we think has an existence of its own, in the same way as every particle of matter has its existence. But the stuff of which thoughts are made has a different formation, which is unintelligible to us. In this sense, it is correct to say that thoughts are things.

From this world of thought, along with our thinking and feeling, come our ideas of truth, goodness, compassion, charity, mercy, law, justice, forbearance, and forgiveness. Creative intelligence must, therefore, have all these attributes in an infinite measure, active on a cosmic scale. "What is here is there also," say the Upanishads.

The possibility that divine compassion and mercy might intervene to avert the catastrophe invited by man's own transgression or greatly diminish its severity is entirely consistent with the concept of an intelligent Creator.

The province of mercy is entirely in the hands of the Lord. Its mystery is inscrutable. The indications are that unexpected events, accidents, and unforeseen upheavals will combine to circumvent the self-destructive plans of rashly contending powers and quell the insurgence of a purblind, rebel intellect, with minimum harm to humanity. But even so, the damage done will be considerable. A limping race will haltingly set herself upon the task of reconstruction to establish a new order on the earth.

That at the height of her intellectual achievements mankind should be poised for suicide has something so unnatural in it that one cannot ascribe it to the normal behavior of an intelligent species. The leading nations are being driven to this entirely irrational course by a hidden psychological impulse about which we are ignorant at present.

We do not grasp the stupendous proportions of the almighty intelligence behind creation. The image drawn is too frequently of a magnified human personality. Our intellect cannot have a correct conception of an omnipotent intelligence that holds the whole of this unbounded creation in the palm of one hand. Any attempt to resist the almighty laws of this inconceivable power, on the part of human beings, is like the attempt of an ant to resist a tidal wave of the ocean. All we can do is fall on our knees with repentant hearts and with eyes bedimmed with tears seek forgiveness for our lapses in order to open the door for grace.

CHAPTER THREE

Scientist-philosopher Carl Friederich F. von Weizsacker, author of numerous books and recipient of several prestigious science awards, including the Max Planck Medal and the Goethe Prize, was one of a small group of leading physicists who worked against those who were attempting to develop an atomic bomb for Germany during World War II.

Director of the Max Planck Institute for Natural Science in Starnberg, Germany, Professor von Weizsacker has carried out extensive research on astrophysics and cosmology, galactic systems and the evolution of stars, quantum theory, quantum logic, and a unified theory of elementary particle physics with cosmology.

In this chapter, excerpted from his Introduction to *The Biological Basis of Religion and Genius*, von Weizsacker presents an analysis of Gopi Krishna's thought, and in doing so contributes greatly to its understanding and its effect.

PROFESSOR VON WEIZSACKER'S INTRODUCTION TO *THE BIOLOGICAL BASIS OF RELIGION AND GENIUS*

In early 1968, some German friends asked me to meet Pandit Gopi Krishna of Srinagar, Kashmir, who at that time was completely unknown to me. I was tempted to make excuses, pleading lack of time. Since my student years I have been fully aware of the fundamental significance of the Oriental tradition of meditation and philosophy. I felt close to it but waited a long time before I studied it seriously. It seemed to me that most of us, who have been born into Western culture, ought first to trace the innermost patterns of our culture until our own development itself would lead us into fellowship with Eastern culture.

The current flood of salvation literature, of traveling yoga masters, and of generally superficial imitations of Eastern practices in Western countries seems to me a rather desperate reaction to the crisis in our own consciousness, a false answer to a valid question.

Fortunately, I did overcome my initial reluctance. When the announced guest entered my room I felt in the fraction of a second:

This man is genuine. He was unassuming and sure of himself, a man who did not show his almost 70 years, who looked his partner firmly in the eyes, and was dressed in the native clothing of a Brahman from Kashmir (that light-skinned social class to which Nehru's family also belongs). He also answered precise questions precisely, in a sometimes surprising way and with a deeply human sincerity, which was often enhanced by a smile. His presence was good for me, and I could feel within me the traces of his simple and good emanations for as long as a month afterward. I received and read his first book, *Kundalini*, which is the story of his life. From my conversation with him and from the book I learned that he had spent almost his whole life in his native Kashmir. He had been a government official for decades. He is married, his three children are now also married, and to this day he has remained the head of his family in the classical Indian sense.

When I recently had the opportunity to visit him for a week in his simple, middle-class home in Srinagar, I saw how much he is an integral part of the society from which he comes. He is a revered leader of the Hindu minority, but he is also respected by the Muslims and has many friends among them. For many years he served as director of a program of assistance for the poor. When one visits a village in his company, many of the peasants recognize him and greet him with enthusiasm. At considerable risk to himself and with great personal courage he has successfully worked for the abolition of outmoded religious customs in his society. Thus, he succeeded in changing old ways so that it is now customary to permit widows to remarry, and he has also been instrumental in reducing the intolerable financial burdens connected with the marriage of daughters. It may not be clear to the Western reader how much of a break with tradition this involves. If one knew no more than this, one would say that Gopi Krishna is indeed an outstanding local leader deserving of our respect and affection.

The basic content of my conversation with him and of his book did, however, turn out to be something quite different. It concerned a shattering, life-threatening experience of a this worldly/otherworldly force that reshapes one's whole personality, the force he calls by its traditional Indian name, Kundalini. I am going to discuss the nature of this experience in another part of this Introduction. Here I am limiting myself to its biographical impact. Gopi Krishna has been meditating since his 17th year, at first out of an impulse for personal purification. When he was 34 he experienced a breakthrough to a new, enlarged, and blissful consciousness. But the process initiated then resulted in a physical and spiritual transformation that threatened his very existence like an all-consuming fire. He was looking for a master (a guru in the traditional Indian sense) but found no one to help him.

Fortunately, his ego managed to stay in control of the processes set in motion, which after twelve years resolved themselves into a permanent inner brightness and into a new sense of vitality. He now felt like a new man endowed with objective gifts that he had never had before, such as the gift of inspired writing; he felt like a man who could turn to his fellow men with a new capacity for help and guidance. He actively discouraged a rapidly spreading movement in his native region to establish him as a famous enlightened one, since he was critical of this kind of fervor; his way of dealing with his fellow men lay in the realm of controllable reality. Yet he was sure that he had experienced the awakening of Kundalini described in classical literature. He studied the writings of the meditative and mystic traditions as one who understood their meaning. After he had spent decades in self-examination he decided to write about his experiences for the world, particularly the world of modern science. His first book was a description of his personal experience. The second book, which is being presented here in Religious Perspectives, constitutes an introduction to the objective lessons he plans to teach in future works.

I myself am writing an Introduction to this book *(The Biological Basis of Religion and Genius)* because I would like to contribute to its understanding and its effect. To do so it is necessary that I also point out its weaknesses. Those of us who read this book as modern intellectuals note a certain naivete on the part of the author. He is a mixture of a wholly traditional and a wholly modern man. His values, particularly the moral values of the tradition in which he grew up, are self-evident for him. He is incapable of even a trace of that cynicism with which every, even the most sincere, modern intellectual has been inoculated with and which has infected the whole world of contemporary thinking.

We intellectuals naively assume that those who lack this inoculation are living in ignorance of something decisively important. That may well be, but in this instance we shall have to move away from our own naivete in order to comprehend the potential insights of another kind of naivete. On the other hand, Gopi Krishna is quite modern in the sense that he deliberately addresses himself to the modern consciousness, particularly to modern science. He is far removed from Hindu orthodoxy, and I have seen him get into irresolvable differences of opinion with Europeans who tried to play the Indian tradition against that of the modern West.

The problem arising here is that his knowledge of European intellectual concepts and of modern science is autodidactic. He does not always clearly distinguish between the customary academic classification of a scientific doctrine and its more subtle meanings. He is therefore not always a competent analyst, but he is something far more important: he is an eyewitness to the truth he represents. Even his sometimes broadly flowing stream of words, a style not unusual in India, is indicative of the way he composes his writings, which are not the result of reflection but flow from the compelling force of a spontaneous, self-repeating awareness.

Gopi Krishna sees the ancient religious writings permeated by hints of a spiritual law. To discover that law he set out on his quest long ago. His contributions to the problem today are not just vague speculations but above all accounts of his own personal experience. His first two chapters give the personal background of this personal experience. According to his autobiography, *Kundalini*, it was precisely the insufficiency of religion and science that agitated him in his younger years. It caused him to search for an inner opening toward a higher, spiritual reality by constant meditation, which he repeated daily before sunrise each morning.

The Experience of Gopi Krishna

"One morning during the Christmas of 1937 I sat cross-legged in a small room in a little house on the outskirts of the town of Jammu, the winter capital of the Jammu and Kashmir State in northern India. I was meditating with my face toward the window, on the east through which the first gray streaks of the slowly brightening dawn fell into the room. Long practice had accustomed me to sit in the same posture for hours at a time without the least discomfort, and I sat breathing slowly and rhythmically, my attention drawn toward the crown of my head, contemplating an imaginary lotus in full bloom, radiating light.

"I sat steadily, unmoving and erect, my thoughts uninterruptedly centered on the shining lotus, intent on keeping my attention from wandering and bringing it back again and again whenever it moved in any other direction. The intensity of concentration interrupted my breathing; gradually it slowed down to such an extent that at times it was barely perceptible. My whole being was so engrossed in the contemplation of the lotus that for several minutes at a time I lost touch with my body and surroundings. During such intervals I used to feel as if I were poised in mid-air, without any feeling of a body around me. The only object of which I was aware was a lotus of brilliant color, emitting rays of light. This experience has happened to many people who practice meditation in any form regularly for a sufficient length of time, but what followed on that fateful morning in my case, changing the whole course of my life and outlook, has happened to few.

"During one such spell of intense concentration I suddenly felt a strange sensation below the base of my spine, at the place touching the seat, while I sat cross-legged on a folded blanket spread on the floor. The sensation was so extraordinary and so pleasing that my attention was forcibly drawn toward it. The moment my attention was thus unexpectedly withdrawn from the point on which it was focused, the sensation ceased. Thinking it to be a trick played by my imagination to relax the tension, I dismissed the matter from my mind and brought my attention back to the point from which it had wandered.

"Again I fixed it on the lotus, and as the same image grew clear and distinct at the top of my head, again the sensation occurred. This time I tried to maintain the fixity of my attention and succeeded for a few seconds, but the sensation extending upward grew so intense and was so extraordinary as compared to anything I had experienced before, that in spite of myself my mind went toward it, and at that very moment it again disappeared. I was now convinced that something unusual had happened for which my daily practice of concentration was probably responsible.

"I had read glowing accounts, written by learned men, of great benefits resulting from concentration, and of the miraculous powers acquired by yogis through such exercises. My heart began to beat wildly, and I found it difficult to bring my attention to the required degree of fixity. After a while I grew composed and was soon as deep in meditation as before.

"When completely immersed I again experienced the sensation, but this time, instead of allowing my mind to leave the point where I had fixed it, I maintained a rigidity of attention throughout. The sensation again extended upward, growing in intensity, and I felt myself wavering; but with a great effort I kept my attention centered on the lotus. Suddenly, with a roar like that of a waterfall, I felt a stream of liquid light entering my brain through the spinal cord.

"Entirely unprepared for such a development, I was completely taken by surprise; but regaining self-control instantaneously, I remained sitting in the same posture, keeping my mind on the point of concentration. The illumination grew brighter and brighter, the roaring louder; I experienced a rocking sensation and then felt myself slipping out of my body, entirely enveloped in a halo of light. It is impossible to describe the experience accurately. I felt the point of consciousness that was myself growing wider, surrounded by waves of light. It grew wider and wider, spreading outward while the body, normally the immediate object of its perception, appeared to have receded into the distance until I became entirely unconscious of it.

"I was now all consciousness, without any outline, without any idea of a corporeal appendage, without any feeling, or sensation coming from the senses, immersed in a sea of light simultaneously conscious and aware of every point, spread out, as it were, in all directions without any barrier or material obstruction. I was no longer myself, or to be more accurate, no longer as I knew myself to be, a small point of awareness confined in a body, but instead was a vast circle of consciousness in which the body was but a point, bathed in light and in a state of exaltation and happiness impossible to describe.

"After some time, the duration of which I could not judge, the circle began to narrow down. I felt myself contracting, becoming smaller and smaller, until I again became dimly conscious of the outline of my body, then more clearly; and as I slipped back to my old condition, I became suddenly aware of the noises in the street, felt again my arms and legs and head, and once more became my narrow self in touch with my body and surroundings. When I opened my eyes and looked about, I felt a little dazed and bewildered, as if coming back from a strange land completely foreign to me. The sun had risen and was shining full on my face, warm and soothing.

"I tried to lift my hands, which always rested on my lap, one upon the other, during meditation. My arms felt limp and lifeless. With an effort I raised them up and stretched them to enable the blood to flow freely. Then I tried to free my legs from the posture in which I was sitting and to place them in a more comfortable position but could not. They were heavy and stiff. With the help of my hands I freed them and stretched them out, then leaned back against the wall, reclining, in a position of ease and comfort."*

This report is the beginning of Krishna's book *Kundalini*. I thought it imperative to cite it verbatim. At the risk of belaboring the self-evident I would like to draw the reader's attention to a few notable features of this report. First, there is the accuracy of self-observation, especially the description of physical phenomena. The author retains his orientation and communicates it to the reader. Year and season, place and hour of the day, bodily posture, and state of consciousness are duly noted.

The physiological location of the phenomenon is the central nervous system: spine and brain. The sensation originates at the base of the spine and, as the result of concentration, moves upward and penetrates the brain like a roaring stream of light. Now, consciousness expands spatially and becomes much larger than the body, corporeality disappears, and there is an experience of light and unspeakable bliss. Time also has vanished—"how long it had lasted, I couldn't say"—and after awhile the circle contracts again, consciousness again becomes aware of its limits, he opens his eyes; the whole experience has taken but a fraction of the time from dawn to sunrise, a space of time particularly short in the tropics. Laboriously he regains mastery of his limbs, arms, and legs; he leans his back against the wall, relaxed.

Further on in the text there is a sketch of the objective prerequisites for this experience: seventeen years of practice in meditation; the objective symbol of divine consciousness in the image of the thousand-leaf lotus crowning the head; the ancient tradition that the "serpentine force" of Kundalini rests at the base of the spine coiled into three and a half windings and that if it is awakened it transforms consciousness.

Against this background it is worth noting that in Gopi Krishna's report there is a threefold interplay of question and answer

---

* *Kundalini, the Evolutionary Energy in Man,* pp. 11-13. Revised edition copyright 1970 in Great Britain by Vincent Stuart & John M. Watkins Ltd., London. Used by permission of Robinson & Watkins.

between human consciousness, the unmoved lotus, and the awakening serpent. Consciousness concentrates on nothing but the lotus. It required seventeen years to purify and fortify one's concentration to the point where the serpent stirs from its slumber. The bliss of its awakening, experienced in the form of physical sensation, distracts consciousness from the lotus and, behold, the serpent recoils and the experience vanishes. Not on itself does the serpent want to focus attention, but only on the lotus blossom. When consciousness finally manages this, the serpent rises up to the lotus like a torrent moving through the seat of consciousness.

If, as a hint for Western readers, I may be permitted for a moment to substitute our metaphysical terms "God," "man," and "nature," which have lost so much of their meaning for us—for the terms "lotus," "consciousness," and "serpent," then we would have to spell out Gopi Krishna's experience as follows: Nature seeks unity with God through man and in the particular man who does not look toward her but only toward God. The man who opens up that path for her is blessed by nature with the torrent of her bliss, with the realization of a new sphere of consciousness.* Obviously, Gopi Krishna did not reflect on all this at that moment, rather he experienced it as an unexplained fact.

Anyone who thinks that the experience opened up a path to happiness for the author has failed to note carefully certain hints already contained in the account we have cited above. After the experience, the author's limbs were stiff and useless. The book goes on to tell how the following day was spent in restlessness and exhaustion, how sleep refused to come in the subsequent night, and how a weakened repetition of the experience the next morning left the author in an even greater state of exhaustion. After a few days he lost his power of concentration and with it also any renewed experience of bliss and his previous capacity for living a well ordered everyday life. What did remain was an ever-growing inner stream of fire in every nerve, sexual excitement, thundering sounds, a maelstrom of copper-colored lights wildly rushing into each other, an unbearable, dry, burning inner brightness by day and night.

---

* Here, it must be noted that according to the conventional tradition of Kundalini Yoga the serpentine power may also be raised to the level of lower centers, hence to lower goals, as for example to the mere purpose of revitalizing the sexual or vital potency of a person. Gopi Krishna himself explains the worldly genius of the artist and the scientist as a raising of Kundalini to the second-highest center. According to tradition, however, only a raising of the power to the highest center leads to the mystic consciousness.

To his horror he was losing even the most elementary feelings of human contact, his love for his wife and children. The account of this development in the book appears to be supported by the fact that it lacks the definite structure of the portion cited earlier. Rather, it describes in trying, confusing, repetitious language the deadly, torturous sensations and struggles that the conscious personality of the author carried on against this maelstrom for two months with unbelievable outward discipline but with a feeling of ebbing strength. (He told only *one* person what was going on within him.)

He tried to understand what was happening to him with every intellectual means at his disposal. In the yoga literature available to him he found a description of the awakening of Kundalini. In spite of constant doubts he came to recognize his own experience with growing certainty. But the literature, which praised the phenomenon as the gift of a higher power, barely hinted at the dangers involved. It told of three channels through which the Power can raise: the central one, called *Sushumna,* which is the one properly intended for it, and two side channels, which Gopi Krishna now identifies with the sympathetic and parasympathetic nervous systems. *Pingala,* the right side channel, is linked with the sun, with heat and excitement. *Ida,* the left one, represents the moon, coolness and restraint. If the power rises up in one of the side channels only, it can be deadly because of "heat" or "cold." In his youth, Gopi Krishna now says, the hot side of his physical make-up had been strongly overactive, while the cool side had been under active.

In his extreme need, which seemed to have insanity as the only possible outcome, it occurred to him that the power might have risen within him only by way of the hot channel. With all his remaining strength of consciousness he therefore concentrated on the left, the cool side. Then, as if it had been waiting for this fateful moment, a miracle occurred.

There was a sound, as if a nerve were tearing. "Suddenly, a silver vein ran crisscross through my spine just like the slithering motions of a white serpent in quick flight, which brought a brilliant, cascading shower of radiant vital force into my brain." He had been saved; sleep was returning to him and he slowly recovered.

His First Attempts at Writing Poetry

Early in 1950 Gopi Krishna experienced a final transition to a stable consciousness, open to, yet not dependent on, the outside world. The transition occurred in connection with his inspired writing. He had completely abandoned his active meditating, but he would occasionally and without effort permit himself to be submerged into the ocean of consciousness surrounding him. He had never had any interest in poetry.

Now he was feeling a desire for poetry. He recited to himself mystical verse he liked, attempted to write, and one day at the center of a bridge in the middle of a crowd of people there flowed "past my eyes like radiant writing in the air, which vanished as fast as it had come, two lines of a marvelous poem in Kashmiri... like a mighty presence rising from nowhere, embracing me and overshadowing all objects around me."

On that same day Gopi Krishna entered a cosmic consciousness that turned whatever he had experienced as explosive and fiery twelve years ago into definite reality which was "like an ocean of life moving from within." I am not going to reproduce the account of this awareness here. I shall return to it later, for this transcends the biographical and properly belongs to the subject itself. But this is the experience that induced Gopi Krishna to write poetry.

The first lines that came to him were a continuation of the couplet that had appeared before his eyes on the bridge. Then he wrote additional Kashmiri poems. A few days later poems appeared in Urdu, then in Panjabi. Gopi Krishna knew all these languages.

> But my astonishment knew no bounds when a few days later I received instructions to prepare myself to receive verses in Persian. I had never read the language nor could I speak it. I was waiting in breathless excitement, and immediately following this forewarning several Persian verses flashed through my brain.... Since the language of Kashmiri is rich in Persian words, I found it easy to understand those that were current in my native language.
>
> After I had exerted a sufficient measure of concentration and effort I finally succeeded in writing down these

lines. But there were many blank spaces, which I was only able to fill in and correct much later.

Next there followed a poem in the German language, a language which even today is completely unknown to him consciously, a French and an Italian poem, and finally a few lines in Sanskrit.

I can feel the inevitably growing annoyance of my scientifically trained readers, for I felt the same way when I read this account. One is inclined to read this story as the twelve-year history of an identity crisis of a sensitive personality, which borders the psychotic. At the same time one must admit that a man who has lived through such a crisis knows a few things, which may be of importance to the rest of us. But why does this story have to end in miracles? Would anything be lacking in a mature and inspired personality if he were to write poems in just those languages he has learned? It was difficult for me to overcome my scientific skepticism, which has been schooled in the psychology of reliable witnesses. I openly admit that reading this particular section of the book I felt for the first time: "Here the imaginative memory is running away with the author; I'd like to see the German poem before I believe it."

But I must honor the facts. Since then I have seen the poem, for it was published privately in 1952. The German poem is everything but a perfect dictation of a—by human standards—perfect intelligence. It is, if one may say so, touching. The poem is written in erratic German, scarcely adequate in expression, reminiscent of a folk song, a naive communication of an unquestionable experience. In view of the cynicism of intellectual critics I don't feel justified in reproducing the whole poem. A few lines out of context may serve as an example:

> *Ein schöner Vogel immer singt*
> *In meinem Herz mit leisem Ton...*
> *Und wenn vergiest der Nachtwind auf*
> *Die grünen Gräser seine Tränen, ...*
> *Dann der Vogel wacht.**

Just as the German poem is German in the way of a German

---

* A beautiful bird always sings
In my heart with a soft voice ...
And when the night wind sheds
Its tears on the green grass,
Then the bird is watching.

folk song, so the Italian poem is written like an Italian folk song: It rhymes *cuore* with *amore*. Although the rhyme patterns are naive, the English poem expresses moral imperatives to the nations of the world in a voice of great prophecy:

> O people of the world unite
> And pave the way to peace sublime;
> Divided you yourself invite
> Disastrous wars, unrest and crime.

What makes this poetic phenomenon possible and what purpose does it serve? I do not know. Honor the incomprehensible!

What followed next in Gopi Krishna's life was the period of intense, sensitive, and wise service to society I mentioned in the first section of this Introduction, a demonstration of restored health and clear thinking. After this period he also studied traditional yoga in search of an explanation of what he was certain he had experienced. In his 70th year Gopi Krishna tried to draw the attention of Western science, particularly of medicine, to the phenomena he had experienced in order to point out their significance. This period is also the point of departure for a later, formally much better, prophetic poem in English describing the horrors of a war that he believes the current course of mankind will inevitably bring about.

According to Gopi Krishna's interpretation, the poem is not intended as an actual prophecy that reads the future as if it had already happened, but it predicts the inescapable consequences of what is happening today. We talked about this at my first meeting with him. At that time he said simply: "The nations of the earth will be united. But war is inevitable." He meant a world war. He expressed what I had been feeling for a long time but had not dared to think about clearly. Indeed, we cannot escape thinking of it that way: War is inevitable unless what is necessary happens. But what is necessary?

In view of the importance of this question we can understand Gopi Krishna's urgent desire to share with the world that which he has experienced as necessary. The story of his life is more than the history of a pathological disturbance with a happy end only if it provides us with empirical data to understand an objective situation. This objective element is more than a simple moral appeal that we already know to be ineffective. The question is, Why do people act morally or immorally? In Gopi Krishna's view, the point at a spiritual law.

What is unique about his view is that this spiritual law is at the same time a biological law. That is why it must be tested in terms of a mode of questioning proper to our natural sciences. He is anxious to have each one of his assertions tested by independent authorities. He is particularly interested in an empirical test. Those who know Western science are aware that it tends to confront almost exclusively only those problems for which it is theoretically prepared, at least in terms of the conceptual framework of the problem. What follows is intended to assist in such a preparation.

The Biological-Medical Aspect

Gopi Krishna's biological view may be briefly summed up conceptually. The spiritual law is by its very nature biological law as well. It is the law of evolution. Although to my knowledge Krishna does not explicitly say so anywhere, he does imply that the lower is designed to develop into the higher and that in fact it does so develop. To conceptualize this process of evolution he uses two concepts taken from traditional Indian thought: *Prana* and Kundalini.

Prana is the all-penetrating, subtle life substance. *Prana* is material, composed of exceedingly fine stuff, as it is occasionally described. Gopi Krishna considers the materiality of *Prana* very important and likes to support this in conversation by citing the well-known line from the Upanishads: " *Prana* comes from nutrition." But at the same time *Prana* appears as a substance belonging to the soul; according to Gopi Krishna, *Prana* is the food of developing human consciousness. Finally, *Prana* is something like the omnipresent energy of the highest cosmic intelligence. *Prana* meaningfully builds all of life according to a plan that is hidden from us, yet partially disclosed to a searching view.

The Western scientist faced with such concepts is apt to admit his confusion that—as long as he is sure of his own conceptual basis—he will casually blame on "those prescientific Hindu views." Our natural sciences today, particularly biology and medicine, are based on a strictly Cartesian separation of matter from consciousness. As long as we believe in the methodological necessity of this separation we are bound to argue, "If *Prana* claims to be matter, then we have to keep it strictly separate from such concepts as consciousness; otherwise *Prana* would belong to the realm of psychology and has nothing to do with physics." Now this point of view is a relic of a way of thinking, which in its basic conception is considered to be highly fragile even by many of those who cannot find anything better to take its place.

Since the formulation of quantum theory, physics no longer holds this point of view but it has obvious problems in formulating a better one. The cybernetic attempt to simulate psychic phenomena with the help of material models is based on a belief in unity that is difficult to articulate. In the last analysis, I do not consider it detrimental that in the practice of behavioral research we do in fact hardly ever succeed in sticking to purely behavioral language and to avoid all "subjective" or "anthropomorphic" expressions. It seems to me that at this point practice is smarter than the theory by which it explains itself. The evolutionary potency is called Kundalini. It is closely linked with sexual potency as indicated by the location of the "serpent" in close proximity to the sex organs.

The evolutionary force functions in two separate stages. In animals it functions directly by way of sexual reproduction. In their case the more highly developed are physical descendants of the less developed. In the case of man there is a development of consciousness, which newly builds up in each individual on the basis of his physical equipment, especially the central nervous system. This evolution of consciousness has its own two stages. Today all men have normal self consciousness in common, but Gopi Krishna takes a hypothetical look at prehistoric times, when our normal consciousness may have been manifest in the higher anthropoids only sporadically and as a deviation from the then normal state.

The higher stage of consciousness even to this day manifests itself only in ingenious and mystically gifted individual persons who often feel lost and homeless among their own fellow beings and in their everyday consciousness, shaped by ideas based on societal norms as H. C. Andersen's "ugly duckling." It is Gopi Krishna's thesis that the development of consciousness is also nurtured by the sexual powers contained in Kundalini. In (his autobiography) he describes how, in his own personal experience, the substance of his seed or its *Prana* penetrates the nervous system and nourishes the nerves that are becoming the instruments of higher consciousness.

The modern scientist is again going to hold his breath at this description and ask himself whether he should continue to follow the argument. Let us try to break down the problem. It has been a thesis of European science since the nineteenth century that the development of animals occurs through lines of physical descent, a thesis which Gopi Krishna as well as other evolutionist Indian thinkers (especially Shri Aurobindo) simply have adopted. But the notion that there is a special "force of evolution" contradicts a dominant doctrine in contemporary biology, the Darwinian theory of natural selection. This conceals a very subtle theoretical problem, which I shall consider later. For now, the modern biologist may acclimate himself to Gopi Krishna's manner of speaking by a change in terminology. The material substructure of development in contemporary genetics is chromosomes. These are passed on from generation to generation through the reproductive cells. In that sense animals have the material "force of evolution" located in their sex organs.

We do not feel that there is a conceptual problem in the assertion that man, quite apart from possible further biological evolution, has consciousness as the basis of his development. It is "the nature of man to have history." Due to the influence of sociological thinking we see this development above all in the transformation and renewal of cultural traditions transmitted by society. Both sides agree that there is such a social development. But Gopi Krishna's interest does not lie in the social interactions through which this development takes place. In a way that may just as well be called personal as biological, he is interested in individual consciousness as the carrier of this development. Here he does depart from the doctrine prevailing in the modern sociologized West in two ways, mildly in one instance and sharply in the other.

The milder departure is in keeping with our classical historiography. He stresses more emphatically than we do at present the historical role of outstanding personalities without, however, isolating them from the social process. This almost certainly reflects, at least in part, the bias of the historiography, which influenced him in his youth. But mature judgment will admit that this is no more than a question of differing nuances. Who can deny the force exerted on the course of history by such diverse personalities as Gandhi and Hitler in this century alone or question the influence of men like Kant and Marx, Plato and Shankara, Christ and Buddha, on the thoughts and actions of men in past centuries?

At the center of his entire argument Krishna places an evolution of the organ of consciousness, which can be described in physiological terms. Our sciences know nothing whatever of such an evolution. This is the field of contest: We enter the fray with a preliminary skirmish by emphasizing first a number of parallels that can be assimilated to our way of thinking and may even be surprisingly similar. Considered from a purely psychological point of view (something Gopi Krishna, of course, does not do), his thesis of the fundamental importance of sexuality in the formation of consciousness directly reminds us of Freudian teaching.

Where Gopi Krishna speaks of an elevation of the seminal fluid in language that must seem purely symbolic to the psychologist, Freud speaks of the sublimation of the libido. The latter is more abstract and somewhat obscures the fact that these are essentially the same concepts. Freud treats libido like a substance to which a principle of conservation may be applied; and what does sublimate mean, if not elevate or rise up? More interesting than this rough parallel, however, is the difference between the two views.

For Gopi Krishna evolution is essentially determined by its goal. For him sexual potency is the "nourishment" of a higher structure. Freud, on the other hand, represents a form of psychological reductionism. The culture he loves and defends is for him "really" sublimated libido, just as for the classical atomist a crystal is "really" a mass of atoms arranged in a pattern and for the biological physicalist a bird of paradise is "really" an orderly system of organic molecules.

I do believe that it is quite difficult to articulate this contrast clearly and that it may possibly disappear altogether on precise reflection. But the trouble with the contending representatives of both points of view is exactly that they fail to engage in such precise reflection.

Gopi Krishna talks about the biological basis of religion and genius, which is the area where his thought may find its principal application. He sees religion primarily in the figure of the religious genius. His theme is not everyday religion but the founder of religion, who has brought about everyday religion in the first place, and the mystic who has left it behind. Even negative manifestations of creativity are included.

Let us speak specifically of rational understanding, particularly in the sciences. It is customary to present science as a system of more or less logical inferences from either axioms or experiences. That is the image of science as a fortress and the way it is defended against criticism once it has been discovered. But it is not being discovered that way. It is a well known phenomenon in mathematics that one "sees" a theorem prior to its proof, an intended structure prior to the formulated sentence and seemingly incoherent segments of a proof prior to the completed proof. In the empirical sciences, Thomas Kuhn (*The Structure of Scientific Revolutions*) has demonstrated the leading role of paradigms that initially define what it is that can be scientifically examined. An individual experience, then, is nothing but a key on a keyboard we have built, which we may press and whose selection we allow nature to make in the process of questioning her. The archaeologist Ludwig Curtius's last word was an admonition called out to a visitor in Rome who saw him in the day of his death: "And don't forget, one only sees what one knows." Science, according to Konrad Lorenz, is essentially the recognition of form, and this recognition of form is the nature of a creative act. We "make" the form by recognizing it; and we recognize it by making it.

From this point let us return to the level of "great" creativity. A great scientific discovery is the recognition of a particularly simple and fundamental form, which heretofore had been hidden in a chaos of appearances and misunderstood theories. It is often described as an inspiration or a special gift of grace, which comes to the researcher when and as it pleases, like an answer from "another authority" and then almost without effort on his part. It is never viewed as the inevitable result of his research effort. Here we find the often disturbing and happy experience: "It is not I; I have not done this." Still, in a certain way it is I—yet not the ego of will but of a more comprehensive self. Those who can sense this may find a like experience in ordinary thinking and acting: How little do we know of the conditions for the success of even the simplest thought, the simplest step or activity?

What Is Evolution?

In the foregoing I have tried to present to the Western reader in as accessible a form as possible Gopi Krishna thought and his conceptual and empirical material, which, stemming from ancient India, often seems strange to us. A certain amount of "spoon-feeding" in the form of my own reflection on the material has been inevitable but this was included as matter of service to the reader. This approach cannot go beyond an effort of submitting the author's theses for discussion and possible examination in accordance with his wishes. In the following I would at least like to indicate how I see these theses in relation to a philosophy of nature and history that I have be trying to develop from exclusively Western premises. Because of space limitations I have to express myself stenographically and, fully aware of the poor style this implies, refer the reader to my own publications.

The opposition of nature and history to designate the qualitative leap from the animal to man in my view constitutes a misleading conception. I prefer to speak of the "history of nature." In this I remain close to the concept of evolution for which, in the final analysis, Gopi Krishna as well as Aurobindo and Teilhard de Chardin are indebted to the evolutionism of the nineteenth century. The spiritualizing of this concept, which we find in all three of these thinkers, seems to me inescapable if man is included in evolution as the spiritual being he happens to be. At this point, however, there is the danger of a conceptual short circuit between vitality and spirit, which keeps many a critical mind from getting too close to this form of philosophy. Trusting in the Spirit which leads us into all truth, I therefore propose to proceed with extreme caution.

First, I do not share the hostility of all the spiritual evolutionists against Darwinism. It seems to me that we should not condemn the theory of selection but understand it.[*] According to that theory evolution, just like thermodynamic irreversibility, is based on the "historicity of time," which manifests itself among other things in the openness of the future and the accomplished fact of the past. The philosophical riddle is time; apart from it there is no need to introduce further riddles into an interpretation of evolution.

---

[*] *The History of Nature*, lectures six to ten (Chicago, 1950); *The Relevancy of Science*, Part I (London, 1964); *The Unity of Nature*, Part III (Munich, 1971).

Specifically, this means that the growth of the number and differentiation of forms does not only fail to contradict the second law of thermodynamics but that, under certain conditions that are fulfilled in the real world, the former may even be derived logically from the latter. We may say that the "energy" of evolution is nothing but the "flowing of time" itself viewed as the inescapability of the future. The "biologism" of the evolutionary thinkers then is nothing but the idea that the historicity of time manifests itself already in the organic sphere of life. Their "spiritualism" signifies, on the one hand, that even the spirit obeys the structure of time insofar as it appears in time. On the other hand, it implies the claim that time itself should be understood spiritually.

An approach in this direction is the attempt—which at first glance seems to lead in the opposite direction—of rendering visible the complete unity of nature by deriving biological concepts from physical concepts. The central concept in a logical analysis of this context is the concept of information. Virtual information is entropy. The growth of forms is a growth of virtual information, hence a growth of entropy. Molecular biology and cybernetics raise hopes for a reduction of biological to physical laws. But does not this elevate materialism to the throne?

Physics and Time

The question is what we mean by "matter." For the physicist this can hardly be defined in terms other than "what satisfies the laws of physics." But what do the laws of physics tell us? Here I can only hint at an attempt to understand physics. The reader, who considers this section a specialty, may pass it by. Physics as an empirical science historically develops into unified theory. I think that we must find the reason why theory as such is possible in the unity of theory and that this unity, in turn, is based on conditions which make experience possible. Experience means learning from the past for the future. It is possible only in time. The structure of time is the basis of unity for physics. This structure must be conceptually analyzed by a logic of temporal propositions and a theory of probability as the form of an empirical prediction of the future. The use of the concept of probability in physics determines the structure of its two fundamental theories, which are mutually related, quantum theory and thermodynamics. They are mutually related insofar as statistical thermodynamics presupposes an elementary theory and also because the concept of measurement in quantum theory cannot be explained apart from the thermodynamic concept of irreversibility. In a stage we have not yet reached these two theories therefore ought to merge into one. Finally, the flanking theories of the structure of space, of elementary particles, and of the universe ought to be derivable as the consequences of a semantically consistent interpretation of quantum theory.

Here, too, the basic approach is temporal, and I now call it temporal finiteness. Quantum theory is a theory of probabilistic prediction of decisions about contingent alternatives (measurements). Up to any given time only a finite number of alternatives are capable of being decided (the finite factualness of the past), but the number of future alternatives still to be decided is unlimited (openness of the future). This results at any given time in a finite dimensional quantum theoretical phase space, which may be represented by the smallest physical objects (elementary particles) in a compact, expanding regular space.

This hypothetical approach is philosophically significant because it accounts for all of physics as a theory of prognosticating the probability of alternatives that can be empirically decided. Even without any further hypothetical considerations it is clear that this falls within the scope of quantum theory. This is often considered a kind of observer-related subjectivism. On the other hand, this kind of physics is undoubtedly inter subjective: different observers can only have experiences that are mutually compatible, unless they are in error. We cannot think of a single observer for whom the future is factual. This "objective subjectivity" is denoted by the concept of information.

Deriving the qualities of "matter" from a count of decidable alternatives may be expected to reduce the concepts of mass, energy, and information to a single unifying fundamental principle of moving form. In this view, the physical world would be—approximating Kant—that which can appear to a finite mind. Insofar as finite mind or consciousness is capable of appearing to itself empirically, it would itself constitute "matter." I have on occasion expressed this in a formula that follows Schelling: "Nature is spirit which does not have the appearance of spirit." But can something, which is a prerequisite of objectivization, still be thought beyond objectivization? Can we think of a totality, which counts us among its parts, *as* a totality? We have reached the problem of One.

The One

To make our approach let us first take a step backward. Gopi Krishna claims that all reality is governed by one law and that this law is at the same time a biological and a spiritual law of evolution. We have expressed the view that the unity of physics as well as that of evolution may be deduced from the historicity of time and finally from a still unknown unity of time. What does unity really mean in this context? Let us take a further step backward. In quantum theory an object may be divided into constituent objects but it does not consist of them. This is demonstrated by the fact that an object permits different, conceptually incompatible divisions (expressed technically: different possible divisions of Hilbert space; Einstein-Rosen-Podolsky-paradox). It is therefore a whole which does not consist of its parts, but rather loses its wholeness in the process of partition. Thus, the atom "is" not a system of nucleus and electrons; we only discover nucleus and electrons when we destroy the atom.

Similarly, this table "is" not a structure composed of atoms. We only find atoms if we radically destroy the table. The area in which the concept of separate objects is valid is precisely the area of the classical approximation in which the phase relationships between objects ("their connections *in* the *Prana*," if we may speak so recklessly) is considered negligible. If we now try to think of the whole world as a quantum theoretical object, then the world is not the multiplicity of objects it contains, but it divides into this multiplicity only for those who look at it with a multifariously objectivizing point of view.* This is but one of the ways to approach the One; we might call it the physical-objective way.

---

* Cf. the last essay in *The Unity of Nature*, Carl F.F. von Weizsacker (Munich).

Christianity and History

There are two questions I would still like to consider, if only in the brief form chosen here: The relationship of what we have said to Christianity and to our own future. Gopi Krishna has the open attitude toward other religions characteristic of enlightened Hindus. Jesus Christ is for him one of the greatest, most compelling examples of religious genius. He uses the conversation of Jesus with Nicodemus as indicative of the meaning of the second birth, the birth from water and spirit.

It is easy for modern intellectuals, who have no contact with the Church, to accept his openness, but this is much more difficult for the Christian theologian and certainly not just on narrow confessional grounds. To be sure, it has been observed often enough that Christians get themselves into a kind of panic when they are asked to recognize the truth of other religions. Since intolerance, even purely intellectual intolerance against " unbelievers," is no longer persuasive these days, some Christians are still looking for the "ultimately decisive" difference between Christianity and the other religions.

I consider this anxious reaction (which in most instances is unaware of its anxiety) as unchristian and as a source of ever new and puzzling misconceptions about other religions and about one's own. It is an entirely different matter to make it clear that differentiations of the historical process cast the great religions and their founders into distinctly different roles and that this is the way it has to be.

There are, however, certain features of the Christian tradition we can already identify, which we have no reason to abandon. Foremost among them is the relationship of Christianity to temporal history. Indians, such as Gopi Krishna, have taken over part of secularized Christian thought in the form of the concept of evolution. Gopi Krishna is well aware of the fact that the worldliness of this concept of evolution places him in opposition to that aspect of the Hindu tradition that seeks only an ascent to and a permanent dwelling place in the One. The philosophy of open time is a Hebrew Christian philosophy to be sure, its relation to the One has remained completely unclear in the Christian theological philosophical tradition.

But when we equate that kind of time with the linear concept of time in chronological history and prognosis, then we have abandoned the level of asking necessary further questions. I do not have the solution to this problem but would like to see it kept before us in the form of a question. The approach to an understanding of this question lies—as with all great theoretical questions—in the practical area.

There is, of course, in Christianity also a proper place for contemplative minds. But only because they too, in their own way, share responsibility for the world and for each single living fellow man.

The Future of the World

In *The Biological Basis of Religion and Genius,* Gopi Krishna merely hints at his expectations for the future. He expects that the present course of the world will lead to disaster, but that opening up a higher consciousness will result in better conditions for mankind and in real development. This pattern of expectation has often appeared during the course of history in a form suitable to the occasion, possibly because it has often been justified. I believe that it is certainly justified today. What counts is that we act in a world that justifies this kind of expectation. The question is how?

CHAPTER FOUR

In the fall of 1970, Gopi Krishna was invited to give a talk in Florence, Italy. He intended to speak extemporaneously, but at about the same time he received a letter from me asking for a brief summary of his views so that a pamphlet could be printed for interested individuals in the United States. Within thirty-six hours of the receipt of the letter, he completed the essay and departed for Europe. More than twice the length of this version, it was privately published a few months later and sent to several hundred scientists and scholars. In 1972, Harper & Row, New York, published *The Biological Basis of Religion and Genius*, with an introduction by Prof. Carl Friedrich Von Weizsacker.

THE BIOLOGICAL BASIS OF RELIGION AND GENIUS

The Shortfall of Religion

Religion is a mystery that has baffled all attempts toward a solution. From prehistoric times, as far back as investigators have been able to trace, man has always been in possession of a religion of some sort. Excavations of fossils of the earlier Stone Age reveal ceremonial burials, thus furnishing evidence that even in the primitive state of culture, belief in survival and the nature of the soul as an entity separate and distinct from the body were prevalent in various forms among the savage populations.

From the study of primitive religions and cults made by scholars, the savage faiths were more or less a bundle of superstition, myth, and ritual that not infrequently assumed horrible and dreadful form. Human sacrifice, sexual orgies, and dreadful forms of self-torture were often common features of the methods of worship. In less developed nations we still come across surviving remnants of these hideous practices of the past.

The reader might be expecting something about the holy

and the sublime, and my introduction, by allusion to some of the odious practices of primitive cults, might appear as ill-timed and irrelevant to the subject. But it is precisely because we have failed to study religion as a whole, from its earliest vestiges to the present lofty ideals of the prophets and sages, in all religions, taken as one composite whole, that we have not been able to discover the law of nature underlying all their infinitely varied manifestations and the religious impulse from prehistoric times to the present. This law is as operative now, when the world is sharply divided between those who believe in the existence of God and those who do not, as it was when religion occupied a position of supremacy and even kings had to bow to the dictates of the Church.

Why do we believe in an omniscient and omnipotent divine power that has brought this world and ourselves into existence when we can find no evidence, perceptible to the senses, to prove conclusively that such a power is real? And why do we strive for perfection and a better order of things when, from our own experience and study, we are irresistibly drawn to the conclusion that from the earliest epochs the earth has been a battleground for a ruthless struggle for existence in which no supernatural agency ever intervened to grant victory or even protection to the believers against those who did not believe in God?

The question is as old as humanity itself, and to this day no convincing answer has been given by any authority on religion or by an illumined sage. Had this question been effectively answered at any time in the history of mankind, the division between believers and nonbelievers would have ceased to exist.

It is too late to ascribe all religious phenomena to the will of God, as preachers often attempt to do. The battle for salvation, which almost all religions impose on their followers, demands that the seeker renounce the pleasures of earth to gain those of heaven. But what the blessings of heaven are and exactly what the state of man would be after his departure to the other world are enigmas that no one has satisfactorily solved.

Even the most eloquent writers on the subject are not agreed among themselves on this issue. Taking the Christian point of view, according to St. Paul, the soul wears a "celestial" or "spiritual" body in the other world as distinct from the "natural" and "terrestrial" body on earth. "Flesh and blood cannot inherit the kingdom of God," he says. St. Augustine, however, declares that "in the resurrection the substance of our bodies, however disintegrated, shall be entirely reunited."

He further clarifies this statement in these words: "Far be it from us to fear that the omnipotence of the Creator cannot, for the resuscitation and reanimation of our bodies, recall all the portions that have been consumed by beasts or fires, or have been dissolved into water, or have evaporated into the air."

Among modern writers there is also a grave divergence of opinion on this issue. According to Dr. S. D. McConnel, the soul builds up, as it were, a brain within a brain, a body within a body, something like the "astral" body, which can persist after death. Bishop Manning is more definite when he says, "When I enter there I shall be myself. This personality, these tempers and tastes, this character that I am forming here will be mine there. I shall be myself and shall be judged by what I am. I shall know my dear ones in the other life. I shall see and be seen. I shall speak and be spoken to."

These few citations are but a small sample to show that the state of man after death and the nature of the other world are still objects of controversy even among the believers. Where then lies the truth? The views expressed about the hereafter and the nature of the soul are almost as varied as there are sects and creeds in India, also. There are many who, after the death of a person, prescribe monthly or yearly ceremonies in which offerings of food, drink, and apparel are made to the priest, who performs the ceremonies in the belief that they reach the departed souls in the other world.

In Islam, too, there is great diversity of views about the conception of the afterworld. According to some authorities, the righteous soul comes to God and lives in blissful proximity to Him, while according to others he first enjoys the reward of his meritorious deeds in a delightful paradise.

Suffice it to say that there are almost as many views about God, the soul, and the beyond as there are faiths and creeds in the world. There are also variations in the gospels of various faiths, and often the revealed teachings and commandments of one flatly contradict those of another, although both claim their origin from the same divine source. Is it possible that the author of this vast creation can be so variable and fanciful that He would say one thing to one, another to a second, and yet another to a third, thereby inciting one to fight the other on the basic issues of life and death?

Nor can we ignore the fact that every major faith is split up into numerous sects and creeds and that each of these divisions has its own ideas and concepts, differing from each other, but all founded on the authority of the revealed scriptures, interpreted diversely to support the views expressed by the founder of each sect. There was a time, however, when no thinker, however great, had the temerity to question the accounts of creation and cosmogony contained in the scriptures. This was not restricted to one faith but applied to all the religions. We are all aware of the time when Galileo, white-haired and bent with age, was made to recant his monumental discoveries in astronomy by the dignitaries of the Church.

We are face to face with a colossal problem when we try to knit together the infinitely scattered threads of religion—say, from the time of Moses to the present day. There is such a vast store of literature, said to have emanated in part from God, and there are so many different points of view that it appears impossible to untie the tangled skein and to locate the thread that now by winding and twisting reflects the appearance of an inextricably confused mass.

Frankly, the intellectual stature of the average man and woman has grown so high, as compared to their prototypes of a few centuries ago, that the beliefs and dogmas of faith that instantly appealed to the latter now fall flat on the ears of the former.

The Error of Science

There is no reason for complacency among scientists in the thought that the intellectual efforts of the past few centuries have culminated in a vast increase in knowledge. There are still large gaps, especially in the knowledge of the mind, which if not filled up, at least to the extent possible now, might result in undoing in a day all that has been achieved with the sweating labor of hundreds of years.

Leaving apart the lacunae in our knowledge of the physical universe—the increasing problems posed by astronomy, the real nature of time and space, the basic substance of the nebulae, or the ultimate form of matter—it is no exaggeration to say that what we know for certain about the mind and its instruments, the brain and nervous system, is still in its infancy. The disproportion in the knowledge of the two worlds in which we live, the outer and the inner, is a sign of abnormality that can have serious repercussions on our thoughts and actions and thereby on the whole life and environment that we create for ourselves.

If we haven't realized that the zest for life and the happiness of mind flow from the inner fountain of our being and not from our material possessions, then we are still lacking in the proper understanding of our own nature. The birds in the air and the beasts in the forests live joyously and contentedly in the environment provided by nature. Because of his more developed nervous system and brain and a more sensitive, unprotected flesh, man needs some amenities, it is true, but beyond the basic needs he does not depend much on his outer belongings for the possession of a happy inner world.

Let us examine this issue a little more in detail. Can there be any denial that for thousands of years a vast majority of the race has drawn consolation and solace at times of acute mental distress and despair and found inspiration and guidance at times of darkness and doubt from the recorded utterances of some famous men and women? When we look at the simple lives of the founders of all the major faiths, the biblical prophets, Socrates and Confucius or others, and the environments that surrounded them, we cannot resist the conclusion that luxury and overabundance are not necessary for the bloom of the inner person. We can even say that their absence is more in harmony with the still unknown laws that govern our moral and spiritual development.

If with all our marvelous achievements in technology, tremendous advances in the arts and sciences, and the provision of undreamed-of luxuries and amenities we have failed to produce even a few men and women commanding the same stature—intellectual, moral, and spiritual—as was attained by most of these historical figures of the dim past in environments of ignorance, hardship, and want, there must be something wrong with our own notions about human life. Our ideas about the measures needed and the environments necessary for our proper and harmonious development must be in error. How can any planning prove fruitful unless we draw a lesson from this experience of the past and try to locate the gap in our knowledge that is making us progressively richer outside without adding a tithe to our treasure within?

Toward the end of the nineteenth century, Professor Tyndall made what he thought was a remarkable statement when he said that he could see the possibilities of life in matter. Before him stalwarts like Cabanis, Buchner, Hobbes, Priestley, Comte, Mill, Herbert Spencer, Heckel, Karl Marx, and after them Freud, Santayana, John Dewey, Bertrand Russell, and others, with all the powers of their genius, directly or indirectly denied independent existence to life and consciousness. The influence of their thought persists to this day, with the result that but few scientists of repute have the inclination to associate themselves openly with societies or groups interested in the occult and the supernatural.

No one can deny the greatness of these brilliant men, but at the same time no one can deny that some of the basic concepts about the mind and matter on which they built their towering structures are now decade after decade eroded by fresh waves of thought, and the day is not far off when with complete erosion they will crumble down, surviving only as curious relics of a less informed past.

What are the fruits of this overemphasis on the soma, on unrestricted material amenities, on the race for possession and power, and on the denial of the spiritual nature of man or the independent existence of consciousness or an almighty, intelligent cause of the universe? Has the race become more noble, more happy, and more peaceful? Or do we notice ominous signs of an almost immediate collapse? What inner torment drives millions of young men and women to seek solace in drugs, alcohol, and almost total abandonment of the modes of behavior that are sacrosanct for the elder generations? Why do others take to occult practices, to spiritualism, to astrology, asceticism, etc., in unprecedented numbers in an effort at self-transcendence to find answers to questions that no amount of temporal knowledge can answer?

In no period of history, even during the darkest age, were there such atrocities, such wholesale massacres, and such bloody wars and revolutions as this century has witnessed. Is there any country that does not prepare for war? Or is there any that is not every now and then torn by internal dissension or shaken by revolts that make a stable environment well nigh impossible?

Disregard of moral values, indiscipline, violence, sexual delinquency, and the like have assumed a position of ascendancy that is reflected in most of the media of the day. Before the very eyes of those whose writings dismantled the walls that were erected by faith to keep man from yielding completely to the animal in him—time-honored conventions, higher rules of conduct, chivalrous ideas, and the ideals of family life, affection, and love—all those sublime attributes of character that distinguish man from the beast are crumbling to dust amid the laughter and derision of the nihilists and the Anti-Christ. The last days of the Romans, who had the most luxurious nation the world ever saw, were marked by certain characteristics that can serve as a warning about the fate in store for our time.

They were (1) the breakdown of the family, (2) the mounting craze for pleasure, (3) extravagant spending, (4) expanding armies and constant threat of attacks, (5) depreciation of moral values, (6) decay in religion, (7) political instability, and (8) immoderate sex.

Considered in this light, who can doubt that modern society is rapidly heading toward the same end? No once victorious nation ever came to a realization, when degeneration set in, that it was decaying and rapidly rolling down the slope, until one day it landed in the mire at the base. On the other hand, its leaders blamed their growing problems and troubles on their enemies, oblivious that the real enemies were their own fast-deteriorating minds. Today's thinkers, rulers, spiritual leaders, and scholars seldom realize that by conforming to the taste and choice of the masses they cannot arrest the process of decay. Degenerative tendencies in art, literature, philosophy, social customs, national character, moral values, and even in religion remain unnoticed by those who fall victims to senescence.

While the leaders of religious thought continue to dwell on the blessings of faith, both from the pulpit and over the media, the unbelievers continue to swell, or new creeds and cults continue to spread. Chaos and confusion become more confounded every day. In the same way, the politicians haranguing on peace see violence and terrorism growing apace, and the moralists, lauding the path of virtue, watch in despair the advancing tide of immorality, powerless to stop it.

What has gone wrong with the world? Why do we find ourselves unable to cope with the growing spate of discontentment and disaffection spreading on all sides? The Communist countries are as much flooded by it as the rest of the world. Why are the promises held by science and technology proving to be sources of worry and fear rather than of elation and joy?

Do not all signs and portents point to the conclusion that sooner or later a global conflagration is inevitable? What will be the condition of humanity when a battered and broken remnant survives, amid the ruins of modern civilization, to carry on the task of history?

Barring the single factor of the influence of modern technology, which alone cannot be so pernicious, all the other factors, such as urbanization, suppression of unconscious urges, heresy, and unfettered freedom of thought and action also operated in the past without causing such explosive situations as we are witnessing now. Social, moral, and political evils assumed overwhelming proportions only when a nation, through a wrong mode of life and thought, fell victim to decay—a grim process of inner deterioration leading finally to senescence and death, the award of Heaven on a collective breach of evolutionary laws. This is the verdict of history.

The greatest tragedy of our time has been that the thinkers, believing that science had found solutions to most of the riddles that confronted them, gave expression to views about the various facets of human life—about the hopes and aspirations of man, his mind and spirit, the aim of his existence, about this world and the hereafter—that in many important respects are as incorrect as were the concepts of the ancients about the physical world. The uncompromising attitude of science toward religion rests partly on the dogmatic attitude of the custodians of faith themselves, insisting on blind acceptance of the teachings contained in the gospels of a creed and partly on the exaggerated stress on divine intervention that more or less characterizes all the religions.

A more considerate assessment would have taken cognizance of the fact that there is no other single factor, including politics, that has had such an influence on the life of man from remotest antiquity to the present day as religion has wielded. No other factor has contributed so richly to the growth of civilization and culture as it. Even a casual study of the major faiths could not fail to bring home that, according to all schools of religious thought, a certain prescribed way of life and conduct and certain prescribed mental and physical disciplines can act as a ladder to lead seekers to God or to states of consciousness in which communion with divinity becomes possible. This systematization of religious effort to gain sublime objectives is at least as old as history.

The most rational way to attest to the truth of religion and to accept or reject its claims would be to test these practices and disciplines after making a comparative study of all of them, and then to pronounce a verdict on the basis of the results achieved. But to this day it has never been done by any group of scientists, dedicating their life to this research alone, in the same way that innumerable groups and societies are doing in respect to the still unexplained riddles of the physical world.

There has been no investigation of the possibilities offered by religion itself. The teachings of the spiritual luminaries of the past have been rejected outright without trial. It has become the fashion to explain the phenomena of the mind in terms of atoms and molecules composing the matter of the brain. Every word that a scientist writes is to be accepted as gospel truth. But every word in a scripture is to be viewed with doubt and distrust. The wheel of fortune that once gave such ascendancy to faith that it became the sole arbiter of what man should believe or not believe, irrespective of the evidence of his senses and the judgment of intellect, now turning round, has reversed the position and made reason the arbitrator, alas, to be guilty of the same abuse.

As time will show, this has been one of the worst blunders ever made by man, because under the loose and sometimes fantastic dress worn by faith lies concealed the greatest secret of existence, a secret that rules the fate of mankind in the same way that the gravitational pull of the sun governs the rotation of the earth. The entire religious literature of the world will be found to be an expression of this mighty spiritual law.

The nature of this law and its implications and possibilities, intuitively grasped by the prophets and sages, are discussed again and again in the revealed scriptures, embellished with supernatural accounts and episodes that prevent the uninitiated from reaching the solid core. To avoid ambiguity, I should like to say at once that it is a biological law as possible of demonstration in a laboratory as the flow of blood.

Evolution Is the Answer

The explanation is that the human brain is still in a state of evolution and that certain specially gifted individuals, such as mediums and sensitives, mystics and seers, child prodigies and geniuses, are but the manifestations of a higher state of consciousness that will be the natural possession of the woman and man of the future.

The phenomena witnessed in these uncommon individuals are often erratic and often beyond their control because there is still a wide gap between the present condition of the brain and the ultimate state of perfection it has to reach one day. Then what we now call supernatural or paranormal gifts will become the normal possession of at least the fully evolved members of the race. Until that time, in the great majority of those who are born with these talents as a natural heritage, we can reasonably expect only imperfect, erratic, or abortive exhibitions, as seen in mediums, psychics, and even in some categories of mystics, due to a combination of circumstances and eugenic factors that continue to remain faulty in the present state of society.

In dealing with religion and every supernormal manifestation of the mind we are dealing with the phenomenon of evolution. The explanation for the amazing tenacity with which mankind has held fast to the teaching of prophets and sages, even at the cost of widespread bloodshed and suffering, lies in this, that the teaching in one form or another, to a greater or lesser extent, contains precious hints about the mode of life and the organization of society necessary to meet the demands of the evolutionary impulse still active in the race.

Although a good deal of the intricate mechanism of the body has become known to science, it is still an unfathomed mystery, especially the province of thought. So deep is the mystery and so unprepared for the disclosure are the learned that hardly anyone would be ready to believe the amazing truth that as a measure of evolution a subtle process is at work in the average individual, resulting in the formation of a biochemical essence of a volatile nature that can be readily transformed into a psychic energy of high potency.

In every form of life, the production of nerve and psychic energy is constantly going on to feed the brain and the nervous system, although the manner in which this is effected is yet not known to science. What I affirm is that the process of evolution leads to the production of a more potent form of those biochemical substances that act as fuel for psychic energy in its various forms and that these processes can be accelerated.

In an infinitesimal dose, lysergic acid diethylamide, popularly known as LSD, can create a revolution in consciousness and may even lead in rare cases to insanity, an apparently incredible performance for such a minute quantity. It would be ridiculous to contend that the most elaborate chemical laboratory on earth, the human body, cannot readily manufacture a substance of this nature under the influence of evolutionary processes active in it. Scientists cannot trace what happens to LSD when it is in the body but can recognize its action by its results. In this analogy, it is easy to imagine that the body can manufacture a substance so subtle that it cannot be detected either, and yet so potent that in the form of radiation it can raise one's consciousness to such higher levels of cognition that other planes of existence and other orders of being come into the range of perception.

What is of particular importance is that the existence of this biochemical substance and its transformation into radiation, either as a natural measure or under the effect of certain practices and disciplines, need not be taken purely on trust but can be observed and verified under the most rigid laboratory conditions. The observation can be repeated time after time until the law is formally recognized.

I am emphatic on this point because I have observed the entire phenomenology of this experience for more than thirty years within myself. Also, the experience is confirmed not in a few but in hundreds upon hundreds of authentic documents, dating from prehistoric times in India, Tibet, China, Japan, and in the Middle East. The documentary evidence is so overwhelming that no reasonable person can disbelieve it.

Why it has not already created a revolution in modern thought is primarily because many of these precious documents are written in what is known as sandhya bhasha, or twilight language, a cryptic form that is intelligible only to one who has had the experience. Now the question arises, how can the phenomena relating to accelerated evolution—or Kundalini—be demonstrated conclusively to meet the demands of scientific research?

What my own experience has revealed is that though guided by a superintelligence, invisible but at the same time unmistakably seen conducting the whole operation, the phenomenon of Kundalini is entirely biological in nature. Probably no other spectacle, not even the most incredible supernormal performances of the mystics and mediums, so clearly demonstrates the existence of an all-pervading, omniscient intelligence behind the infinitely varied phenomena of life as the operations of a freshly awakened Kundalini.

It is here that man for the first time becomes acutely aware of the staggering fact that this unimaginable cosmic intelligence is present at every spot in the universe and that our whole personality—ego, mind, intellect, and all—is but an infinitely small bubble blown on this boundless ocean. But to suppose that even a particle of this ocean of consciousness can ever become extinct or cease to be is more absurd than to imagine that there can be night on the sun.

With the awakening of Kundalini, an amazing activity commences in the whole nervous system, from the crown of the head to the toes. The body is now transformed into a miniature laboratory, working at high speed day and night. In the Chinese documents this phenomenon is described as the "circulation of light" and in the Indian manuals as the "uprising of shakti," or life energy. Nerves in all parts of the body whose existence is never felt by normal consciousness are now forced by some invisible power to a new type of activity, which either immediately or gradually becomes perceptible to the subject. Through all their innumerable endings, they begin to extract a nectarlike essence from the surrounding tissues that, traveling in two distinct forms, one as a radiation and the other as a subtle essence, streams into the spinal cord.

A portion of the essence floods the reproductive organs, which also become abnormally active, as if to keep pace with the activity of the entire nervous system. The radiation, appearing as a luminous cloud in the head, streams into the brain and at the same time courses through the nerves, stimulating all the vital organs, especially the organs of digestion, to adjust their functions to the new life introduced into the system. The awakening of Kundalini denotes, in other words, the phenomenon of rebirth, alluded to in plain or veiled terms in the religious lore of mankind. A more powerful and direct connection is now established between the individual and universal consciousness.

This phenomenon of transformation or rebirth is alluded to by Christ in metaphorical language in his dialogue with Nicodemus when Christ says, "Verily, verily, I say unto thee, except a man be born of water and of the spirit, he cannot enter into the kingdom of God. That which is born of flesh is flesh; and that which is born of the Spirit is spirit. Marvel not that I said unto thee, ye must be born again."

The intense activity of the sexual organs is clearly perceptible in the case of both women and men. The ceaseless flow of the reproductive substances into the spinal cord, the vital organs, and the brain, and also the altered activity of the digestive system, and even of the heart at times, can be easily observed with the help of the information contained in the ancient literature on the subject.

The statements of the kind that during the process the semen dries up with the suction, or becomes thin, the male organ shrinks, or that the sexual appetite is lost, contained in the old texts, convey important bits of information for those engaged in the investigation. An ancient Chinese work, *The Secret of the Golden Flower*, contains unmistakable hints about this process, which no one with some knowledge of the subject can fail to notice. And yet C. G. Jung, in his commentary on the book, entirely preoccupied with his own theories about the unconscious, despite the unambiguous nature of the statements in the work, finds in it only material for the corroboration of his own ideas and nothing beyond that. The same thing happened in a seminar held by him on Kundalini, of which a written summary is available in the Jung Institute. None of the scholars present, as evident from the views expressed by them, displayed the least knowledge about the real significance of the ancient document they were discussing at the time.

The Mechanism of Evolution

If paranormal achievements and a transcendental state of consciousness are possible for some men and women, they must be possible for others, too, provided the biological factors in the case of the former are present in the latter also. God or nature cannot be partial to those who possess the gifts and endow their minds with these extraordinary attributes as a mark of special favor. A more rational explanation would be to ascribe a biological cause for them and to find out by study and experiment where the secret lies. No one can deny that human consciousness itself is the expression of a biological organ and that, apart from the organism, it is never perceptible in any form.

Until the nature and properties of life energy or prana, serving as the fuel of thought, are determined, scientists will continue to be baffled by the phenomena of mind and consciousness in the same way as the ancients were mystified by the aurora borealis, lightning, thunder, etc., until the mystery was solved by the discovery of electricity. The most practical way to study this elusive substance, more marvelous than any substance of the physical world, is to investigate Kundalini. With the present methods of observation, it would not be difficult to follow the track till conclusive data about the new field of research are collected. The domain of the conscious is so amazing, however, that there will be no cessation of mysteries and surprises till the end of time.

Positive evidence about the inner changes can be furnished by the successful initiates themselves, even at this stage. The change occurring in consciousness can never be imagined by one who has not had the experience, however. During recent times, Tennyson, Wadsworth, Proust, Bucke, and others had experiences somewhat similar to those of the mystics, without undergoing those rigorous disciplines usually associated with spiritual unfoldment. When research is started, it will be found that in the past, too, this "gratuitous grace" has been a common feature of mystical experience, as if those who had it were already fashioned for it from birth or needed but a slight stimulus to gain it.

The extremely diversified accounts of religious experience are due to the variation in the mental level, ideas, and cultural development of those who have it. For a thorough investigation, it is necessary that a team of scholars and scientists, comprising skeptics and believers both, should take up a course of exercises for a sufficient period, in a spirit of dedication, as is done in other scientific objectives, with due regard to the ethical standards necessary for it. Then they could evaluate the results. Even one case of awakening would be sufficient to determine its biological nature and to observe the various changes and developments that occur. As has been mentioned, the metabolic processes of the body are highly accelerated, and an inner process of brain-building and streamlining, somewhat akin to the processes occurring in an embryo in the womb, takes place until consciousness is completely transformed and a superior type of mind is born. What achievements might be possible with an awakened Kundalini once the feasibility of the transformation is empirically demonstrated and the biological factors become known to science is impossible to say.

When transformed, the man or woman must become a genius or a virtuoso of a high order, with exceptional powers of expression, both in verse and prose. Or they must possess extraordinary artistic talents. Some of the ancient prophets and seers are examples. Precognition, powers of healing, psychic talents, and other miraculous gifts may develop simultaneously along with genius. An intellectual with a healthy constitution and noble attributes of character can develop into a spiritual prodigy, a person of such unique gifts and talents that he or she can shine as an idol before the eyes of the multitudes, with a power of fascination and appeal possessed by only the most magnetic of people. In this way, the metamorphosis effected can bear striking testimony to the efficacy of processes generated by Kundalini.

The evolutionary mechanism is so constructed that at a certain stage of maturity it can be stimulated to such intense activity that the evolutionary cycle can be completed in one's lifetime, raising man to the next higher stage of consciousness decreed for him by divine ordination. There is no difficulty in a scientific investigation when the spheres of the operation are known. The biological reactions in the body are unmistakable. The ceaseless suction of the seminal fluid and its flow into the spinal canal and nerve junctions of the vital organs and the brain cannot remain undetected.

The halo or aureola shown around the heads or figures of saints and illumined sages is symbolic of the inner illumination experienced in the metamorphosis of consciousness. There is a noticeable change in the digestive and excretory functions of the body during the course of the transformation. From both the subjective and objective sides, the phenomenon is as possible of verification as any other function of the human body.

Why should such an overwhelming importance be attached to this research when the ultimate object of the awakening of Kundalini is merely a change in consciousness, which, as the past record shows, can be effective only in an extremely limited number of cases? Why should the phenomenon be of importance or interest for the whole of the human race? Because gigantic revolutions in human life and thought were effected by only a handful of spiritual geniuses during the historical period. This factor alone presents a phenomenon of such magnitude that it makes research on Kundalini a pressing need of the times. But there are other equally important factors that make Kundalini virtually the arbiter of human destiny, and for that reason by far the most powerful driving influence on the life of man. No attempt made by the intellect can penetrate the veil or solve the mystery of creation because the veil itself is a creation of the intellect. It is only by self-transcendence that light begins to penetrate into the darkness, dissolving the problem.

The present rapid multiplication of sects and creeds, which the orthodox custodians of the various faiths are powerless to stop or even account for, owes its origin to the mounting pressure on the brain caused by the religious urge and is the inevitable fruit of civilization and leisure. Only an awakened Kundalini can ease it. Those who seek solace in occult practices of any kind, in drugs, in prayer and worship, or in any other form of spiritual effort and who eagerly hunt for teachers for guidance are often without knowing it yielding to a subconscious urge to rouse Kundalini. It is an urge almost as powerful as that which makes a healthy young woman long for a child.

Even in the Communist countries in the next few decades, the ever-increasing pressure of the inexorable evolutionary processes will break the fetters forged by political ideology that suppresses healthy expression of the religious impulse. If this outflow is still denied, it may result in the same violence as was previously used to prevent it. History will follow in the reverse direction unless the law is recognized.

Since Kundalini is the fountainhead of the religious desire in man, it means that a mode of life and conduct, or a system or society, that puts the brake on its legitimate activity can never be conducive to peace and happiness. Rather it must lead to psychic and physiological disturbances both in the individual and in the group. The religious impulse, unlike the reproductive urge, is not static but dynamic in its operations. In other words, it is not appeased by the same kind of nourishment over and over again but demands a change in diet, according to the evolutionary stature and the intellectual acumen gained. When this is denied, it gropes blindly for other vicarious foods to satisfy the hunger gnawing inside. The multiplicity of creeds therefore is nothing to be wondered at. The tendency will continue to spread until the right food is found.

Mental disturbance and psychosis are, at the present state of our knowledge about this nerve mechanism, not infrequently the possible consequences of a sudden arousal of Kundalini. Practices aimed at arousing Kundalini sometimes result in abruptly forcing open the central channel and the connected compartment in the brain at a time when the system is not yet attuned to such a development. In such cases terrible ordeals await the initiates, through which only some survive. Rapid flights to higher levels of consciousness cannot be without some degree of risk, unless the mind and body have been attuned to them.

As pointed out in the opening lines of this chapter, primitive religions were a bundle of superstition, revolting forms of worship, savage ritual, and myth. Since the evolutionary impulse is part and parcel of the psychosomatic organism of man, it is only natural that its expression should correspond to the psychological level of the people. We should not expect the religion of the barbarian and savage to have the refinement and sublimity that permeated throughout the historical period of the civilized nations.

And yet at the same time we should not expect that the religious concepts and ideas prevalent thousands of years ago would continue to hold the same attraction and appeal for a higher intellectual level of people. Revolt in some form against the obsolete ideas and forms of worship or ritual is, therefore, just a natural outcome of the psychomental evolution of the race. The growth of countless novel cults and creeds is indicative of the first impact of the tide and the eager search of the masses for a more satisfying spiritual food than the one provided by the older faiths.

The question that arises here, as a natural consequence of what has been stated, is that if Kundalini is the source behind genius and high intellectual or artistic talents, it must also be the factor responsible for the evil geniuses of history. This is something that our scientists should know about. The same biological device in the body that has the capacity to raise man to the stature of a god, with supernormal gifts and virtues, like saviors and sages, also has the power to fashion him into a monster. The highly talented military commanders, dictators, and demagogues who drenched humanity in blood were as much a product of Kundalini as were the illumined saints.

No amount of material wealth and prosperity can save mankind from the depredations committed by gifted amoral men, pursuing ambitious goals, in whom Kundalini is awake in a malignant form. Their hold over the masses being irresistible, their power of organization unmatched, and their military skill unequaled, even one specimen of this class can play havoc with the whole of humanity. The only silver lining in the dark clouds threatening us at present is the recognition of science, after a thorough investigation, of the almighty law. We can no longer afford to play with fire and allow our ignorance of the awful law to result in the continued birth of evil geniuses fatal to man's survival.

A wrong mode of life, disharmonious social and political environments, improper food and drink, immoderation and intemperance, and also excessive worry, anxiety, and fear, unrestricted ambition and desire, greed, selfishness, envy, jealousy, and hatred, acting adversely on the system, interfere directly with the proper manufacture of the precious fuel for the high-potency radiation that is at the bottom of all extraordinary or supernormal exhibitions of the human mind.

Lacking healthy nourishment, the psychic energy takes on a stunted, distorted, or diseased form, in the same way that lack of proper food in insufficient measure stunts, distorts, or damages the health of a suckling babe. This is the reason why revelation came to guide mankind. Every prophet and seer born on earth came, knowingly or unknowingly, to draw attention to this law.

The signs and symptoms of degeneration we notice now and that marked the closing phases of all the premier civilizations and victorious empires of the past point conclusively to a deterioration in the physical and mental assets of a people or nation. Disproportion, deformation, or distortion in the psychic radiation is the cause of the appearance of not only the sadistic geniuses who caused horrible slaughters from time to time but also of many forms of neurosis and insanity.

Professor Zaehner, in his book *Mysticism: Sacred and Profane*, touched a very important point in citing the instance of John Custance, a certified manic-depressive, who was prone to mystical experiences during his manic periods. Huxley, in his book *Heaven and Hell*, also cites the case of Renée, a schizophrenic who has given an autobiographical account of her own passage through madness. She calls the world of the schizophrenic "the country of lit-upness," of which the illumination for her is infernal—an intense electric glare without a shadow, ubiquitous and implacable.

The growing flood of mental troubles, which is a curse of modern civilization, is nature's forewarning that the evolutionary process is going wrong. What I assert is that one single law is at the base of all inexplicable phenomena of the mind. Only one remarkable series of changes, caused in the psychic energy that serves as fuel for thought, is responsible for all the varied and complex phenomena that present at this time insolvable riddles to science. The greater incidence of insanity among the men and women of genius and the seeds of eccentricity in many of them establish the existence of a common link between the two. Research into Kundalini implies, in fact, an investigation into almost all, at the moment, obscure phenomena of the mind.

The Divine Possibilities in Man

There is every likelihood that from the sides of both religion and science eyebrows will be raised and open doubts expressed at what I say. But this will only be a transitory phase, because every important discovery in the realm of knowledge almost invariably took the world by surprise. But when the destined hour arrives, circumstances so transpire that, however incredible the disclosure might have appeared in the beginning, soon after a day comes when it becomes the most talked-about topic of the day. In my humble view, there is nothing that can counteract the overhanging threat of nuclear holocaust like the knowledge of Kundalini.

Once the possibility of a spiritual rebirth with the arousal of this mighty power is accepted, Kundalini Yoga will provide the most sublime enterprise for the pure-minded and intelligent adventurous spirits of the age. The finished products of Kundalini must transcend the normal limits of the mind. If this transcendence does not occur, the visionary experiences are either a delusion or a myth. Even those who have sporadic glimpses of the ineffable but for a few times in their life are usually men of genius or of high intellectual stature. Those in a state of perennial ecstasy must essentially have uncommon intellectual talents, paranormal gifts, and an altered rhythm of the nervous system. In their case, the enlarged consciousness persists even in slumber, for which reason such sleep is called "Yoga Nidra," or the sleep of Yoga.

The marvelous power reservoir of Kundalini, the unmistakable symbol of the divine in man, opens up new horizons of such sublimity, joy, and glory that even a modest description would appear incredible unless a few transformed adepts support my assertions to convince scholars of the golden future ordained for humanity.

The human mind is so constituted that no luxury and no treasure of the earth can assuage its burning fever, seeking an explanation for its own existence. All the heavy weight of this inscrutable mystery, all the questions posed by intellect, all the suffering of the harrowing ascent of evolution, all the pain felt at the injustice and misery prevailing in the world, all the disappointment of shattered dreams and broken hopes . . .

All the anguish of eternal partings from near and dear ones, and all the fear of ill health, decay, and death vanish like vapor at the rise of the inner sun, at the recognition of the inmost self, beyond thought, beyond doubt, beyond pain, beyond mortality—which once perceived, illumines the darkness of the mind as a flash of strong lightning cleaves the darkness of the night, leaving man transformed with but one glimpse of the inexpressible splendor and glory of the spiritual world.

May this sublime knowledge become accessible to all. May there come enlightenment and peace to the minds of all.

CHAPTER FIVE

On October 6, 1973, the op-ed page of *The New York Times* featured this unusual article, unusual in that it was perhaps the first time that the subject of higher consciousness was ever discussed in its pages. "Beyond the Higher States of Consciousness," the *Times*'s choice of headline, was an excerpt from a book of questions and answers by Gopi Krishna titled *Higher Consciousness: The Evolutionary Thrust of Kundalini*, published the following year by Julian Press, New York.

BEYOND THE HIGHER STATES OF CONSCIOUSNESS

Even with its nuclear arsenals and contamination of air, water, and earth, it is not science that has become destructive; it is the distortion of the human intellect that is responsible for the present unsafe situation of the world.

Knowledge can be both constructive and destructive. The ultimate arbiter is the human intellect. This is why revelation has always been a necessary instrument for the spiritual progress of the race. Intellect, unable to see centuries or even only a decade ahead, cannot determine the evolutionary needs of mankind. It is liable to make serious errors in calculation at any time.

Human life is so complex and the course of evolution so full of bewildering situations that only a cosmic intelligence can guide it rightly to the destined goal. Can even a whole galaxy of the highest intellects, in every branch of knowledge, make an accurate forecast of what would be the state of mankind after the span of only the next quarter century? Or even what changes will occur in the current concepts of science, politics, and religion?

If not, doesn't it plainly signify that the race is drifting toward an indeterminable goal at the mercy of forces of which it has no control?

The error of science has been that it has entirely ignored the spiritual side of man and devoted all its attention to the physical and organic fields. The outcome is that mankind faces a threat of annihilation on one side, or death with poisoned air, water, and earth on the other, and of mental distortion on the third.

On the political side, it has become a seething cauldron of aggression, violence, lust for power, and hate. On the spiritual and moral side, we see confusion rampant everywhere. There are as many ideas, concepts, systems, and doctrines as there are scholars or teachers expounding them.

It is not surprising, therefore, that science has failed to create that homogeneity and that clarity of thought that are essential for the harmonious progress of mankind in the social, political, and spiritual fields.

Science today is suffering from the same distemper of mind that affected faith during the period of her supremacy, namely dogmatism, vanity, and arrogance. It is amazing to what extent even scientists can be led astray by vanity. They understand very well that all we know about the visible cosmos is but a drop in the possible ocean of knowledge. Not a year passes when they are not forced to revise their opinions about certain issues.

But with all this uncertainty, most of them display a dogmatic attitude toward mind and consciousness. It is chiefly because science has been one-sided in this investigation—ignoring the spiritual side of man—that it has failed to bring about that wholesome transformation in the mental and moral sides as it has in the physical.

The neglect of the material side brought about the fall of the once highly honored sovereign faiths of mankind. In the same way, the neglect of the spiritual side is now tending to undermine the position of ascendancy gained by science.

In either case, it was the intellect that failed to assess the position correctly and to err in overemphasizing only one side of man and neglecting the equally important other side.

Therefore, it is not science itself but the overweening vanity and shortsightedness of savants and scholars—or, in other words, a faulty intellect—that is responsible for the destructiveness of modern technology.

The first thing that should be done to bring about a harmonious development of human beings and the eradication of present-day irrational beliefs in the spiritual realm is to embark on a scientific investigation into consciousness.

There is a huge volume of literature available in both the East and the West describing methods for attaining the higher states of consciousness and the nature of these higher states. A documentary research into these volumes, followed by systematic experimentation, can, I am sure, lead to an understanding of the biological relationship between expanded states of consciousness and the brain.

When this is achieved, the next step would be to find the laws underlying this relationship. Enough material would be available—when this is done—to enable scholars and scientists to understand the nature of the changes imperceptibly occurring in the brain and consciousness.

It is not only by experimentation on the methods leading to higher states of consciousness, but also by the observation of the psychic forces responsible for genius, mediumistic faculties, and insanity that these evolutionary processes can be understood.

The all-inclusive nature of sex energy has not yet been correctly understood by psychologists. In fact, the very term reproductive, or sex, energy is a misnomer: Reproduction is but one of the aspects of the life energy, of which the other theater of activity is the brain. The cephalic activity is so slow and subtle as to be almost imperceptible. But this activity is the cause of genius, uncanny psychic powers, and also insanity.

Once this fact is empirically demonstrated, we come to a turning point in our present concepts about mind and consciousness—even about matter and the universe as a whole.

The first harvest of this change will be the beginning of a new science dealing with subtle intelligent energies in the cosmos. When this happens, the gigantic physical world—now dominating the whole mental horizon of science—will be relegated to its proper position. It is but the visible peak of an infinite creation, of which the unbounded major part is sunk below the surface of the space-time ocean, forever hidden from the sight of man.

It is only in higher states of consciousness that a fragment of the submerged portion comes into view, causing a state of wonder and exhilaration that is beyond description. It is only when the evolving human organism and the cosmos are viewed in right perspective that the appropriate ways of life and conduct, favorable for this transformation, can be devised by science.

Try as we might, without a clear knowledge of the goal ahead, we can by no exercise of the intellect determine the right pattern of life essential for mankind on the evolutionary path: a united world, abolition of war, demolition of armaments, disbandment of armies. An environment more in harmony with nature. A life more natural and simple. Removal of barriers between man and man, inculcation of altruistic and humanitarian principles, moral education, social equality, and universal brotherhood. These are some of the basic factors that contribute to the harmonious progress of mankind.

This may appear idealistic or even fantastic and impracticable to many people. But the conclusion is unavoidable. At its present intellectual stature, the alternatives facing the race are either self-caused annihilation with dreadful agony for myriads, or knowledge of and obedience to the laws of evolving consciousness.

CHAPTER SIX

In the beginning of the 1970s, millions of Americans were thinking about taking up the practice of meditation, and many thousands had already begun. For some, the results were worthwhile; for others, they were not. Gopi Krishna attempted to explain the reason for this disparity in a book published in 1975 by E. P. Dutton, New York, and titled *The Awakening of Kundalini.* This chapter is an excerpt from it.

IS MEDITATION ALWAYS BENEFICIAL?

There are many intellectuals who believe that the states of illumination many thousands of people are seeking are but the inner mental states bordering on the subconscious. They hold that these states can be evoked in hypnosis or during the alpha and theta phases of biofeedback. "A yogi can learn to control his brain waves in a matter of years," say Karlins and Andrews in their work *Biofeedback*, adding that "the average person using biofeedback training can learn to control his brain waves in a matter of hours." They quote Dr. Johann Stoyva as saying that information feedback techniques might be able to teach the "blank-mind" state, typical of Zen and Yoga, within "months or even weeks."

Stoyva's own experience of alpha, they say, "was like a flowing gray-black film with a luminous quality." At another place: "As the technology for measuring and training brain waves becomes more sophisticated, unpracticed meditators will have the opportunity to duplicate the physiological states of Zen and Yoga." This is a misconception.

The gravity of the error lies not in misjudging the nature of mystical ecstasy and the phenomenon of illumination closely associated with it, but in completely overlooking a factor that is of paramount importance for human welfare and safety. This is the factor of evolution or, in other words, of the resistless change in human consciousness caused by an equally resistless, though still imperceptible, microbiological change in the human brain.

We see unchallengeable evidence for this transformation when we compare the relics of ancient cultures, three to five thousand years old, with the culture of today. But as a group, biologists are not prepared to concede that the human brain is still in a process of organic evolution, for they see no perceptible symptoms of such a process. True, there are no discernible signs in the brain to attest to this transformation. But then are we able to decipher all the cryptic language of the cranium, and is it not still almost a complete mystery to us?

Until very recently we could not even find any visible organic signs of such a glaring pathological upheaval as that of insanity, and even eminent psychologists believed it to be purely psychic in nature. Even now the biological origin of insanity is completely obscure. On what evidence then do the erudite pass their judgments, when the nature of bioenergy and the microbiology of the brain are still a closed book?

The very first experience of the beatific state brings the realization home to one who has it that the nature of consciousness varies with different individuals. The difference between a blockhead and an intellectual is in the depth and volume of consciousness of each. Each point of awareness, representing a human being, has its own spectrum, its own brightness, depth, and volume, and in this way each varies from the other. The consciousness of the enlightened person is virtually illuminated, and he or she lives—both in the waking and dreaming states—in a resplendent world of light.

Consciousness is a sovereign reality of the universe. Its range of manifestations is infinite. Just as there are subhuman states of consciousness, so there are also transhuman states. Mystical consciousness or enlightened awareness marks the lowest limit of the transhuman variety. There have been historical personages who had it either occasionally or as a perennial possession from birth.

We see this state of illumination gradually increasing when we rise from the lowest to the highest stratum of the human mind, both conscious and subconscious. Every individual is enclosed in a watertight shell of his own mind and is entirely debarred from having even one fleeting glimpse of that of another. This strict isolation makes each individual invest others with the same kind of consciousness that he has himself, with more or less intelligence, sensitivity, etc. This is a fallacy. There is a difference in the very structure or spectrum of each individual consciousness caused by the difference in the biological organism through which it is expressed.

The very texture of illumined consciousness is thus distinct and different from others. It is not only that one has visual feasts of light and color or an extended awareness, but also wholesale transformation of consciousness must occur.

During the course of genuine mystical experience a higher dimension of consciousness intervenes, eclipsing the normal individuality, partially or wholly, for a certain period. It then seems as if a new world, a new order of existence, or a superhuman being has descended into view. There is an unmistakably enhanced perception of lights, colors, beauty, goodness, virtue, and harmony, which lend a superworldly appearance to the whole experience.

Do we not see this greater apperception of light, color, beauty, harmony, ideals, moral values, and creative joy in the great geniuses of mankind, the great painters, sculptors, musicians, writers, philosophers, poets, mystics, and reformers? Transcendental consciousness, adorned with all these attributes, is but a step ahead and must be clearly understood as such to chart out the direction in which the evolution of consciousness is taking place before our very eyes.

If it is possible to produce geniuses of all these categories with guided meditation, biofeedback training, drugs, hypnosis, letting the mind go, or other practices of that sort, then enlightenment cannot fail to respond to the same treatment to produce Christs, Buddhas, or Platos in lavish numbers in the years to come. If not, then why all this confusion?

Biofeedback and Mystical Experience

Biofeedback equipment is designed to identify certain phases of consciousness. The technique has come into use because some scientists who are experimenting on consciousness are under the impression that the alpha and theta states provide the matrix from which mystical experience and creative talent are born. It also provides an avenue for the cure of mental and even bodily ailments and for acquiring greater mastery over the mind. By means of a signal that can take the form of light or sound, biofeedback provides an index for identifying different stages of consciousness, namely (1) alert wakefulness; (2) stilled, passive, relaxed or vacant states; (3) the somnolent states preceding sleep; and (4) deep sleep. They are designated as beta, alpha, theta, and delta, respectively. Alpha and theta are slower-paced waves and are associated with inward attention, problem-solving, creativity, etc.

In order to point out the error involved in this supposition, it is necessary first of all to differentiate between the alpha and theta states and the state of concentrated attention that precedes mystical ecstasy. According to the *Yoga Sutras* of Pantanjali and every other time-honored manual of Yoga, the mind has to pass through two stages of concentration, namely dharana and dhyana—that is, a primary state of concentration and a more stabilized and prolonged form of it. Only then can it attain to Samadhi or the mystical trance. There are detailed directions in all Yoga treatises on how this state of unbroken fixity of attention can be achieved. The target to be attained is that the observing mind and the object contemplated should fuse into one. This can occur in only two ways: Either the object dissolves into consciousness and only the seer remains intensely conscious of himself, or he loses his own identity and becomes one with the object on which the mind is fixed.

The rigorous forms of pranayama, mudras, and bhandas, peculiar to Hatha Yoga, are all aimed to enhance the effect of concentration on the brain and nervous system even farther in order to accelerate the awakening of Kundalini. With gradual practice, the mind is trained to fall into deeply absorbed conditions that, in samadhi, attain a depth that makes the seer oblivious to his surroundings, though far more intensely aware within.

The aim of the practices is to keep only one object or one line of thought before the mind to the exclusion of every other object or chain of ideas. In order to achieve one-pointedness of the mind, a great deal of voluntary effort is necessary, and the practitioner has to keep himself always in a state of alertness to prevent his mind from slipping into passive or drowsy states or into other streams of thought and fancy. There is a world of difference between a passive, inwardly focused mental condition—where the ideas are allowed to meander and drift, as is the case in the state preceding sleep—and the alert, attentive, centrally focused state necessary for concentration in all its forms.

This is clearly brought out in the *Bhagavad Gita* at various places. In verse 25 of the sixth discourse, for instance: "Little by little let him gain tranquillity by means of reason, controlled by steadiness. Having made the mind abide in self, let him not think of anything. . . . As often as the wavering and unsteady mind goeth forth, so often reining it in, let him bring it under the control of self."

This point is further elucidated by Krishna in reply to the query of Arjuna, in which the latter points out that the mind is extremely restless and as hard to curb as the wind. "Without doubt, O mighty armed," says Krishna (VI: 35), "the mind is hard to curb and restless, but it may be curbed by constant practice and by dispassion."

The cultivation of a one-pointed mind, as a prelude to attaining God-consciousness, is also repeatedly emphasized in the Upanishads. "Taking hold of the bow," says the *Mundaka Upanishad* (II: 2, 3), "one should fix on it an arrow, sharpened with meditation. Drawing the string with a mind absorbed in the thought of Brahman hit, O good-looking one, that very target which is the immutable."

The citations can be multiplied indefinitely to show that the practice of meditation, undertaken in all Yoga disciplines, has to be active in nature and that the mind has to be kept fully alert, focused only on one thought or image. The discipline has to be continued until the mind becomes habituated to concentrated application on one image or subject for prolonged periods. This state of one-pointed attention and absorption is better developed in the highly intelligent and talented mind and is a prominent characteristic of every form of genius. On the other hand, the vacant, idiotic, and insane minds lack the power to focus their attention intelligently on any subject for a sizable duration of time. The irony is that some teachers of Yoga and other meditational techniques, by their own admissions and demonstrations, confirm this erroneous view of the scholars.

Those who declare certain kinds of Asanas or a certain amount of control over their respiration, heart action, and other metabolic processes to be Yoga—or, in other words, the summum bonum of this time-honored discipline—fall into the very trap in which many scientists are gripped at the moment.

There are others who prescribe negative forms of concentration, forbidden by the ancient masters, which allow the mind to think loosely or wander ceaselessly during meditation, leading to passive, somnolent, or quiescent states indicated by the alpha signal in biofeedback. They say that the visionary experiences or creative flashes that sometimes occur in this state, as they do sometimes in dreams, also, are the landmarks of genuine mystical experience.

Misled by the annunciations of professional Yoga teachers, some scientists equate the transcendental state of mystical ecstasy with self-induced, quiescent, daydreaming, vacant, or passive states of the mind. In this assessment they fail to notice that in all the descriptions of mystical ecstasy there are certain very prominent and unmistakable symptoms that are not encountered in the alpha or the theta states.

These are (1) vivid sensations of light both within and without; (2) a feeling of extreme rapture that is reflected in the whole appearance of the individual; (3) often streaming tears at the majestic and sublime nature of the spectacle; (4) a sense of intimacy or proximity to an infinite presence or a celestial being; (5) contact with an infinite fount of knowledge; (6) horripilation; (7) a sense of unbounded wonder and awe at the surpassing vision; and (8) intellectual illumination with Jnana—that is, perennial wisdom.

During the period the ecstasy lasts, the awareness is highly intensified and enlarged. The individual becomes more fully conscious within than he ever was before, and the impact of the experience is often so powerful that even a single excursion into this ineffable territory remains indelibly imprinted on the memory to serve as a landmark through the rest of his life. The genuine mystical experience deals a shattering blow to the ego and melts down the walls that segregate the individual from the rest of his fellow beings.

The narcissistic and phony forms of Yoga or other disciplines, on the contrary, inflate the ego even more and isolate more completely the individual from the resplendent One in All. This is the reason why the truly illuminated are humble, unpretentious, and even childlike in their behavior, indifferent to worldly greatness and fame.

Unenlightened professional spiritual teachers are often self-centered, dominating, and ostentatious, eager for a following and the adulation of crowds. In one breathless moment of inner illumination wrought by the successful practice of Yoga, the whole personality of a man can undergo a radical change for life. "He who is happy within, who rejoiceth within, who is illuminated within," says the *Bhagavad Gita* (4: 24), "that yogi, becoming the eternal, goeth to the peace of the eternal."

In raising these issues, I do not want to cast any doubt about the therapeutic value of biofeedback training or of hypnosis or of those methods of mind culture that prescribe passive, empty, or fluidic states of mind for the practice of meditation. Nor do I want to raise questions about their capacity to bestow calm and relaxed states of mind or even to induce visionary or extrasensory states with weird features and colors, like the ones described by scientists engaged in this investigation. But this weird or exotic imagery, color, shape, or feature, unattended by other symptoms, is not mystical experience at all. These same experiences are sometimes encountered in dreams or with drugs. They signify neither the beatific state nor a contact with cosmic consciousness. When once this is clearly grasped, then only can there be any hope of a well-directed investigation into the still little-understood mystical ecstasy and other allied phenomena.

Mystical Consciousness vs. Drug States

Other psychic researchers equate mystical ecstasy with LSD experiences and the hypnotic state. They assert that the LSD state is very similar to mystical experience or that they can induce the mystical trance into their hypnotized subjects with proper suggestions. If these mistaken ideas are allowed to spread unquestioned, they are likely to rob religion of all its divine color and reduce it to the babblings of individuals prone to delusory states of mind with drugs, autohypnosis, or promptings from the subconscious in relaxed or semi-awake states between wakefulness and deep sleep.

An enterprising writer, R. Gordon Wasson, has identified the Soma of the Vedas—the drink of the gods, which bestowed immortality and led to ecstasy and the highest inspirational states—with the mushroom *Amanita muscaria,* or fly agaric in English. This brilliant red mushroom with white spots is said to be familiar in forests and folklore throughout northern Eurasia. The juice crushed out of it, the author believes, was used by Vedic seers copiously as an inebriant, and this soma juice is lavishly mentioned in various hymns as the source of inspiration of the Vedic poets.

"The most astonishing of candidates for soma was exposed by Sir Aural Stein, the explorer-scholar, as rhubarb," Wasson says.* "According to Stein himself, no Indian in recorded history has made a fermented drink of rhubarb, though, of course, with the addition of sugar or honey the juice lends itself to fermentation. Stein must have forgotten either his *Rig Veda* or his sense of humor." Wasson further states that in 1921 an Indian had advanced the notion that soma, after all, was nothing but bhang, the Indian name of marijuana, cannabis sativa, hemp, or hashish. In a flash of inspiration, he now replaces both of these with a "mushroom" fermentation.

The Wondrous Mushroom, by R. Gordon Wasson, McGraw-Hill, New York, 1980.

How far Wasson's own opinion is worth credence will be clear when it is pointed out that soma is also the name of the moon, which is associated with the luster in the head created by Kundalini. In every depiction of Lord Shiva, the crescent of the moon is shown invariably on one side of the head. The Vedic hymns, when read with clear knowledge about Kundalini, show that the drink of immortality is the ambrosia mentioned in the tantras and books on Yoga, whether Indian, Tibetan, or Chinese.

This nectarean substance flows into the head as a radiant, living energy, and then circulates in the body on the arousal of Kundalini. The Vedic hymns mention the attendant signs of thunder, light, and sounds, and symbology of the bull, sky, and the nectar; also the moods of ecstasy and inspiration that characterize the ascent of the divine fire into the brain.

There must have been a fermented drink, too, used as a stimulant even by the priests, just as we have alcohol today. But no priest or divine or other ecclesiastic of our time has waxed eloquent about it as the bestower of immortality and the vision of gods. This lack of knowledge about the phenomenon of Kundalini, and that it has been at the base of the religious and magical practices and concepts of antiquity, has been responsible for causing confusion among scholars in their attempts to interpret the ancient texts. There is similar symbolism in the tantras also where the word "wine" is mentioned with a double meaning. It is the common beverage often used in tantric worship and also the drink of divine intoxication, poured by an awakened Kundalini into the brain to cause the intense rapture and bliss characteristic of the ecstatic state.

Wasson himself seems to have forgotten to draw the correct inference from the hymn in the *Rig Veda* (X: 85:3), which says, "One thinks one drinks soma because a plant is crushed. The soma that the Brahmans know—that no one drinks." Brahmans means the knowers of Brahman or cosmic consciousness. The word "soma" has an esoteric meaning also. It refers to that vitalizing internal beverage with unlimited power of rapture that nature has provided as an incentive to the evolutionary effort in the same way as it has provided the transport of love as the incentive for the equally important procreative act of man.

In Sufi poetry there is the same play on the words "grape" and "wine." The Taoists call it the "elixir," the Indian alchemists "parada" or "mercury." Mircea Eliade has made a similar error in regard to the "nectar" that is said to drip down the throat from the palate from Khecheri Mudra and holds it to be saliva, implying that the ancient masters, who show such a deep knowledge of human anatomy, had not the acumen to make a distinction between saliva and the flow of an exhilarating essence in the region specified.

Again, a similar error has been made by C. G. Jung in his *Psychology of the Unconscious*, in interpreting a Vedic hymn referring to the fire produced by the friction of two sticks. He treats it as an allusion to coition, while the terms used clearly point to the fire produced by Kundalini. Meanwhile, what has been stated is enough to show that lack of sufficient knowledge of the esoteric aspects of ancient religions can ensnare even the most powerful intellect, not initiated into the mystery, into drawing wholly erroneous conclusions.

If the present-day trends in science continue to grow, the day is not distant when the state of religion in the countries that still follow some kind of faith would be no better than what it is now in the Communist lands. It will reduce the precious spiritual heritage—the Bible, the Upanishads, the *Bhagavad Gita*, the Koran, the Discourses of Buddha, and the inspired utterances of other saints and mystics—both in importance and value and deprive them of all the lofty ideals of their grandeur and worth.

The very fact that the existing major faiths almost everywhere have been a most dominating factor in the life of mankind for thousands of years should make scholars pause and consider that there must be some inexplicable reason at the bottom. What made vast multitudes accept their sway for such long periods of time and still do the same even in this rational age, in spite of all the apathy and even antagonism of sundry luminaries of science?

This point must be made with some force because of the momentous issues involved. The various systems of Yoga are designed to accelerate the evolutionary changes occurring in the body, to raise the brain to a supersensory level of cognition. This is the natural aim of all healthy religious disciplines and practices. The whole fabric of religion owes its existence to the instinctive response of surface consciousness to the demand of the evolutionary impulse, operating in the deepest recesses of the human psyche.

Whatever progress has been achieved so far in every branch of knowledge and skill has been gained by dint of rigorous mental effort-study, reflection, and concentration of the mind. Steady application of the mind, done voluntarily in full wakefulness, day by day by countless men and women, has made mankind what it is today. Is there a single man or woman of talent who rose to distinction without herculean effort?

The Goal of Meditation

A mind intensely concentrated on a single object is like a pinioned bird that cannot move its head. In this condition it can only see the object immediately before its eyes. There is then no possibility of its soaring in ever-widening circles to infinity. A state of abstraction like that of a mathematician solving a problem, or a painter drawing a likeness, is actually what is to be cultivated. An arrowmaker, so engrossed in his work that he fails to see the king passing by, is a classical example mentioned in the ancient manuals.

The aim of concentration is to stimulate a dormant reservoir of psychic energy to feed the brain. Mere pinpointing of the mind in itself is not illumination. It is only when there is a flow of this energy to the brain that the mind can slip its tether of the body and observe its transformation into an oceanic entity with amazement and awe.

The sensation of light or fire or inner illumination is a distinctive sign of the flow of this psychic force. The intellect continues to function in the background. Otherwise how can the condition be assessed and described? If intense concentration or pinpointing of the mind were an indispensable precondition, then other forms of Yoga—for instance, the Yoga of selfless action, or devotion and intellectual discrimination (the "wisdom of Plato")—would be entirely ineffective in inducing the mystical state.

In that case, how can we account for the experiences of those who have sporadic flashes of illumination? There is a whole army of talented men and women who, without any regular spiritual discipline or practice of Yoga, had the experience thrust upon them in a way that left a permanent mark on the whole course of their lives. The impact of the experience was so powerful that it outshone other extraordinary incidents of their lives. They include outstanding scientists and scholars about whose acuteness of perception and accuracy of observation there cannot be any doubt.

They include such figures as Pascal, Tennyson, Wordsworth, Emerson, Charlotte Brontë, Walt Whitman, Richard M. Bucke, George Eliot, D. H. Lawrence, Nietzsche, and many others. Their descriptions of the extraordinary state possess certain features that, for one who has had the experience himself, affixes the seal of authenticity. A few sentences from some of them should clarify what I mean.

"I was in a state of quiet, almost passive enjoyment, not actually thinking, but letting ideas, images, and emotions flow of themselves, as it were, through my mind," says Bucke. "All at once, without warning of any kind, I found myself wrapped in a flame-colored cloud. For an instant I thought of fire. . . . Directly afterward, there came upon me a sense of exultation, of immense joyousness, accompanied or immediately followed by an intellectual illumination impossible to describe. . . . I saw that the universe is not composed of dead matter but is, on the contrary, a living Presence. . . ."

The experience of Arthur Koestler is somewhat different but refers to the same, sudden transformation of consciousness: "This cliché had an unexpectedly strong effect. I saw Einstein's world-shaking formula, energy equals mass multiplied by the square of the velocity of light, hovering in a kind of rarefied haze over the glaciers, and this image carried a sensation of infinite tranquillity and peace. . . . The sensation of choking with indignation was succeeded by the relaxed quietude and self-dissolving stillness of the oceanic feeling."

Nietzsche's version seems even different, but on closer scrutiny conveys the same significance and points to the same enlargement of consciousness. "Has anyone ever observed that music emancipates the spirit, gives wings to thought? . . . The gray sky of abstraction seems thrilled by flashes of lightning; the light is strong enough to reveal all the details of things; to enable one to grapple with problems, and the world is surveyed as if from a mountaintop. . . . And unexpected answers drop into my lap, a small hailstorm of ice and wisdom, of problems solved. Where am I?"

This expanded consciousness does not only come with a sense of bliss, of stillness and peace, an oceanic feeling or the awareness of an infinite presence, but many times with problems solved and riddles answered. It has come through history and will continue to come to the end of time with new masterpieces of music, poetry, and art, new discoveries of science, and new horizons of philosophic thought. It is a mistake to isolate mystical experience from the creative impulses of the mind. Consciousness is growing in an ever-widening circle and, in this process, continues to pour into the lap of humanity all that is precious in literature, art, and science. Every high intellectual and every genius, gifted with creativity, is very close to the border from which the mystical province begins. The vision and the experience can come at any time.

Genuine samadhi or transcendental experience is like stepping into a wonderland where consciousness itself, and not the sensual world, becomes the fascinating object of contemplation. The mind and intellect are immovably held in the observation of a breathtaking display that is beyond anything experienced on earth, even in dreams. Mark the words of Tennyson when he says, "I felt my soul grown mighty and my spirit with such a vast circumference of thought. . . ."

In looking at the objects around him, he now sees something new that he never observed before. He perceives the difference in the forms, the temporal durations, and the distances as distinctly as he did formerly, perhaps even more distinctly than he did before. But at the same time, he sees all these things strung on consciousness as the pearls of a necklace are strung on a thread that runs through them all. Consciousness now becomes the primordial reality for the mystic in the waking, dream, and trance states. This is the reason why all authorities on higher states of consciousness in India agree on the point that Turiya—the transcendental state—covers all the other states of consciousness.

The enlightened consciousness that sees the divine in every object and every nook and corner of the universe, therefore, does not lose the sense of form but perceives everything distinctly as before. On the contrary, another faculty is added to the mind that enables it to perceive what it never saw before—the throbbing world of life, of inexpressible streams of consciousness flowing on all sides, like the transparent waters of a pellucid lake that allows the numerous aquatic creatures and plants subsisting under its surface to become distinctly visible without the least aberration in their forms. The sense of awe and wonder, of a fulfilling experience, of unbounded joy and the conviction of immortality, flows from this breathtaking transformation witnessed in oneself. Wherever the enlightened consciousness looks, it sees a projection of itself diversified into the countless objects it beholds.

This isn't all. When the external contacts are excluded and the consciousness broods on itself, it soon slips the anchor of the body and, extending in lustrous waves of undifferentiated awareness, assumes the proportion of a boundless ocean in which the melted ego retains just enough individuality to feel itself one with a stupendous universe of being that has no beginning and no end. It is a superficial knowledge of mystical experience that can cause one to believe that superficial methods such as drugs, hypnosis, guided meditation, mantras, or passive sleep-like states of mind can lead to enlightenment. Mystical experience, even when sporadic, denotes a leap into a wider dimension of consciousness, which is the evolutionary target of the human race.

In perennial mystical consciousness, the position of the subject and object remains the same, with this difference: Subjective consciousness now dominates the scene. The differentiation of form, whatever its physical basis, from the point of view of our mental processes depends primarily on the potentiality of consciousness to assume multifarious forms to interpret physical events about the real nature of which we know nothing except what is revealed to us by our mind.

What is remarkable in this subject-object nature of the world, and the observing consciousness, is that while all we see, imagine, scan, or weigh is constantly fluctuating, the mirror that reflects every image and every thought remains the same. The same subject-object relationship between the world and the human observer continues to exist even in the case of the enlightened consciousness, except with this difference: The role of consciousness, as the reality behind the phenomenal world of name and form, becomes obvious.

The panorama stretching to the last limit of the horizon and the void of the ambient sky, besides all the physical objects crowded into it, seems to be filled with an immanence, a glorious inexpressible presence, calm, serene, and blissful, unaffected by the most violent events and upheavals. It is like the deep bed of an ocean that remains undisturbed even in the most furious storm, lashing the surface waters into a violently agitated mass of racing waves.

For the enlightened, therefore, the divine and the world of forms exist side by side without causing the least confusion. The change in depth of the observing consciousness reveals a subtle new world, a living, throbbing world of unutterable beauty, harmony, happiness, and peace.

"By each of these disciplines," says Plato in *The Republic*, "a certain organ of the soul is both purified and reanimated that is blinded and buried by studies of another kind; an organ better worth saving than ten thousand eyes, since truth is perceived by it alone."

This is the divine eye that sees the one in many and unity in diversity. This is the divine flame burning everywhere to light the universe of suns and earths. This transcendental organ of the truly enlightened cleaves the darkness—*avidya*—of the normal mind to introduce a new feature in the consciousness of the observer. The phenomenal world seems no longer to be a monstrous cauldron of revolving masses and clashing forces but the planned creation of a cosmic intelligence ruling every atom of the colossal host.

CHAPTER SEVEN

Gopi Krishna's last visit to the West was in 1983, when he was invited to participate in a conference held in Davos, Switzerland, by the International Transpersonal Association. His paper was in two parts, the first dealing with the demands imposed on the human brain by evolution, and the second about Mahatma Gandhi and the widely publicized episode involving him and his nineteen-year-old grandniece, Manu. Due to the limitations of time, however, he was unable to read the second part. But the paper had been duplicated and copies were distributed to the participants. This chapter, then, is Part II of the Davos speech.

A PARADOXICAL EPISODE IN THE LIFE OF GANDHI

One aspect of Kundalini that would bring the phenomenon into focus, especially among scholars, concerns one of the most remarkable personalities of our time, Mahatma Gandhi, who brought independence to India. It shows how Kundalini acts as a divine instrument in shaping human destiny and how unique individuals, fashioned by her, become instruments in causing mass upheavals to change the fate of empires and the multitudes under their sway.

There was an episode in the life of this extraordinary man of which no satisfactory explanation has been provided so far. The authors of the book *Freedom at Midnight*, on which the Gandhi film is based, describe this episode as a drama whose unique dimensions eventually scandalized some of his oldest associates, alarmed millions of Indians, and baffled the historians who tried to comprehend all the intricate facts of Gandhi's complex character.

The drama centered around a nineteen-year-old girl, Gandhi's grandniece, Manu. The girl, orphaned at an early age, had been brought up by Gandhi and his wife as their own granddaughter. On the death of his wife, Gandhi promised to be a mother to the girl and actually cared for her as mothers do. One day, when nineteen, Manu shyly confessed to him that she had never felt sexual arousings normal in a girl of her age. Gandhi himself had taken a pledge to be a Brahmachari—that is, to abstain from sex—and had taken this decision to his wife in 1906. After the vow was taken, Gandhi did all in his power to obliterate the faintest signs of erotic desire in himself. For years he experimented with different diets to choose one that had the least effect on his libido.

As the result of his rigid control, he came to believe that he had killed the last vestige of sex in himself. But his confidence was shattered thirty years later when he noticed himself in a state of erection one night. He was greatly depressed at the thought that he had not been able to achieve the goal for which he had battled so long. The perfect Brahmachari, in the view of Gandhi, was a man who could lie by the side of a Venus, in all her naked beauty, without being physiologically or mentally disturbed. He firmly believed that the sublimation of his sexual energies would give him the moral and spiritual power to accomplish his mission in life.

After listening to the confessions of Manu, Gandhi decided to put himself and her to the test. With this idea in his mind, he announced his decision to Manu that they would share the same pallet and sleep together, like a mother and daughter, without the least idea of an erotic nature. Manu agreed and the plan was put into effect. But soon rumors began to float and scandals to spread. As his confidence in his mastery over himself grew, Gandhi extended the range of physical contact with women. He nursed them when they were ill and allowed them to nurse him. He had his daily massage on his bare body done by young girls, and in that state gave interviews or consulted with his party leaders.

As the word of what was happening spread beyond the limits of the Ashram, the news caused an intense shock to the party leaders, face to face with a critical situation at the time. Gandhi confronted the rumors in an evening prayer meeting. His words calmed his immediate associates, but the calumny continued to spread. Emissaries came from Delhi to protest against this strange behavior, but Gandhi flatly refused to deviate from his course. Finally it was Manu herself, perhaps on a hint from one of the emissaries, who persuaded him to abandon the practice with the assurance that in all other matters she would continue to act as before.

This riddle in the life of Gandhi has not been satisfactorily answered so far. In the case of a scrupulously conscientious man, like him, who staked his life for his principles not once but several times and did not yield, even in the face of death, it would be unfair to suppose that he had libidinous aims that he deliberately concealed under the pretext of acting as a mother to Manu. It is, indeed, a puzzle why Gandhi himself should have been so insistent on her sharing his bed in order to steel himself or her in the discipline of Brahmacharya, as he must have been conscious that such behavior on his part could be misunderstood and create scandals seriously inimical to his reputation and mission. We cannot imagine that a shrewd public leader like Gandhi could be so naïve as not to be aware of the consequences that could ensue from his strange behavior.

This paradoxical episode in the life of Gandhi is easily explainable in the light of Kundalini. As the result of a favorable heredity, his own ideas, and, perhaps, even practices, Kundalini must have started to stir in him even before he ceased his relations with his wife—that is, the energy must have started to flow into his brain. In other words, he must have felt that he was becoming urdhva-retas, which in Sanskrit means one with an upward flow of reproductive energy.

In the first phases of awakening, the demand on the energy is so much that sexual appetite is lost and the male organ shrinks. This is clearly brought out by Arthur Avalon in his book *The Serpent Power*. Gandhi, too, must have experienced it. This is patently clear from his own remarks that "the sexual organs of a real Brahmachari begin to look different. They remain as mere symbols of his sex, and his sexual secretions are sublimated into a vital force pervading his whole being."

The first phase of the awakening can last for months and years, depending on the constitution, heredity, life-style, and behavior of the subject. The awakening of the power signifies a new activity in the brain leading to an expansion of consciousness that ultimately terminates in the mystical vision. The opening of the brain center does not occur at once, because that would be calamitous and can end in instant insanity or death. But in benign cases it occurs by slight degrees, each small expansion followed by a period of adjustment, time after time, until the maximum possible for the subject is achieved. After each adjustment, when the demand on the secretions diminishes, the partially or completely lost virility is restored.

The attempt of the mechanism of evolution is to adapt the body to the expanding new activity of the brain so that the flame of extended consciousness is maintained undimmed, with the combined activity of the organs and tissues, as is the case with normal consciousness. For this vital purpose, every single drop of the reproductive fluids is sucked up and used as the driving force for the changes wrought. For this reason, although from the outward appearance the male member appears to shrink, there is, on the whole, a heightened activity of the reproductive organs to supply, for inner consumption, as much of the secretions as possible.

In this process there occur periods when the demand on the generative secretions is so great that the subject needs constant stimulation to increase the supply of the reproductive juices. This stimulation is provided by an erotically pleasing object.

The tantras and other works on Kundalini clearly acknowledge the need of an attractive female partner in the practices undertaken to awaken Shakti. The real reason for this lies in the demand of the brain to condition itself for the manifestation of a more extended state of consciousness. If this demand is denied, due to some fault in the reproductive system, or if the precious essence is wasted in pleasure, the results that follow can be disastrous.

Gandhi, as the leader of the independence movement of a subcontinent carrying a population of more than four hundred million, with a hundred problems constantly on his head, needed an enormous consumption of psychic energy to keep himself in a state of balance and calm. The expansion in his consciousness, which had already started, added vastly to the problem. Only a man of iron resolve could maintain his composure in the crises that surrounded him on every side. The drain on his procreative organs, to sustain his brain in such a situation, must have been terrific. It is no wonder, therefore, that this great son of India needed a stimulant to keep up an uninterrupted supply of the food his brain needed.

Most probably Gandhi himself had no inkling of the transformative process at work in him. This needed a life's experience of a powerfully active Kundalini. The adjustments must have taken a much longer time in his case, on account of the severe ordeals he had to undergo, the extremely austere way of life he led, the load of tasks he had to do, and the fasts he kept. He was cast into a severe fit of depression thirty years later when he noticed that he was still prone to sexual arousal, because he was unaware of the cyclic operation of Kundalini.

Gandhi could never know of the real reasons for his attitude toward Manu. He submitted to the organic need of his brain without knowing why he was so insistent in acting as a mother to his grandniece. Compared to the colossal task he had on his shoulders, this little episode of his affection for Manu and his preference for daily massage have no significance. Nature accomplishes her great tasks in her own way and leaves shortsighted mortals wondering how it could happen. But for this subconsciously motivated behavior, which he himself could not consciously understand, it might not have been possible for this great soul to carry out the herculean task that had been entrusted to him.

The experiments on Kundalini will keep the world breathless with wonder for centuries to come. Every great historical event, every great revolution, and every war that has occurred in recent times has been the result of a ferment in the brains of the leading figures involved, resulting from the activity of Kundalini. When this power begins to act, every facet of the personality in which she acts is known to her. The rigid, unbending Gandhi, who would not deviate from his principles, had to be tackled in his own way. In order to keep the overtaxed brain supplied with the fuel needed for its sanity, stimulation was indispensable. How could it be provided consciously, in the existing frame of his mind, against the principles he had cherished all his life? For this reason, the subconscious came into play, as it does in the life of many of us, to impel to actions unconsciously, which otherwise we would refuse to do.

There are certain peculiarities in the life of Gandhi that

unerringly point to the conclusions I have drawn. He was married at the age of thirteen, entering the delightful rose bed of wedded life with exuberant joy. It seems he had a strongly marked erotic side. This is brought out by a curious incident. One day, while massaging the legs of his dying father, whom he dearly loved, Gandhi was seized by a sudden burst of sexual desire that made him tiptoe to his room and wake up his pregnant wife. A few minutes later, while the two were still swimming in pleasure, a servant came to inform him that his father had died. The incident left a deep scar on the mind of Gandhi and could have provided one of the reasons for his vow of continence at the age of thirty-seven.

The pledge was not confined to the subdual of erotic desire alone. To Gandhi at this age it meant control of all the senses; restraint in emotion, diet, and speech; the suppression of anger, violence, and hate; a simple, austere life; and the attainment of a desireless state close to the ideal depicted in the *Bhagavad Gita* of a self-controlled sage. The most significant feature of the transformation is the age at which it occurred. As already indicated in my books, the usual time for a spontaneous arousal of the power is about the age of thirty-five, with a margin of a few years this way or that. The desires and impulses that arise are the same as those that stirred in Gandhi.

These include an accentuation of religious fervor, or a strong urge to turn from the world and devote oneself to a spiritual or a noble cause. Note the somewhat identical stirrings in the crowds that devote themselves intensely to spiritual disciplines. There are other traits exhibited by Gandhi during this period that leave no doubt that the energy had begun to operate in him. At the time when some of the incidents mentioned occurred, Gandhi, now seventy-seven years of age, was facing stresses that demanded a more abundant supply of the psychic fuel to save his aging brain from giving way under the strain. When Kundalini occupies the last center in the head, a continual stream of sublimated reproductive energy irrigates the brain, reducing greatly the pressure on the generative organs or removing it altogether. Instead of causing tensions that need release, it now opens a fountain of creative joy in the head that puts what was formerly thought to be the peak of delight into shade.

It is our own distorted vision, born of weakness, that makes us think that sex energy is too profane an object to be used for the holy communion with God. The breasts of a mother serve as a delightful object of erotic pleasure for the husband or lover, but at the same time they provide life-saving nourishment to her child. No one ever contends that the milk he imbibed from his mother's breasts in infancy was impure. In formulating her plan, nature does not care for the petty idiosyncracies of the human mind. The same divine power that brings a human child into being drives it at a certain period of life to the act of procreation and, when the time is ripe, fills it with the urge for self-awareness, as it had once filled it with erotic desire, to lead it ultimately to the vision divine.

I have presented the case of Mahatma Gandhi because it is typical of an active Kundalini. The aim has been, in the first place, to show the tremendous influence that the power exerts on the life of individuals and, through them, on the life of multitudes. Secondly, to throw a glimmer of light on one of the infinitely varied activities of this divine power to help those in whom it is astir, or might stir up in the future, to regulate their lives. Thirdly, the aim is to clear this great soul of the shadow that was cast on him toward the end by the episode described.

The union of men and women, on the earthly plane, for procreation or enjoyment is human. But the same union on the superearthly plane, to help the soul win back its glory and freedom, is divine.

At some time, I would like to discuss this subject at greater length, with illustrations drawn from the lives of other distinguished men and women in whom there is clear evidence to show that the power was active from an early period of life. These would include both Freud and Jung, who contributed so richly to the science of the mind but had no inkling of the mysterious force operating in them to which they owed their fluency of expression, vast knowledge, and deep insights. Had they known it, much of what they have written would have remained unsaid. Such is the bewildering play of Kundalini. She is the inscrutable Maya-Shakti, the author of this magic show of life, a dream and a reality both.

CHAPTER EIGHT

Gopi Krishna believed that validating the metabolic activity and the altered states of consciousness resulting from it would not take long, but he felt there was a great urgency in getting the research under way. This is the reason why, despite his reluctance to leave his new home in Dehra Dun, where he was anxious to begin work on a new book, he accepted the invitation to address the International Transpersonal Association at its 1983 conference in Davos, Switzerland. The title of his speech precisely states his purpose, because, as he told those in attendance, "the world is asleep while a crisis is mounting in every human brain." From Davos he went to Canada for a brief visit with friends and then to New York, where, in November, he met with Native Americans who wanted to know about his prophecies for the new age.

ACCELERATING BRAIN EVOLUTION:
The Only Path to World Peace

The awakening of Kundalini can occur in many ways, which will form the subject of future research. Here I would mention only two. One is the slow, imperceptible awakening effected by meditation and other moderate disciplines that come under the name Raja Yoga. The practitioner is usually not aware of the transformation that occurs in the cerebrospinal system until, in a successful case, an expansion of consciousness attended by indescribable happiness and beatific visionary experiences inform him or her that a change has occurred within. They often attribute this change to dormant powers of the mind coming into play, or to divine favor, or, as many psychologists believe, to the outflow from one's own subconscious.

What is not known or even suspected is that the expression "awakening of Kundalini" in the language of science denotes accelerated evolution of the brain and the activation of a dormant area in it known as brahmarendra. The arousal, through the forceful methods of Hatha Yoga, can be explosive and sudden. In that case, the cerebrospinal system leaps to a new, bewildering activity, creating chaos in the mental world of the subject.

Lightning starts to flash in his system and his whole inner being becomes a turbulent pool of light, with glistening silvery or golden threads marking the paths of the nerves through the body. An authoritative work on the subject, *Panchastavi*, describes the inner scenario in this way:

> Located between the four-petaled and the six-petaled lotuses (Muladhara and Swadishthana) at the end of the cavity of pudenda (that is, between the rectum and the genital organ), coiled three times, beaming with unbounded splendor like that of the sun, fire, or lightning, Thou, O Kundalini, dost first pierce the six-petaled lotus, then the ten-petaled (Manipura), then the twelve-petaled (Anahata), then the sixteen-petaled (Visuddha), and then the two-petaled (Ajna-Chakra), on Thy way to Brahmarendra, O Parvati, Daughter of the Himalayas, our obeisance to Thee.

The fascinating cartographs in the Hatha Yoga books, with their chakras, lotuses, and the figures of deities, are not merely a figment of imagination or creations of the subconscious. They represent a figurative rendering of the lightning effects perceived in the interior when the power starts to operate. Luminous currents dart here and there through all the body or rise into the brain to cause an expansion of the personality and fill it with a splendor that is awe-inspiring to behold. It is for this reason that in the Taoist manuals the awakening is known as the circulation of the light.

The secrets of Kundalini have never been disclosed openly so far. What I am revealing is not knowledge picked up by study or gained through reflection but gathered from my day-to-day experience for years on end. There are valuable hints scattered in the tantras, shakti shastras, and books on Hatha Yoga, but direct experience is necessary to understand them. The fact that the awakening is attended by luminosity in the interior, particularly in the head, and sounds in the ears, is repeatedly mentioned in these treatises.

In describing the gifts acquired, the words "high talent" or "genius" are not used in the ancient texts, but what is stated is that the recipient of the favor from the goddess becomes a great poet, a great logician, a great mathematician, a great repository of knowledge, or an eloquent speaker. Similarly, the attainment of miraculous powers or psychic gifts known as "siddhis" is invariably spoken of. From this it is easy to infer that in those cases where extraordinary talent or psychic powers are manifested as a natural endowment, it can be safely assumed that Kundalini is active to a greater or lesser degree.

Traditionally, the practice of Hatha Yoga is considered to be dangerous because, in the case of miscarriage, it can lead to insanity or death. The practitioners are forewarned of the danger in the texts. There is a borderline class, known as Avahoots in India and Mastanas in Persia, who combine extraordinary clairvoyant gifts and loquacious tongue with schizophrenia or manic-depressive psychosis in varying degrees. They are often highly venerated and sought after. Crowds follow them wherever they go in the fond but false belief of gaining some boon.

Specimens of this category sometimes pose as spiritual teachers to instruct others, while themselves unaware of their own aberrations. The irony is that even scholars are often carried away by the fervor of the moment and lend credence to what they say. The ill effects on the mind, caused by a miscarriage of Hatha Yoga practices, can also be true in the reverse way, which means that certain types of mental disorder might be due to a malefficient activity of Kundalini. This is an issue of great importance for healers of the mind.

The practice of Yoga of whatever kind and the arousal of Kundalini, in the final stage, lead to samadhi or mystical experience. Samadhi, too, can be of two kinds: one brought about by self-hypnosis, arrest of breathing, or vacuity of the mind caused by forced cessation of thought, or by making the mind blank. This kind of samadhi, except for certain visionary experiences, euphoria, or other benefits occurring through suggestion, has no transmuting effect on the personality or of opening a new channel of perception in the brain.

The other kind of samadhi denotes a revolution in the brain itself, leading to the formation of a luminous sheath known as the shining body, and as the solar body, which operates either for occasional brief intervals or in a perennial form as the interior self of the initiate. This inner transformation, involving the subtle areas of the brain, is not possible without the activity of the psychosomatic mechanism of Kundalini.

The cases of spiritual illumination have been rare in history. Mystics like Kabir, Rama Krishna, Rumi, or Eckhart have been few and far between. It is sometimes amusing to see the crowds of claimants to enlightenment who pose as spiritual teachers, counting their followers in the thousands, or even hundreds of thousands everywhere. Not a few of these adherents are men and women of learning and intelligence in search of guidance on the spiritual path.

I am curious to know whether there exists any criterion or a standard by which an enlightened individual can be distinguished from highly intelligent, versatile, but unilluminated claimants to this state. If there is a criterion, how has it been set up and how many people are aware of it? If there is no criterion, how has it been assumed that all that is said or written on Yoga or Kundalini today is correct?

If no standard has been set up and no thorough study made of samadhi or mystical trance, it means that the world is still groping in the dark about a phenomenon repeatedly observed during the past five thousand years and on which all of the current religions of mankind are based.

Kundalini, the evolutionary energy in human beings, is operating now as it operated in the past, to produce spiritual luminaries, oracles, prophets, sages, clairvoyants, philosophers, poets, musicians, painters, scholars, scientists, and other leading minds of mankind. But what is of importance for the world to know is that the operation of this divine power is influenced, to a considerable extent, by the environment, the traits of character, the frame of mind, and the life-styles of the populations or individuals in whom it is active, creating exceptional personalities for the race. Most of them are benign, but some are malignant.

Words are hardly adequate to express the staggering magnitude of the traditional concept of Kundalini, as presented in the tantras and shakti shastras. Her other name is Prana Shakti, the creatrix of the universe. As a small sample of the tributes paid to her as Prana Shakti or cosmic life energy, the following two verses from *Panchastavi* will be illustrative of what I mean:

> Thou art luster in the moon, radiance in the sun, intelligence in man, force in the wind, taste in water, and heat in fire. Without Thee, O Goddess, the whole universe would be devoid of its substance.

> Those starry hosts that roam the sky, this atmosphere which gives birth to water, this Shesh-nag [a mystical serpent] which supports the earth, the air which moves, and fire which shines bright with leaping flames, they all, O Mother, exist only by Thy command.

An intellectual treatment of Kundalini based purely on study or on one's own ideas about it without actual experience is not possible. This is brought out in the commentary on the very first verse of *Sat-Cakra-Nirupura*, on which Arthur Avalon's *The Serpent Power* is based. Sings *Panchastavi*,

> O Goddess, Thou art the Shakti [power] of Shiva [the Creator], who has the moon on His forehead, Thou art His body, the senses, the mind, the intellect, the power of action, and the doer of deeds. Thou art desire, rulership, and also delusion. Thou art His refuge as also the veil that hides the reality. What is there that doth not spring from Thee?

Another famous work on Kundalini, *Saundarya Lahari*, ascribed to the philosopher Shankaracharya, refers to this almighty power in the same reverential terms. Kundalini is the gayatri in the Vedas, the supreme mantra that every twice-born Hindu must recite with his morning ablutions. The syllable *om* is the symbol of the same power. As Prana Shakti, Kundalini is the architect of all forms of life in the universe. She is our thinking, our speech, our imagination, our creativeness, the energy that brings us to life, guides us in infancy, fills us with fire of love in adolescence, with ambition and the desire for adventure in youth and then slowly withdraws the vigor she had bestowed unto the last breath, when a mortal ceases to be an actor in the drama of life.

Kundalini will continue to remain a mystery till the end of time. Even when some secrets of this power and the methods to awaken it become a part of human knowledge, this marvelous element of creation will still continue to be beyond the reach of our intellect.

What I wish to make clear is that the phenomenon of Kundalini in its subjective aspect cannot be explored by any methods known to science. The only way would be for pioneers to make the experiment on themselves. Nature has interposed a barrier here that does not allow human intellect, concerned only with material objectives, to enter the holy precincts reserved exclusively for the enlightened mind. But there are physiological symptoms by which the phenomenon can be recognized at once.

One of them is the highly increased activity of the reproductive organs in both men and women. In the males, the activity can be easily measured, but in females, because of the very form of the organ, it is not so easy to do. From the experiences narrated to me by several women who had the awakening, however, it is clear that subjectively, and to a great extent objectively, too, the experience is similar.

Civilization and Kundalini are complementary, one accompanying the other. After many years of close observation, I have come to the conclusion that in the language of science, Kundalini represents the mechanism of evolution in human beings. Civilization is not possible unless this power has been activated to the extent that people are able to create and to conform to the conditions demanded by a civilized mode of life. It has been a great error to suppose that mankind could have moved even an inch beyond the thinking and behavior of the primate or subman unless there were, by some natural process, an upgrading of the brain.

The brain of the prehistoric man of, say, twenty thousand years ago, which could only articulate a limited number of words and live almost like an animal, without any idea of the ocean of knowledge that has grown since then, could not be the same as of the humans today. If this is conceded, it would mean that the mind can act independently of the brain. This would imply in turn that part of our thinking can be done without involving cerebral matter, which is to say without a corresponding activity of the neurons. Acceptance of this idea would spell the death of the Darwinian or neo-Darwinian theory of evolution and the origin of life.

Evolutionists who favor the Darwinian hypothesis are in a dilemma when face to face with the reality of the striking improvement that has occurred in the performance of the human brain. This is a change of such a massive character that no one can deny it. Why I am emphasizing this aspect of our progress is because the mighty psychic force responsible for this evolution has its own laws, and these laws must be known and obeyed if the race wishes to survive in peace.

The phenomenon to which I wish to draw attention now has, so far as I know, never been made a subject of study or discussion before. My own treatment of it might be startling and even unrealistic to critics, but it has to be kept in mind that the idea is broached for the first time and needs calm reflection or even further study by others before it is subjected to fire. But the truth has to be told.

It is only time and the experiments, which will be done in the future, that will show how far I was correct and what inner transformation had enabled me to uncover this law.

We all know that there have been many civilizations and cultures in the past, and after a long or short period of progress and prosperity, they came into evil days and vanished forever. This happened to the civilizations of Egypt that built the wonderful pyramids and temples, and the Indus Valley civilization that was so advanced that they had planned cities. Women used ornaments of fine workmanship and beauty aids to enhance their charms, as they do today, and there were toys for children to play with. The same fate overtook the Chinese civilization that built the Great Wall, wonderful palaces, and underground cemeteries for kings with clay soldiers, horses, and carts, lifelike in size, to defend the corpses when they were buried.

The Indo-Aryans excelled in metaphysical thought and contributed greatly to the advancement of knowledge in the sciences and arts. Then there was the Greek culture, with its great systems of philosophy and marvelous works of art and architecture. After that came the Romans, with their control over most of Europe and some other parts of the known world, where they built roads, bridges, and other facilities for civilized life. This was followed by an efflorescence in Arabia that penetrated to near and distant lands.

We now have the European culture, based on Greek and Roman prototypes but far in advance of any of the past ones on account of the transformation wrought by the discoveries of science and the marvels of technology. The point is whether this last crowning civilization, with all the highly advanced knowledge of science and the arts, would survive, if not forever, at least for thousands of years to come, or vanish like its predecessors, leaving only some relics here and there to show the grandeur it had attained.

This civilization has no external aggression to fear, as did the Romans and the Greeks, except perhaps from another planet, and it is too widespread and too strong to be in fear of vandals or barbarians as potential foes to reckon with. But strange to say, it has created a monster of its own by the very exuberance of its resources and the intellect, and that is the nuclear missile and the bomb.

The point is, why did the ancient civilizations deteriorate and vanish? Why, when at the height of wealth, power, and domination, should whole nations, dynasties, or families fall? Why shouldn't the progress continue, generation after generation, with the resources and the knowledge gained? Why should the present world, with all its wealth, knowledge, resources, and skills, its media, wise men, clever politicians, and giants of science, find itself in a precarious position almost on the verge of collapse if a world war breaks out?

Instead of setting a good example of love for their neighbor, essential for peaceful coexistence, why should the most advanced nations spend billions of dollars every year stockpiling a fiendish weapon only to destroy themselves? Have all the resources of human wit or, say, of diplomacy been exhausted to find a formula for peace? No. Because the urge for domination in the more advanced nations has become stronger than the basic urge for self-preservation. For an intelligent species that can employ the most destructive forces of nature to carry out its designs, this is a most ominous symptom. Has anyone answered this riddle? No.

Again, why is the glamorous world of today, provided with

easements and luxuries never known before, out to destroy itself not only by fighting a nuclear war but also by polluting to a lethal degree the planet on which it lives? The reason is because the knowledge of Kundalini or divine law of evolution is still a sealed book to the learned.

Civilizations rose and fell, families prospered and then went to ruin, individuals rose to power and then mingled with dust because of the ignorance of the cosmic law ruling the life of man. For those who believe in God, or a cosmic intelligence, it would be blasphemous to suppose that the universe has been created without purpose or plan, or that the race has been brought into existence only to eat, drink, and make merry with the extravagant expenditure of the resources, both mineral and organic, of the earth. There must be a reason why intelligence has been granted to mankind and why a whole planet with all its wealth has been placed at her disposal.

For any profound thinker, apart from the materialist, it cannot be a mere coincidence that there is a highly intelligent species with unbounded ambition, a fertile imagination, and an inventive brain at the top of the organic kingdom. It can't be an accident that she is placed in command of prodigious resources with no other claimant to dispute. There are scholars who talk on the origin of the universe, the wonders of the sky or galaxies thousands of light-years away, but when confronted with these questions of immediate concern to mankind, turn a deaf ear.

The alternatives are that either mankind will continue to stay on earth, using these resources more and more for her own pleasure and luxury, or with further advancement of technology, a segment of the race would migrate to other planets to people them. Continued residence on earth, with no outlet for extraterrestrial adventures at the present height of her intellect, would lead to stagnation, decay, and final death.

I am not dwelling on this issue as a topic for speculation but a stern reality, for mankind has arrived at the parting of the ways, where she can survive and progress only with full awareness of the invisible, superintelligent force that rules her destiny. The ideas I am expressing come from a massive book before my inner eye, which opens and shuts of its own accord, permitting a glimpse of only that which I am ordained to reveal.

If there is a purpose in creation, it can never be that the race has progressed to this breathtaking degree as a self-won achievement for which there is no reason or rhyme in the cosmic plan. It must surely be our lack of understanding that leads to this erroneous conclusion. If there is a purpose, it can't be that the highest embodied intelligence should surround herself with luxuries and idle away her spare time in pleasure and fun or that all her days and nights should be spent in satisfying her basic needs.

If this were permissible, then the vanished cultures of the past would not have begun to deteriorate at the very moment when they touched the zenith of prosperity, abundance, and luxury. It wouldn't have happened then that the imperial nations of the past would start to collapse when they were at the peak and then beget degenerate offspring who brought disgrace to the once-illustrious names. The historical instance of the horrible taint in the blood of the Roman emperors, beginning with Julia, the daughter of Emperor Augustus, and evidenced in Caligula, Claudius, Agrippina, Nero, and the rest, is but one of many to show what a curse attends unbounded wealth and unbridled power for which the ambitious sweat and bleed.

The purpose for which man has come is engraved on his forehead, stamped on his brain, and ingrained in his blood. What an average human being longs for most of all is plenitude, peace, happiness, a loving partner in life, health, freedom from ill luck, respect of his fellow beings, a long life, and a peaceful end. Immoderate ambition, insatiable erotic hunger, unrestrained lust for heroics or leadership, or a consuming desire for fame mark the character of only a fragment. No revealed scripture commends these traits, for they signify a deviation from the model of a harmoniously evolved personality.

The goal of humanity pictured by religion is of a superior kind. Every man and woman has to strive for self-perfection until he or she gains the inner kingdom or vision of God. The purport is clear. Satisfaction of the basic needs or pursuit of pleasure and luxury are not the targets of human life. Ambitious temporal goals are not equally feasible for all. They inevitably lead to competition and rivalry, which cut at the roots of compassion and love, replacing them with envy and hate.

Enforced equality, as a political measure, provides no incentive for hard labor and independent planning, except the interest of the state, which, after a time, ceases to inspire. Spiritual goals that prescribe austerity, sacrifice, and surrender generate admiration and gratitude. They have a greater appeal to the heart and a more elevating effect on the mind. The poorest altruist who gives what he or she can for a good cause is richer in the heart than the richest magnate who takes away for himself what he can from the world.

It may take ages, but the glorious consummation cannot but come to pass. A truly progressive mankind, free of retrograde conservatism and dogma, would arrange her social and political orders in a way that everyone has plenty and peace, living in harmonious surroundings, charming and clean, with war eliminated, poverty removed, disease controlled, decay arrested, and life prolonged—the inner being of everyone a bubbling fount of joy. This is the picture I see of the future of mankind.

No vicissitudes of time, no machination of the overambitious and power-crazy, no stockpiles of nuclear weapons, no destructive war, and no diplomatic maneuvers of the high and mighty would obstruct the fulfillment of this purpose. Every event that befalls, every weapon that is devised, and every battle that is fought, instead of blocking the way to this lofty goal would tend to bring it nearer and nearer. Such are the inscrutable laws divine.

Shortsighted mortals, for their own selfish ends, place hurdles in their path with their own hands, which sometimes calamities come to remove.

What I say is not a wishful dream. I am not speaking from the clouds. Note what a change has occurred between the uncouth Stone Age man or his unsightly wife and the handsome men and lovely women of today. From this it is easy to imagine what further transformation may occur in the not-too-distant future if the evolutionary beautician is allowed to accomplish her task. The beauty and vigor and fragrance of bodies perfected by Yoga is repeatedly mentioned in the ancient writings.

Longevity, extended youth, and freedom from disease are also added. The average age span of the more evolved race will be extended to one hundred twenty years. In and out, the future man and woman would conform to the highest ideals of beauty, grace, and nobility of which we sometimes dream.

Mankind has to stay for hundreds of thousands or even

millions of years on the earth. The era of science has only begun and is hardly two hundred years old. If the expenditure of the earth's resources or the use of machines continues, on the same scale, for hundreds of years, demanding less and less effort, both mental and physical, and adding more and more to luxury and indulgence, it will not be humans but a monstrous species that will inhabit the earth after only a couple of centuries.

The cureless toxins of decay will invade the brain, leading to aberrations, deformities, and perversions that have been a repeated feature of the decadent aristocracies and ruling dynasties of the past. No amount of scientific knowledge can grant us absolute power over life and mind. They have their own secrets and their laws. Surfeit and overindulgence act on them as lethal poisons act on the body. No human effort can alter this law.

Continued evolution of the human mind cannot be taken lightly or treated as a process that can go on by itself without our racking our brain about it. The transition from human to transhuman consciousness would create such a host of intricate problems for mankind and entail such care and attention that with all her resources of knowledge and skill she would find it hard to carry the load of duties and responsibilities involved.

It is for this reason that Kundalini is addressed as Mother, for it is only through her grace that the brain can be saved from cracking under the pressures exerted on it, when there is a conflict between the demands of evolution and the unwholesome life led by self-deluded human beings.

The tempo of progress can serve as an index to show at what speed the brain is upsoaring. The greater the speed, the more urgent is the need to put our house in order to avoid a conflict.

The world is asleep while a crisis is mounting in every human brain. Had the discovery been made in time, the state of the world would not be what it is at present. There would be better planning, healthier living conditions, a united mankind, more advanced social and political orders, and widespread awareness about the target of human life and the methods to achieve it. What we have is intellectual confusion and chaos, a Tower of Babel in which everyone is crying at the top of one's voice to make oneself heard. The cries mingle together into an incoherent roar that save for its loudness has no saving wisdom to impart.

With the first experiments on Kundalini, many of the current systems of thought, many of the concepts of science and the assumptions of psychology will come tumbling down to earth. The reason is that the universe we perceive is only a creation of consciousness. In one dimension it is all there, with its atoms and molecules, books and charts, suns and planets. In the other, it melts away like a vanished dream. But the mystery isn't over. The universe of consciousness now unfolded is a greater wonder and presents a more unfathomable mystery to solve.

Mankind, when arrived at this stage, would not be at the journey's end but begin another lap of it entirely beyond our imagination to conceive. One of the most amazing features of our time, in the eyes of our progeny, would be the blindness of the intellect that assumes that what it perceives with the senses is the totality and not just the tip of an iceberg of which the bulk is beyond our power to discern.

The leading personalities of our day are far in advance in quick-thinking political acumen and temporal knowledge of the greatest thinkers of the past. But many of them are pygmies compared to the spiritual giants of those times. The former present a disproportionate appearance in their psychic buildup, invisible to the normal eye, making them oddities on the astral plane, the result of lopsided evolution of the brain.

The millions of known cases of mental disorder, in spite of the crimes committed by some of them, are not a menace to the race. The danger comes from the crowds of smart, highly efficient people whose instincts are not balanced and who lack the moral counterpoise to offset the enlarged ego, boundless ambition, and immoderate greed of the highly intelligent mind. Keeping in view the picture of this mental disproportion, count now the number of abnormals occupying the highest seats of power among the nations of the world.

Remember that there will be in a few years no less than twenty nuclear states and that even one abnormal person at the head of any one of them can ignite a fire that would set the earth ablaze.

The only possible way to save the world from this grave danger is to gain knowledge of the evolutionary mechanism and the conditions needed for its healthy operation to create the harmonious personalities that can bring peace. The only method to gain this knowledge, apart from what is contained in the spiritual literature of the world, is to undertake extensive studies of the phenomenon in various places around the world.

There are many fields of study and research in the various departments of science, but none of such urgency and importance as the research on Kundalini. Nature has left no other door open for the study of the mind or other intelligent forces of nature, because further evolution of the brain is needed before entry can be gained to the supersensory planes of creation. It is only the accomplished products of Kundalini who will be able to guide the race beyond the intellectual level now reached by her.

CHAPTER NINE

This chapter, with some additional material from an interview, is an abridged version of an essay in *The Awakening of Kundalini*, published in 1975 by E. P. Dutton, New York. It had originally been presented as a paper at the 1973 Conference of the Association for Humanistic Psychology held in Council Grove, Kansas. "In all my writings," he said, "I have sown the seeds of what I consider to be the most pressing need of mankind—namely, information about the evolutionary mechanism in human beings, slowly drawing the race to a golden future of harmony, peace, and happiness."

ABOUT PSYCHIC PHENOMENA, PSYCHOLOGY, PRANA, AND FREUD

The idea of Kundalini is mentioned in a veiled way in the Bible, and there are clear mentions of it in books on alchemy and other esoteric disciplines. In the beginning of this century, an American writer, James Morgan Pryse, traced references to Kundalini in several passages of the Bible. For some years past, this ancient doctrine has penetrated even into the exclusive precincts of science, and some eminent scientists have come to know of its implications in the context of the current views about religion and mystical experience.

There is, however, a general attitude of incredulity in the context of the present attitude of science toward religion and the supernatural. This attitude has resulted in a curious situation. What we generally see is extreme skepticism on one side and extreme credulity on the other. Considering the climate that has prevailed so far, I welcome the rather rigid attitude from the ranks of science. Too ready a response to a new and unexpected idea is not to be expected of a seasoned intellect. A thorough probe is necessary.

What appears to me paradoxical is that some scientists should lend credence to various occurrences, as for instance telekinesis and the possibility of mystical consciousness with the use of drugs—both still debatable propositions—and should hesitate even to accept as a hypothesis that there does exist a dormant source of a still unidentified biological energy that is at the root of all such bizarre phenomena.

Can anyone deny that there must be an explanation in psychosomatic terms for all the transcendental and paranormal phenomena of the human mind? If the phenomena are accepted, then the existence of a causal source for them must also be admitted. They just cannot occur at random, due to causes that must always remain beyond the probe of the intellect.

If this position is not accepted, it means that both psychic phenomena and the beatific vision will, to the end of time, continue to puzzle and mystify without any hope of a rational or even suprarational solution of the problem.

Without the corroboration of a single great mystic, many scientists have taken it for granted that the conscious, semiconscious, or deep-sleep states induced by drugs, biofeedback, autohypnosis, or restraint of breathing and blood circulation, represent or are on a par with mystical experience—this despite the fact that they have not even tried to define in the phraseology of science what "mystical experience" means.

There is such a deep gulf of difference between the mystics known to history and the specimens produced by these methods that it does not need any special effort to distinguish between the two. The evidence furnished by all these subjects of investigation—psychic displays, hypnosis, mind-altering drugs, breathing exercises, other forms of Yoga—however trivial they might be, would tend to furnish material to enable scientists to formulate views about this still uncharted realm.

But since we know that mystics have been credited with all states and faculties—namely, psychic powers, including telekinesis, clairvoyance, precognition, healing, altered states of consciousness, trance conditions, and the like—why shouldn't mystical experience form the taproot of the research and the other occupy a subsidiary place to it?

With research on psi extending now to more than a century, have we come any nearer to the understanding of the force responsible for them? Has any psychic healer, clairvoyant, medium, or yogi been able to specify the force that is working in him? Do they not generally ascribe their extraordinary gifts and performances to a control (like the demon of Socrates), to concentration of mind, to pranayama, to the favor of a guru, divine grace, and the like?

From avowals made by persons of all these categories, not one of them has been able to furnish a rational or a convincing explanation for his or her feats or an accurate knowledge of the power working in them. Is not this study enough to convince investigators that they must look for the explanation somewhere else and not work in a rut in the exploration of a mystery that has baffled all great intellects of the past? How can the subjects of these extraordinary phenomena, who are themselves mystified by them, enlighten the men of science who investigate their surprising or weird displays?

I am concerned over the issue for several reasons. It is high time now that scientists accept the existence of bioenergy (prana), the intelligent force behind all chemical actions and reactions of a biological organism. Here we deal with a new dimension of matter and consciousness. The experiments made in Russia and other places to locate bioenergy (apparently the cosmic orgone energy of Wilhelm Reich) are yet in a very rudimentary state, but as has always happened in the sphere of knowledge, if the idea is based on a solid foundation, the experiments will be successful and the elusive medium will be located one day.

What I suggest is that an investigation on Kundalini provides a most practical way to study the action of bioenergy in the transformative processes set afoot in one in whom the energy is aroused. We have numerous historical instances to show that conversion and transformation of consciousness are possible under certain circumstances. But how does it happen? What are the biological factors responsible for it?

As already mentioned, the first symptom of the awakening that I experienced was a sensation of light in the head. It was not as if I were seeing the light or that I had an inner vision of light, however. Rather, it seemed as if a stream of liquid light were entering my brain. It still persists to this day.

During the first days following the awakening, it was distracting, but slowly it began to acquire an enrapturing condition. Now it is fascinating to a degree I am not able to express. From the first day, after the power was aroused, I felt this stream of liquid light moving through all my nervous system, in my stomach, in my heart, in my lungs, my throat, and in my head, taking control of the whole of my body. That was a most marvelous experience for me, as if a new life energy had taken possession of my body.

It was intelligent, purposeful, an energy that knew what had to be achieved and was aware of all the conditions and rhythms and effects of my body. It knew every organ intimately and behaved in a manner that continued to sustain me through each day, even though I was thinking that I was perhaps heading toward a lunatic asylum, for months and years.

This experience is mentioned in many esoteric books. It is described in one of the most authoritative books on this subject, *Sundalarhi*, written by Shankaracharya. Some thirty-six commentaries have been written on it, and every syllable has been explained by commentators. From the first line to the last, the author expresses his humble submission to the same power to which he attributes his life and all that he has gained—his genius, his breath, and everything that he owns on earth.

In fact, the moment this energy begins to circulate in the body, man's pride falls to the ground. He then sees for the first time that he is not the master of the body but that there is an energy, a life energy, superintelligent and loving as a mother. It is this energy that keeps our body in shape, that digests our food, and that, when we sleep, tones up the brain and clears it of poisons. It sustains us in illness and, when an accident occurs and, say, a bone is broken, or there is severe injury in the internal organs, it at once knows what is to be done. The person may be unconscious, but things are happening inside his body to sustain life.

It is this that is the mother energy, the intelligent energy that maintains the flame of life in every living organism.

Now, according to current concepts in psychology, it is held that the subconscious mind or the unconscious maintains the autonomous functions of the body. Actually, it is this superintelligent energy. This is what I want to make clear. Our mind is also a product of this energy. It enters the brain like an electric current, and then the brain begins to function. It enters the heart, and the heart begins to beat. It enters the stomach, and it begins to digest. It is an energy that is a marvel of marvels.

My own humble contribution to the ancient tradition of Kundalini—not as a speculative hypothesis but as the direct outcome of my own experience—is that this dormant reservoir of bioenergy is not only responsible for mystical experience and the still baffling psi phenomena but is also the presently unlocated and still disputed evolutionary mechanism in human beings, as well as the fountainhead of genius and extraordinary talent.

Let us take as an example the studies of the phenomenon of sleep. Only two decades ago, some of the dramatic disclosures now made were not only unknown but also may not even have been believed. Even with all the research done so far, the mystery of the REM phase, peculiar to mammals, stands unsolved. There must be some solid reason behind it.

It has been observed that deprivation of REM sleep for a period of several days in succession has a tremendous effect not only on people but even on animals. They become abnormal and behave in strange ways. There occurs loss of attention and avoidance of work in human beings. A man of steady character may become irresponsible and flippant, behaving in a manner as he would never do in a normal state.

Why I am very much concerned over the issue is that just as deprivation of REM sleep creates certain abnormal conditions of the mind, in the same way, deprivation of a healthy environment at an advanced stage of human evolution creates abnormal tendencies in the human mind that are impossible to remedy unless the environment is changed.

The problems that now face parents did not exist fifty years ago. From where has this tidal wave of unconventionality, distaste for work, craving for drugs, unrestricted sex, etc., invaded the earth? Do we not see in the present revolt of modern youth some of the features that attend prolonged deprivation of REM sleep? Without the investigation of sleep and dreams, it would not be possible to ascribe a sudden change in behavior of an individual known to us caused by insufficient

REM sleep as the real cause, and we would naturally grope in the dark to assign a reason for it.

In the same way, because of our ignorance about the evolutionary needs arising afresh at every step of the ascent, we are prone to ascribe other reasons for sudden changes in behavior of people. It may be that just as in the case of change in character due to loss of REM sleep, the real cause could not be diagnosed fifty years before, fifty years hence what I now assert about the sudden change in behavior of a section of modern youth might be explained in the light of the research conducted during the interval.

The reason for concern lies in this: Deprivation of the needed environment and a healthy way of life compatible with evolutionary needs can have a subversive or distorting effect on the mind. We can see the indications in the growing scale of teenage suicides and the growing scale of mental disorders.

With even slight aberrations in their mental equipment, of which we have seen several examples in the rulers and dictators of the current century, mankind can never abide in safety or peace under its leaders or presidents or kings, in any form of government, in the years to come. This unavoidable conclusion regarding present trends cannot but cause concern to every farsighted human being.

Kundalini is the guardian of human evolution. When aroused in a body not attuned to it, without the help of various disciplines, or not genetically mature for it, it can lead to awful mental states, to almost every form of mental disorder, from hardly noticeable aberrations to the most horrible forms of insanity, to neurotic and paranoid states, to megalomania, and, by causing tormenting pressure on the reproductive organs, to an all-consuming sexual thirst that is never assuaged.

I am not telling a fairy tale conjured up by my imagination but have experienced the hard realities of this yet little known phenomenon not only on myself but also have met it in the case of scores of other people and treated some of them back to sanity and health.

In the ancient books on spiritual awakenings, mind is held to be the product of this energy or prana. Prana is the life energy, and it is also responsible for the mind and the intellect. It has to be understood that prana is the energy that maintains and sustains life in all its forms. It is the Holy Spirit, and it is responsible for all the phenomena of life, even our intelligence.

In the normal condition, prana keeps us tied to this world, just like normal human beings. In this normal condition, prana enables us to function with our thoughts and feelings in a normal way. But when it is aroused, then its attempt is to change this average mortal into a superhuman being with a transcendental state of consciousness. And it achieves this purpose by transforming the brain and the nervous system as well as the internal organs. This is what occurred to me.

It took me twelve years to reach a new dimension, where I could be certain that a very radical change had occurred in my interior—twelve years of daily remodeling; and all the while I was watching it helplessly as it acted in my body. Even now, sometimes, I watch it.

Specifically, some of the changes I noticed taking place were—that is, from the very start—that I was day and night living in light. The first thing that happens is that the bioenergy that feeds our brain and in the normal individual is not visible, becomes distinctly perceptible.

Suppose you are now trying to visualize some distant city, such as New York. You then see New York in the normal way, as I myself used to see it before this occurrence. But now if I try to visualize a place I have seen, I see it bathed in light. I see it against a bright background in the back of my head. My imagination is now glowing, virtually glowing like an everburning light, and all my thoughts, all my reasoning, all my calculations are done in this light. So there is a radical change in the mental stuff. It is changed, and one lives in a world of light.

The very first verse of *Panchastavi*, an ancient and highly esoteric work on Kundalini, makes it clear. It calls the energy by two names—the abode of light and the abode of sound. Both of these are present in me. I constantly have music in my ears. The *om* signifies this sound. I hear it like the murmur of bees or like bells that are ringing at a distance, or like a stream that is gently flowing. It is a beautiful music, always present in my ear. And an effulgent light is always present in the back of my head. It is constantly there.

This light pervades my visual field of perception, both internally and externally—internally in dreams, and when I am imagining something, and when I am sitting and turn my attention inward. Or, if I close my eyes, I see a starry sky glowing, just as on a clear night you see a sky shimmering with the starlight. And when I turn my vision outward on the world, I see everything bathed in a silvery light, like an enchanted place. For me, the world is now a paradise, an enchanted place in which to live.

Let a team of open-minded scientists, in the service of knowledge, call by means of wide publicity for personal histories of people who have had or are having Kundalini experiences, and the results, I am sure, will be a flood of letters from people in all spheres and walks of life. Many of these will, no doubt, be fictitious from hysterics and cranks, but there would still remain a large percentage of genuine cases that can provide incontestable evidence for what I say.

Though I am aware that any allusion to any ancient work on a religious subject is anathema to some scholars, who think, like the intellectuals of sundry vanished civilizations of the past, that they have reached the end of knowledge, I am purposely reproducing this verse from a work more than a thousand years old to show that what I am stating has confirmative evidence of the past. The verse, from *Panchastavi*, mentions the gift of genius and, what is as important, the flow of the gleaming radiation and the potent generative fluids from the muladhara chakra—that is, the reproductive region—to the brain through the spinal cord. The language is metaphoric, but the allusions are clear:

"Flawless, exceedingly sweet and beautiful, soul enchanting, uninterrupted flow of words [in speech or writing] manifests itself on all sides in them [devotees blessed with genius] who keep you, O Shakti [energy] of Shiva [universal consciousness] the destroyer of Kamadeva [Cupid], constantly in their mind.

"They see you shining with the stainless, pale luster of the moon in the head, seated on a gleaming lotus throne, sparkling with the white glitter of snow, sprinkling nectar on the petals of the lotuses both in the muladhara [the root center, close to the organ of generation] and Brahma-Rendra [the cavity of God in the head, corresponding to the ventriclar cavity]." (3:12)

The sparkling radiation is white like snow. Sometimes it is likened to camphor and sometimes to milk. The ambrosia is the nectarlike reproductive secretion that, at the highest point of ecstasy, pours into the brain with such an intensely pleasurable sensation that even the sexual orgasm pales into insignificance before it. This unbelievably rapturous sensation—pervading the whole of the spinal cord, the organs of generation, and the brain—is nature's incentive to the effort directed at self-transcendence, just as the orgasm is the incentive for the reproductive act. In the later stages, the sensation ceases and a perennially blissful consciousness becomes a permanent or occasional feature of the successful initiate's life.

The bliss of ananda, repeatedly mentioned in Yoga manuals and other spiritual books, refers to the transformed rapturous consciousness created by the flow of the bioenergy drawn from the nerves feeding the reproductive system and spread all over the body. The distinguishing feature between this bioenergy and that normally feeding the brain is that the former appears like a glowing radiance in the head, spread around the body, and, when the attention is directed inward, spreading far and wide to reveal a throbbing world of lustrous, intensely blissful life.

The single-pointed attention of the talented writer, poet, musician, scientist, and painter or thinker, and the moods of intense absorption experienced during the creative periods, attended by a sense of satisfaction and even joy, felt by every creative mind at its handiwork, both depend on the operation of Kundalini. The gifted child who neglects his play or other form of amusement and sits absorbed in some book or an experiment or a work of art, is blessed with an emanation from the same source. In mystical experience, the beatific state, transcendence or samadhi, the same bioenergy, rushing up in a much more powerful stream, creates the transports of inexpressible bliss and the intensely absorbed state of ecstasy.

In all the authoritative books on mystical experience, as has been said, two symptoms, light and sound, are mentioned repeatedly. Also mentioned are inspiration and revelation. They are considered to be the signs of one being born again. And then there is bliss, or inner happiness, which is indescribable. One can imagine that he becomes a king overnight. He certainly will be very happy, but that happiness can only be for some time, whereas in the case of genuine spiritual rebirth there is an ever-welling fountain of happiness. This is one; the other is that it is attended by music in the ears and light in the head—an entrancing, absorbing light.

Also, one gains deeper insights, knowledge, inspiration, poetry, and in some it may be art. These gifts come spontaneously, from inside, even if one has had absolutely no attachment nor any aptitude or predilection for such things.

For instance, I began to write poetry, like a child. I felt an irresistible urge. Now I must write poetry. Somehow I was taught. My ears and brain were working together so that ultimately I composed some good pieces in my own language and in other languages, too.

There is the case of Janaka, who started to write transcendental poetry from the age of eight and astounded his teachers and his parents. It must have been a case of the prana being awakened from birth. Prana awakened is the fount of genius. It is the fount of creative gifts in man. To what extent it will lead in the future I cannot even dream at present. It may lead to such discoveries of science as are totally beyond our thought at the moment.

There are two phases to spiritual rebirth. The first is when the energy is working to adjust the inner organs and the brain to the new condition. During that period, any physiologist can see an unusual activity going on in the body. For instance, for years my pulse rate was about a hundred, just like a baby's. My elimination, also, was like a baby's. My appetite increased during one period to an enormous extent, so that I could eat almost ten times what I was normally eating. But during those days my body had already adjusted to some extent, and my elimination remained normal. I gained weight, of course, but at the same time, what was more important is that I survived. I say I survived because I had made a mistake. I had again begun meditating, though my body was not yet adjusted to the former awakening, and I opened the center in the brain farther.

Now the opening of this center needs a greater flow of the new bioenergy, otherwise there is either insanity or death. The bioenergy flows into the brain from the reproductive organs, and one can easily see the sensations and feel the flow all the time.

This I have confirmed from other people, also. In the beginning stages, the flow of this energy into the brain creates such an irritation of the nervous system that there are constant orgasms going on inward. I was frightened, thinking that something abnormal had happened to me. Such a condition can be easily observed if there is a genuine case of a Kundalini awakening. No scientist can doubt it afterward. It can be most easily verified in a laboratory, because during the first days there is a very strong pressure on the sexual organs. One can feel them moving with tremendous activity. It is as if an all-out effort is being made to produce as much sexual fluid as possible, to be absorbed into the organs, the nerves, and the brain, so that the new nerve energy might be able to circulate without causing disturbance.

It is like this. Suppose we have an infection. The body then tries to throw it out and the organs work with increased activity. There is a higher temperature, and the heart beats faster. It is the same after the awakening. In the beginning stages, it seems as though a foreign element has entered the body and the reaction follows. Ultimately there is a battle between the energy and the organs, and they are subdued. The nerves become accustomed to the new activity, and then a person becomes normal again. Now I am just like a normal human being. I don't perceive the energy flowing through my nerves unless I turn my attention inward because they have become accustomed to it. But in the beginning, the sensations were very acute, and I was constantly disturbed.

Now I would like to change my drift a little. In the case of insanity and psychosis, one almost invariably finds the people affected complaining of sensation, burnings, terrible lights, fire, noises, etc. This is the prana acting in a morbid way, when the nervous system is not in the right order, or when the heredity is not favorable, or when the life is not well disciplined. Then the bioenergy, which is now set into motion and flowing, is never able to adjust the body.

I passed through almost every stage during the course of my experience, but there was one thing of great importance. Heaven bestowed on me a tremendous power of mental endurance. Every day I witnessed in my own self something I can only ascribe to insanity, and yet something was assuring me, "Be patient. This will end in a beautiful way. You have to endure this torment for a short time." This especially happened in dreams. When I was terribly agitated, all I had to do was recline on a bed. Then I would feel the silver energy going (even now this happens) into my brain and soothing me. And soon I would fall asleep.

So somehow my system was already ripe for the experience. If it had not been, I would not have survived. This readiness of my system I ascribed to the life of my father and mother. They were ideal people, so whatever I have gained, I credit more to them than to myself. It somehow seemed that it was a predestined combination. My mother was the third wife of my father. One had died, and one was not mentally sound, and then he married a third time, and there was a difference of something like, maybe, twenty years between the ages of the two. But somehow, in my case, it created the eugenic factors so that my nervous system and brain were able to adjust to this powerful energy, which otherwise could have ended in disaster.

The nature of mental illness, so far as my experience goes, is subject to verification. What is known as human personality—the living, thinking "I"—is a certain spectrum of the prana. This ephemeral "I" or ego or personality, which thinks, imagines, and feels, is a spectrum of prana that reflects the eternal light as a dewdrop reflects the sun. Everything happens by the reflection of that eternal sun.

What we perceive is the reflection of that light through the spectrum of prana, and it is different in every individual. There is a specific spectrum for apes, another for baboons, and still another for elephants, etc. It is this spectrum of prana that is the heredity also, and it carries life on from generation to generation. Evidence in support of this can be seen in sickness.

For example, a person is terribly ill, and after three weeks, when the illness grows worse, he has delirium, and his personality is totally distorted. All of his body and the organs try to maintain its purity, but death occurs when the pranic spectrum can no longer be kept in its proper condition. This is the reason for death. Disease occurs when the body becomes impure. The bloodstream and tissues become poisoned, and the pranic spectrum loses its original condition. We have a fever, or we have this or that, but in fact it is the prana that is first affected.

Scientists hold that the effort of the body is to maintain the purity of the blood, but it is really the pranic spectrum, and when, due to certain conditions of the body, or due to a morbid awakening of Kundalini, or because of an inferior organ, such as the liver, kidney, or the heart, the pranic spectrum cannot maintain its purity, a psychotic emerges. In that case, it is a disorder of the imagination, of the will or of thought, because the prana is in a disoriented condition.

There is a very close relationship between the psychotic and the mystic. In a mystic, there is a healthy flow of prana into the brain, and in the psychotic the flow is morbid. In fact, the mystic and the psychotic are two ends of the same process, and the ancient traditions class mad people as mad lovers of God, or something divine. Some of them in this category have clairvoyant faculties. In many clinics, there are people who are mad but who pose as geniuses, poets, spiritual teachers, or as clairvoyants.

C. G. Jung, in *The Secret of the Golden Flower*, records certain cases in which the insane made drawings that resembled the mandala, the circle used in tantric practices. Naturally this means they had the same tendencies in their subconscious as the tantric worshipers had. In their case, they are distorted. What the mystic feels as joy, the psychotic feels as terror. What the mystic sees as blissful light, the psychotic sees as a blinding glare. What the mystic feels as cool and fresh, the psychotic feels as fire. So it is the same energy, now distorted, that burns the brain.

What actually happens is that terribly poisoned prana goes into the brain, and the suffering is awful. Why some people who are insane commit suicide is because they cannot bear it. They cannot tolerate the mental torture they experience.

As has been mentioned, prana is the purifying agent of the body and mind. The most important psychological change in the character of an enlightened person would be compassion. He or she would be more detached, have less ego, and without any tendency toward violence, aggression, or falsehood. The awakened life energy or prana is the mother of morality. It has been this evolutionary energy that has created the concept of morals. All morality springs from it, not from an expediency of our social structure.

This means there is definitely a biological basis for morals and values. It is the activity of this life energy that guards our morals. When it is awakened, its first effort is to clean the mind of evil desires and passions, of anger, malice, envy, and jealousy, even of excessive ambition and desire.

In my view, one distinguished psychologist or biologist, or

even a great physician or surgeon, blessed with the same experience that I have or that fell to the share of the great mystics of the past, could prove instrumental in causing a revolution in thought, as Sigmund Freud did. Freud, however, showed excessive, even mistaken emphasis only on one aspect of the life energy, which he called libido. This sexualized "élan vital" is, in terms of Freudian psychology, the archstone of human life. It is the foundation of man's character; the bedrock of his mental traits; the guardian of his family life; the fountainhead of poetry, drama, romance, and chivalry; the bestower of genius; the mainspring of his love, loyalty, attachment, and devotion; the architect of his civilization; and, at the same time, the demon of his envy, jealousy, hate, and aggression. When repressed, disoriented, or frustrated, especially in childhood, it may take the monstrous form of mental aberration, perversion, neurosis, and insanity.

Perhaps no other psychologist had such a tremendous influence on the thinking of mankind as Freud. Do I not represent Kundalini in the same terms without the extremism of Freud? Is not Kundalini also the sexual life current? I even define its somatic character. Where lies the difference then between what I say and what is generally accepted by all Freudian psychologists of today? The main point of difference between us is this: The ubiquitous libido of Freud is not merely the eros but much more, namely the central fount of life energy, which acts both for propagation and evolution.

The moment this is accepted, the angularities and extremes of the Freudian hypothesis disappear. The frantic, even morbid efforts made to interpret everything in terms of sex can be plainly traced to an error. While the multisided effect of the powerful sex impulse can be clearly noticed in many spheres of thought and act, other influences also come into play, as for instance the urge to power and wealth, the desire for name and fame, the thirst for self-knowledge, the lure of the supernatural and the occult, and the like, which have profoundly shaped the life of man.

Since mystical experience and the concepts of religion did not dovetail with his hypothesis, Freud quietly set upon the task to uproot the whole edifice of religion and the supernatural. To him they were nothing more than pathological states of the mind, a regression of childhood narcissism that sets store on an illusion to gratify itself. These formulations, one can plainly see, have had a pernicious effect on the thinking of a large percentage of modern psychologists. For many of them it is even difficult to extricate themselves from the chains forged at an early age to bind their mind firmly in disbelief and doubt. Had Freud, like Dr. R. M. Bucke, even one glimpse of the transcendental, his whole pattern of thought might have changed and his prodigious influence caused a healthy revival of spiritual science.

Freud's concept about libido is of a psychic energy drawn from the libidinous tendencies in human beings, which is to say the reproductive energy, but only from a psychic point of view. He does not say that it has organic roots. This is what Wilhelm Reich emphasizes, that this libido must have roots in the organic structure of the body.

We know our bodies depend upon food and that there must be some way by which organic energy is transformed into psychic energy. It is not purely chemical energy, nor is it purely electrical energy. It is something about which science is still puzzling over. Therefore, Freud's concept of libido was restricted only to its psychic sphere, with no explanation and no description given of its somatic base. I believe that in the seminal energy of human beings there are two ingredients; one has a subtle, volatile, organic base, which can at once be converted into psychic energy of greater potency, which streams into the brain in the form of liquid light, and also a grosser, biological part, which also goes to the brain through the spinal canal, and there it supplies nourishment to the cells when the process of Kundalini rejuvenation is going on.

What my experience tells me is that in the whole organic structure of the body and in the cells there is a vital element and that the nerves collect it and concentrate it in the reproductive fluids of both men and women, and that when Kundalini is activated, a reverse action takes place. The vital element is then separated from the grosser elements and, as a radiation, it then streams into the brain to give rise to the phenomena associated with mystical ecstasy.

Research on this energy is essential for psychologists to know the nature of the mind. At the present moment, psychology deals only with the observed phenomena of the mind but not its nature or what energy feeds the brain, or how it is related to the body, or how the body acts on it, or how the mind acts on the body. Research on the phenomenon of Kundalini will for the first time reveal how energy is supplied to the brain, and that it is superintelligent.

The actions and reactions of our muscles, and what happens in sleep are not done mechanically by the cells, but an intelligent energy courses through our body, acting and reacting in such an amazing and bewildering way that the intellect cannot even trace it. This will be the first lesson for psychology.

In fact, psychology will begin from the time the research on Kundalini begins. At present it is not a science, because it does not know the nature of life energy. It only records some observed data about dreams, about sleep, about mental disorder, or about habits, or about the fact that there is will or imagination and feelings, etc. But it gives us no hints about life at all. So the study of psychology will really begin from the day research is made on the phenomenon of spiritual rebirth or mystical experience. At present, psychology is a disputed realm. Different psychologists have different theories. Some believe in a soul, others do not.

The day is not distant when the transpersonal trends in psychology and psychiatry, already started, will completely sweep away the sacrilegious area of his speculation. There is no answer in any system of modern psychology to the challenge posed by the revolt of the rising generations and the entirely unexpected trends of thought met in them. Why this upheaval has occurred is not difficult to understand. We all know what happened whenever a political system became despotic and oppressive, a social system exacting and corrupt, and a religious system excessively authoritarian and dogmatic. There arose a demand for revision and reform. Political revolutionaries, reformers, and prophets appeared on the scene. The old system was overthrown, often with dreadful bloodshed, suffering, and pain, and a new one installed in its place.

The same may happen to the present overbearing and dogmatic trends in knowledge. There may be a revolution, which has already started, and it may not stop until radical changes are effected. "The attempt to combine wisdom and power," said Albert Einstein, "has only rarely been successful, and then only for a short while."

It amuses me when I see scientists, justifiably proud of their knowledge, summarily dismiss what I say as unrealistic, even preposterous. What is a mystery to me is that on what grounds do they base their instant judgment? Does what I say violate any biological principle or law? In the present stage of our knowledge of the brain and the nervous system, is it abhorrent for a man of science to assume the existence of a living energy responsible for the phenomenon of life? If not, where lies the harm in accepting what I say as a working hypothesis for empirical verification? The idea, I agree, is entirely novel and is broached for the first time. But that is no reason to assume beforehand that it cannot be true.

If a new idea that has a certain amount of plausibility is viewed with suspicion and mistrust from the very start by men of learning, then how can knowledge grow? "I know nothing except the fact of my ignorance," said Socrates, in spite of his prodigious knowledge compared to the standards of his day. Time has proved him correct to this extent, that we now know much more. How can we know that something similar to what I affirm would not disprove, in the years to come, many of the views about the mind and consciousness voiced proudly by the savants today?

What Freud did in his day some scientists and psychologists are even now doing with regard to the inexplicable phenomena connected with religion and the occult. The neurotic and psychotic, with all their changing moods, eccentricity, erratic behavior, fear, anxiety, hate, violence, aggression, awfully depressive or excited phases, persecutions, delusions, obsessions, and fixations have, like a normal man, a personality of their own. A personality alienated and distorted, no doubt, but a personality nevertheless.

Each case of mental disorder has a well-marked character of its own, and, apart from the appearance of the body, can be recognized by his or her peculiar mental traits, as we can recognize normal men and women by theirs. This definitely points to a basically altered neuronic structure or composition and also to alterations in the bioenergy supplying the brain.

I am positive about this because I have myself come across some cases in which neurosis and insanity appeared soon after the awakening of Kundalini. I am also in touch with cases in which the arousal has led to frightening or mind-shattering experiences. The libido, to use the name adopted by Freud, must have roots deep in the biochemical structure of the body. The fact that it can affect human behavior in drastic ways, and even violently change the whole pattern of life, is clear testimony to its influence on the chemistry of the body. Its expression through the evolutionary channel—that is, the brain—is subject to the influence of countless factors connected with the life, environment, and the family history of an individual.

When even slightly tainted or stained, due to various causes such as a wrong mode of life, unhealthy environment, faulty heredity, shock, frustration, repression, tension, and numerous other factors, it becomes the direct cause of mental and nervous derangement. It is hard to believe that any psychologist, with a somatic bias in his beliefs, can disassociate consciousness from the condition of the brain. If the mind is abnormal, the brain, too, must be a shareholder in the abnormality expressed. According to the latest research, there is a confirmation of the position that the horrifying visions and auditions of the insane have their root—in certain kinds of disorder—in subtle changes in some neuronic structures in the cranium. The real root, as has been said, is an impure or toxic condition of the prana.

The susceptibility to mental distemper, noticed in the men and women of genius, and the extreme care enjoined on yogis in every detail of life in the ancient scriptural lore arise from this reason. When pure, the bioenergy released by Kundalini causes the transports of ecstasy and the flow of genius, and when toxic, the nightmares of insanity.

It may be interesting to note that after my awakening, my dreams were in fairylands. According to Freud's interpretation of dreams or books on dreams from other authors, they appear to be very strange and bizarre occurrences, sometimes giving fear, sometimes creating distractions, etc. In my case, generally, the dreams are in fairylands, in vast spaces, in the sky, on the oceans, or of other forms of life, of other beings, as if I live on a borderland between this world and the other. And in my dreams, the other world, too, is revealed to me.

I never have a nightmare, never a frightful dream. Somehow my system is now kept clean, and the joy that wells up in me during the day is also present in my dreams. These facts are all mentioned in the ancient books, the sacred teachings or scriptural lore.

The men and women who have undergone this transformation and now have this expanded consciousness and bright imagination are known to be in the samadhi state, the state of oneness with cosmic consciousness. All the great mystics who have written on the subject have given their own symptoms openly and plainly. That is the tradition. And from their descriptions, one can compare one's own condition. So I feel no reason to doubt that what I experience is a normal state. Though very rare, it is a real state and one that has been responsible for all the mystical experiences of which any record is available.

I feel that I now have the same experience that the great Christian mystics, Sufis, Taoists, and Yoga adepts have written about, but with this difference: In my case, as in many others, the mystical condition is perennial. It is constantly present. In some cases it comes in flashes, in spontaneous spurts in varying periods, maybe from a few minutes to an hour or two in duration. But in my case, it is now a perennial condition.

This has given me the conviction that the human mind is evolving toward this state as soon as the human body can maintain the brighter flame of consciousness. The inference is obvious, that the human race is proceeding toward this higher dimension of awareness.

THE SPLENDOROUS EDEN IN WHICH I LIVE

We never realize, when looking at the brow of a friend or stranger, that inside the osseous dome the whole universe is contained in but one particle of divine substance, smaller than a grain of salt, smaller even than the smallest fragment we can see.

It is not to the pineal or the pituitary gland that I refer; it is not to any part of the brain material, but to the wonder that builds it in the womb and uses it as its instrument to enact the drama of life in every individual.

The wealth of knowledge the future voyagers shall bring in the days ahead, to enrich the race with spiritual treasures, is beyond conception. The world still has no awareness of the real marvel of the brain, and the quest to know more about it will never end as long as humanity is allowed to stay on earth.

What skies will open before her, what horizons melt, what barriers she would overcome, what tempests brace, what sights would meet her eyes shall be the saga of the future. It will be

CHAPTER TEN

In 1983, Gopi Krishna agreed to write an article on creativity for the magazine *Impact*, published by UNESCO, but he was unable to complete it before his death. Much of what is included in this chapter comes from the notes he made for it, and also from other unpublished work.

"I don't claim that my poetry or my prose possess that excellence that is the hallmark of genius," he had written at one place, "but for one who had never been a poet or a writer all his life, the sudden acquisition of the gifts, at an advanced age, as happened in my case, is not an ordinary occurrence, and I view it in the same way as Newton viewed the fall of an apple, as indication of the universal law of gravity. What I have to say about creativity or genius is not intellectual or theoretical but born of my own experience. And I can say with confidence that I have observed myself as meticulously and dispassionately as an empiricist would observe an object under his study in his own laboratory."

packed with romance, adventure, transport, and delight, before which all the sagas of the past would fall into shade.

What I have learned is that the brain, the most precious possession of every man, woman, and child on earth, is in a state of organic transformation, carrying the entire race toward a glorious destination. The Creator is far, far away. The Lord of this infinite creation, though everywhere, is yet farther away than the last limit, if any, of the universe. There are countless planes of consciousness and countless barriers of the sensory walls to be crossed before He can be reached.

But the Almighty can be experienced by the puny human mind. His glory is spread everywhere, and in the illuminated state, this glory is perceived more clearly than in normal consciousness. This is what actually happens. What I have learned is that the human encephalon already has embedded in it the scroll or blueprint of man's future destiny, and what is even more fantastic, it also has built into it the key to his rise to another dimension of consciousness.

It is in this new dimension that, for the first time, light begins to dawn on his own mystery. Even if I write a dozen books, it will not be possible to narrate in detail the highly exciting and adventurous life that I live within. From December 1937, and after every few years, the panorama in my interior changed, and I found myself in a new world, each time with its own allurements and its own problems.

The most beautiful palace on earth, with mirrors, crystals, and gems, everywhere reflecting the milky luster of hundreds of fluorescent lights, would be a poor simile to portray the splendorous Eden in which I live and breathe. It is a fairyland beyond the conception of the most imaginative writer. My experience, understood in its true color as the entry into another dimension of consciousness, presented to me a new vision of human destiny.

This is a multifaced, multidimensional, and multitudinous universe. Humanity lives and dies in but one out of innumerable planes of consciousness that exist in it. Our sensory equipment is only for this one particular plane of existence. Creation does not consist of what we call spirit and matter alone. The universe we perceive is but one out of myriads running parallel to each other, sometimes occupying the same space, formed of diverse, what we name material, components each imperceptible to the other.

Each has its own layout, its own expanse, boundaries, plan, its own dwellers, order, values, rules, and laws. It is clear that there are other channels of knowledge that come into operation in transcendental consciousness.

In describing my experience, I must make it clear at the outset that my mind does not work in the same way it did before 1937, or as normal minds do. My inner being has been completely altered, and now my observing self or "I" is always encircled by a halo of light, which extends on every side to an unmeasured distance or as far as my imagination can reach. Whatever visual images there are have a lustrous formation visible against a background of mellow light. It is an incredible state of being. I see my whole body and surroundings permeated by this luster, a living radiance that fills all the space within and outside of me.

I have no words to express the sense of sublimity I feel when looking at a beautiful panorama of nature, or the azure sky glowing with the light of the sun. There are moments when I realize with a thrill, which permeates to my inmost being, that it is not an earthly vista I am looking at but divinity transformed into the fascinating spectacle I see.

In my autobiography, I have described my fluctuating mental condition in the beginning. This fluctuation was due to alterations occurring in my pranic spectrum. It was this slow transformation of the element constituting my personality that ultimately resulted in the state of radiancy in my interior that I never possessed before.

After my first experience, however, I oscillated between life and death, sanity and insanity, for nearly twelve years and experienced the indescribable ecstasies of the mystics on the one hand and the agonies of the mentally afflicted on the other. For part of this period my mental state became so acute that, when retiring to bed at night, I was never sure whether I would rise alive or sane in the morning. But almost by a miracle my reason and judgment remained unimpaired, which allowed me always to evaluate my mental condition day and night. I clearly saw my own organism battling with a new situation in my interior, as if a new and powerful psychic energy were operating in my brain and nerves in place of the former, much weaker current, whose passage I could not feel at all.

But the powerful energy now circulating in my system filled my head with a silvery luster and darted through my nerves and organs in flashes of light. At the same time, I started to hear an inner cadence, varying in tone and pitch, from time to time, which has lasted to this day. This play of sound is known as unstruck melody in all the books on Kundalini, and it is an unmistakable sign of the awakening of this power.

Inner light is an invariable feature of mystical experience. In the mystical trance, the subject finds his visionary experiences bathed in a heavenly luster and sometimes hears voices or sounds coming out of empty space around. After nearly twelve years of uncertainty and suspense, I found myself well established in a new state of perception resulting from a continued biological transformation that had occurred during this long period and of which, in my ignorance, I could not make head or tail, as the whole province of this extraordinary potential in the human body is still shrouded in mystery.

I now came to realize that every panorama of nature had a beauty for me that I had never noticed before. Every landscape or scene I observed, and every object I saw was bathed in a milky luster that enchanted me, and I could hardly take my eyes from it, so fascinating was the spectacle at times. My ears were always listening to an enrapturing melody, except at times when I had some health problem. Then the sounds became somewhat discordant and harsh, as if to warn me that something was amiss in my interior. This helped me times out of number to assess the condition of my health and to take precautions in time.

At last I arrived at a fairly stable mental condition, but the process of expansion still continued, almost imperceptibly, without causing any disturbance or anguish, except during rare periods of ill health. Finally a stage came in the evolution of my mind where, whether sitting in my room or in movement outside, whenever I turned my attention upon myself, I experienced the same oceanic expansion, the same thrill, the same wonder, and the same radiance as I did on the day when Kundalini irradiated my brain and wafted me to lustrous planes of eternal being for the first time.

It is only now that I am able to assign a reason for this

unbalanced state of mind that defied all my efforts to understand at that time. The awakening of Kundalini does not only mean the activation of a dormant force in the body, but also an altered activity of the entire nervous system and the opening of a normally silent center in the brain. The repeated allusion in the Yoga texts to the central conduit, designated as Sushumna, and the outer channels, Ida and Pingala, to chakras or nerve plexuses, controlling the vital organs—lungs, heart, liver, kidney, digestive tract, etc.—and to particular areas in the brain, like the Brahmarendra, provides clear corroboration for what I say.

What I would wish now, with all my heart, is that this transformation be recognized and accepted as a possibility for every individual. I believe it is often to this transformation that the books on alchemy and occultism refer in the West and those on Yoga and the tantras in the East. My conclusion is that the brain has a potential unknown to science that can radically change the personality of a human being.

Though I have received communications from hundreds of honest people narrating their experiences of Kundalini and expanded consciousness, save in extremely few cases, the narratives fail to draw a correct picture of this extraordinary state.

Those who wish to confirm whether their own experience of altered consciousness conforms to the accepted pattern should make a study of the accounts of a few of the great mystics known to history.

A normal person, turning his attention upon himself, after closing his eyes, disregarding the impressions coming through the senses, perceives an area of awareness primarily around his head. It extends to the whole periphery of his organic frame when he brings his attention to bear on it. The same individual, when reflecting on an issue, with his eyes closed, makes it the focus of his attention within the small area of his awareness, or in other words, in the inner recesses of his being or self. This narrow, body-dominated area of awareness is the private sanctuary of all human beings. It remains alive and alert from childhood to death. In it every one of us lives, perceives, thinks, reflects, imagines, feels, fancies, and dreams. This is the inner man or woman of whom we only see the outer raiment of flesh but whom we never glimpse intimately by any means whatsoever—an elusive element that no one has been able to grasp so far.

This inner, intimate sanctum of awareness is dominated by the ego. Every individual experiences himself as a unit of awareness, always conscious of his body and his own individuality, name, face, form, color, parentage, home, country, race, occupation, faith, creed, and the rest. Every person is a type by himself, in some particular way differing from the rest, with his own quota of intelligence, humor, love, feeling, good and evil traits, and all other characteristics that go to make up a human being. With all these differences, the one thing in common to all normal people is this ever-present sense of "I-ness" and the area of awareness surrounding it. This area, in turn, surrounds the body and, except in states of deep absorption, whether on external objects or inner events, is intimately aware of the corporeal frame.

For the purpose of our discussion, it is not necessary to make fine distinctions among mind, consciousness, and awareness; otherwise we will end in confusion. Every person, with the perennial backdrop of ego or "I," thinks, feels, or experiences, etc., in his own unit of consciousness or awareness or mind. When the subject of transhuman consciousness is more fully developed, new terms or phrases will have to be added to the existing languages or a new language will have to emerge to portray what current semantic devices are not able to express correctly.

The Sanskrit language is already more expressive in this respect, but scientific terminology to cover all the different aspects and shades of this transformation is necessary. It is sure to come into existence in the course of time.

With the arousal of Kundalini, this unit or circle or pool of awareness, consciousness, or mind starts to expand. What does this mean? It means that the individual ego, with its small periphery of awareness, always perceptive of its close link with the body, begins to grow wider and wider and the idea of the body dimmer and dimmer, until it seems that one is floating in space, unfettered by the mortal frame. It seems as if the body has melted away or receded to a distance, where it is almost lost to one's perception. Consciousness now dominates the whole scene, clearly perceptive of the transformation that has occurred. There is no interruption in the continuity of observation, as happens in sleep. The intellect functions even more clearly than before, observing the amazing metamorphosis with wonder and awe, uprooted from the position it held before.

To explain my point, all I need say is that there is a tremendous unused potential in the human brain. In order to make use of this potential, close cooperation between the nervous system and all the vital organs is absolutely necessary. A person has to change to the roots of his being to possess a mind that can penetrate to the deeper layers of creation. In the case of some—for instance, born mediums, clairvoyants, seers, and the illuminati—the organism is already conditioned that way from birth. In those who have to develop the faculty, a transformation has to occur in the deepest levels of their mortal frame.

The explanation I am offering to account for all paranormal phenomena may well cause surprise and even incredulity. The parts of the body—namely, the brain and the nervous system—or the force that operates through them—namely, life energy or prana—are still fringe subjects. Science has slowly come to the same conclusions to which I have been irresistibly led by my experience. The indications are already there, but more time is necessary for a closer accord.

For instance, only recently the existence of a hitherto unidentified nervous system regulating the activity of certain organs has been announced. Also, a team of Russian scientists has reported that the thoracic duct, which contracts and relaxes, plays an important role as a second heart in the organism's vital activity and that it works all the time, pumping five to six liters of white blood a day. A controversy is now on whether or not the finding of the Russian team is correct. We are not concerned with what the final outcome of the debate would be, as for our purpose it is sufficient to note that the existing knowledge about the body, which is considerable, is still far from complete. Therefore, a dogmatic attitude resistant to new ideas and discoveries about the potential present in it is, on the face of it, irrational and unscientific.

The practice of every form of religious discipline is designed to cause this altered activity of the cerebrospinal system. There is no other way to gain supersensory perception or a higher dimension of consciousness. This altered activity of the brain and the system has been at the bottom of every case of illumination, seership, and genius in the history of mankind.

For the purpose of this thesis, it is necessary to reiterate the view I have expressed in my previous works, that a slow process of evolution is at work in every member of the human race to effect this alteration, generation after generation. The aim is to reach a climax where a superior consciousness will bloom in the distant progeny. The process can be accelerated with certain psychosomatic exercises, making it possible to reach the climax in a single life. It is on this possibility that all healthy spiritual disciplines are based. There is also a possibility of a fortuitous combination of favorable hereditary factors, resulting in the birth of a more evolved specimen, with the characteristics peculiar to illumination or to seership or to an intellectually gifted mind.

Science has still to account for the phenomenon of enlightenment, which has been responsible for the greatest mental revolutions in history. It also has to solve the riddle of genius, to which all the material and intellectual progress made by mankind is due. The wonder is that the world is still at a loss about the source from which all art, science, philosophy, ethics, religion, and all other knowledge has been born. But what is even more surprising is that while the learned assiduously devote all their time and energy to add to this already vast store of knowledge and art, they show but little interest in discovering the source from which it all comes.

The activation of the cerebrospinal system until a higher dimension of consciousness is manifested can occur in several ways. There can be a slow process of arousal, so gradual and imperceptible that the practitioner of a discipline is not able to notice any marked change in his normal awareness almost up to the last. What he might notice is a change in his thinking and behavior; an urge to meditate or pray; a preference for solitude; a greater regard for principles; abatement of passion, ambition, and desire; diminution of ego and pride; a growing love for his fellow human beings; and an impulse for self-introspection, with a growing sense of inner peace and detachment from the world.

An unmistakable sobriety in thought and serenity in behavior in such a person soon become apparent even to a casual observer. He wins the confidence and respect of those who come in contact with him. Steady and self-reliant, one in whom the practice of a spiritual discipline proceeds in a healthy way, he soon becomes independent in his opinion and judgment and is not easily influenced or diverted from his course by the changing trends of the day.

The aim of the evolutionary process is to create a more noble, more sober, more far-seeing, more sensitive, more compassionate, and more loving individual. Those who think that their practice of Yoga or another spiritual discipline has come to fruition, or that their Kundalini has awakened, would do well to assess their progress by a critical examination of their own thoughts, acts, and behavior to know how far their evolution conforms to the standards set in the great religious scriptures of the world.

The first signs of success are a greater regard for truth; a greater measure of self-mastery; steadfastness; altruism; the absence of envy, malice, and hate; and a greater sense of empathy with all human beings. The climax of the practice—namely, the vision of God or cosmic consciousness—can be sublime and blissful only when the personality of the seeker evolves in the right direction as a result of the changes brought about in the organism.

The reason why all great spiritual teachers, including the founders of the major faiths, have laid greater emphasis on the cultivation of noble qualities than on meditational techniques is obvious in light of this fact.

A healthy, well-balanced, normal mind is far more preferable, from the point of view of survival, than an unbalanced or unhealthy paranormal one. Every step taken in the upward direction must be attended by a corresponding improvement in the thought and behavior of the person. This correspondence has special relevance to the problems of our time. Mankind is in a critical state because a good many of the leading minds lack some of the essential qualities needed for balanced evolution. The thermonuclear devices and the present precarious condition of the world are the grim outcomes of this disproportionately evolved personality.

There are countless people who, with the practice of Yoga or other forms of meditation, experience luminous phenomena in their interior or even when looking out. They often ascribe them to a new psychic development in themselves. They see flashes of light or colors or bright halos around objects or lustrous figures or designs, and the like, attended by sensations in the spine as if some kind of an energy is rising through it into the brain. I receive numerous letters from different parts of the world claiming experiences of this kind and seeking my opinion about them. In many cases, the correspondents believe they have aroused Kundalini and that the lights they are perceiving or the sensations they experience result from it.

There are many in whom these phenomena occur even without the practice of a spiritual discipline. That in most cases of both these categories, the lights and the sensations result from Kundalini admits of no doubt. But whether or not the development is healthy and would lead to a harmonious state of expanded consciousness is often open to question. For those who have these experiences, the only correct way to evaluate them and to assess the possibility of their success is to measure how far their thinking and behavior have changed for the better, and how far they have gained in inner strength and character than before.

If the assessment is favorable, one can be sure that one's evolution is proceeding on the right lines. If the assessment is not favorable, reappraisals of the discipline undertaken and of one's own mode of life are called for.

We now come to the other type of activation, where the practice of a spiritual discipline leads to a sudden arousal of the power, as happened to me. In such cases, mental and physical disturbances often become unavoidable. The reason is a sudden change in the functioning of the brain. The activation of the normally dormant supersensory chamber creates a revolution in the entire organism. The brain now needs a more powerful psychic fuel to perform its new, highly enhanced functions. The organism works feverishly to bring about this adjustment. I suffered and sometimes blundered because I had no inkling of the upheaval that had occurred.

The true proportion of the change that spiritual disciplines are designed to cause in the brain is not generally understood. It is not that a good life has to be led and meditation practiced in order to propitiate a deity, to win a peaceful and happy mental state in tune with the reality. The actual position is that with the practice of these disciplines, a mechanism in the brain springs into action, causing a revolution that can act as a bolt from the blue on the mental world of the individual, especially when the onset is sudden and unexpected. This is particularly true with hazardous Hatha Yoga practices. The sudden onset of this activity, as the result of heredity or misdirected Yoga practice, can become the cause of intractable forms of psychosis that defy all attempts at cure.

This fact, too, has a special relevance to the conditions existing today. That an abrupt activation of the evolutionary organ, or its malfunctioning, can lead to certain types of mental disorder is an issue of paramount importance, needing immediate atttention on the part of science. The obvious inference is that the evolution of the mind does not occur only at the level of the psyche, as held by some scholars like Sir Julian Huxley or Teilhard de Chardin, but has its roots deep in the psychosomatic organism of man. In other words, the human brain is still in a process of organic evolution toward a target of which we have no awareness at present. Research on Kundalini will confirm this.

The still persisting organic evolution of the brain raises issues that are of staggering importance. We show little concern about what is happening in our cortex because we are entirely unaware that it is still evolving in a definite direction, toward a predetermined target. We are unconcerned because we still do not know that nature is insistent that, more than wealth or possessions, we should leave, as our contribution toward human progress, a more enriched and healthy mental endowment for our progeny. We are unconcerned because we are ignorant of the fact that in spite of our present advance in knowledge, we are recklessly violating a most stern law of nature, which rules our destiny, and that the present dangerous condition of the world is the direct result of our wanton disregard for this almighty law.

I have no words to convey the magnitude of the error that lies behind our current thinking about the mind. If mankind is growing in intelligence and if this obvious growth results from an organic evolution of the brain, there must be a system in this upward drive based on certain conditions similar to those that govern the growth of all organic forms of life. It cannot be a random process, acting capriciously, carrying one brain in one direction and the other in another, or choosing some and discarding others at its own fickle will and choice. But it must be a uniform process operative in every member of the race, under biological laws that shall become known one day.

All forms of life on earth are provided with survival mechanisms and, in the case of gregarious types, with group instincts that guide them in the habitat they choose, the food they eat, the shelters they build, the societies they form, and the mode of life they lead to conform to the pattern ordained for them by nature. Generation after generation, these creatures follow the same instinctual behavior, and have been doing so for hundreds of millions of years. The issue here arises: Has man, because of his intelligence, been left absolutely free to choose his habitation and to live in any manner that suits his pleasure or need, or has nature imposed certain conditions about which we have no accurate knowledge at present?

If there are no conditions attached, it means he is even free to destroy himself. If he is free to destroy himself and actually effects his own destruction, it means there is no almighty power governing the behavior of intelligent forms of life.

This raises important ontological issues. If man destroys himself, it would mean that the whole aeonian drama of his evolution, enacted for millions of years, has been in vain, that he is just as waste a product as the dinosaurs. The inference would then be clear that either terrestrial life is the result of an accident or the creation of insentient forces that have no plan and no design. Or, if there is an intelligent Creator of the universe, He is totally unconcerned with what happens in it. In either case, the conclusion would be the same, that there is no almighty power to take cognizance of man's behavior and to override his decisions when they are in sharp conflict with the laws ruling his destiny.

It does not stand to reason that the creation of an infinitely intelligent and omnipotent Creator can be without design or that, out of the existing countless forms of life, man alone is exempt from conforming to the ordinances of nature. This does not stand to reason even if we hold that life is the outcome of an accident, because there is no creature in the organic kingdom whose behavior is not governed by strict biological laws. It might be that we are ignorant of our own profundity.

It is only now that we have begun to learn more facts about the inexplicably mysterious senses in some lower forms of life—

for example bees, bats, ants, migratory birds, etc.—and this has made the mystery even deeper than before. Can it not be that there are ever more profound depths in the human psyche of which we are unaware at present? This unawareness, in turn, could be the reason for the behavior that has brought us to the brink of disaster at this particular time.

Coming back to the issue of evolution, it is obvious that if the brain is still in the process of organic growth to reach a predetermined target, it means that there is purpose in human existence and that evolution is planned.

If evolution is planned, it follows that there is intelligence behind the whole phenomenon of life on earth. In that case, there cannot be uncharted freedom for man alone out of all other creatures on earth. There must be curbs and controls that do not allow him to interfere in his own evolution. There must be impulses and instincts that come into play when he attempts to break away from those natural curbs on his behavior.

It would be puerile to suppose that the all-knowing intelligence, which has planned this evolution, would not be prescient of the fact that, at a certain stage of his intellectual progress, man would be in possession of forces capable of destroying the entire species, and even the whole kingdom of life on earth.

This technological leap to almost unlimited power of destruction must have been foreseen and provided for. The possibility of divine intervention in the affairs of man, at times of acute crisis, to prevent him from doing irremediable harm to himself or causing his own destruction has, therefore, always to be kept in mind. I say this firmly because the time for the demonstration of spiritual law has come.

CHAPTER ELEVEN

In response to the many requests he received asking him to prescribe some form of meditation technique, Gopi Krishna dictated this brief suggestion. It was on his last trip to the West, in 1983. After his death eighteen months later, "A Prayer to the Lord" was found among his unpublished papers.

ON MEDITATION

I am not taking any disciples or giving guidance, because if guidance is to be given it should be individual. Different people are at different levels of evolution already. They have different constitutions and temperaments. Here we do not have a mechanical pattern. It is not a machine that we are going to transform—it is the human being.

In every hermitage in India, the gurus had to pay individual attention to their disciples. It has been a practice throughout the centuries. For years the disciples had to live in the ashram so that the guru could know them thoroughly, and *then* he could give them guidance.

But there are two ways to take on the path to enlightenment. One way is drastic. Intensive. The other way is slow. The slow way, every one of you can adopt. And that slow way is—it is in all religions—in the first place, to have a healthy body and a healthy mind, and slowly to develop yourself in human attributes. The first attribute is love. Universal love; love of the family, love of friends, love of the universe—even love of the enemy. Then to develop compassion. When we are seriously ill or in some terrible difficulty, we wish that others would sympathize with us. And we are happy, we feel consoled, when someone comes to us and expresses his sympathy for us. We feel very much soothed. We should understand that others need the same thing. So an attitude of compassion and love is essential.

Then devotion. Truth. Honesty, patience. Perseverance. I do not say that they can be cultivated in one day, but the attempt should be there, and nature is forgiving. But the attempt that has to be made first is to develop ourselves, because these are the characteristics of illuminated consciousness. When the man or woman is purified, all these attributes develop in him or her so that, if we consciously develop them, we are coming nearer and nearer to the higher stage.

Then there is regular prayer and worship, and if we meditate, that meditation, too, should be a prayer. Mechanical meditation is a hindrance rather than a help. So this is the path. This is the safest, the simplest, and the easiest path. First cultivation of ourselves. Giving up the self as much as possible. But this does not include giving up any basic urge or appetite, but moderation. Moderation in food, moderation of enjoyment, moderation of activity, and moderation of entertainment. Excess of eating or not eating, excess of activity or not activity, any of these extremes is to be avoided. The middle path, as Buddha says. The middle life, but with these characteristics, to be like a child—as Christ has said, without smartness, without cleverness to gain the advantage over my own friend or neighbor or brother.

Here in all these disciplines we are trying to seek audience with the Lord of the universe. Our ego must be melted first. And all that we do must be in a spirit of prayer, or a humble solicitation to grant us the interview. We can never force ourselves into the presence of the almighty. No drop can become an ocean. We have to seek it with submission, with humility, to be like children. This sophistication has to be given up. Our hearts are to be purged of all impurity. And we have to mingle our ego with dust.

It is a very tough journey. But if one has a deep urge inside and very little ego, if one is true and honest, loving and sympathetic, charitable and compassionate, he is sure to bring success. He or she is sure to awaken one day to his own glory. Even if for a moment, even if for a few minutes, his or her life is transformed. He knows that he has won. But this is the life described in all of the religious scriptures of mankind. The revelation has been the same. There are no shortcuts or back doors on this path. Man has to evolve, physically, mentally, and spiritually, to win this crown. There are no magical things. It is painful for me to find in the books, written in these times, a completely incorrect picture of this state. It is not a magical thing. There are no magicians. There are no hidden people or gurus somewhere in secret. You have already been given the teaching by the greatest illuminated sages born. Christ, Buddha, Shankaracharya, Muhammed, all the mystics.

And you can compare that with what I have said. This is the acid test of any teacher who comes forward to teach. He or she must conform to the tradition. The path is the same. It is one for all mankind. And this path will lead—*is* leading—to one world, one humanity, one goal, and one happiness. The time has come, in spite of all the power and the strength of the material forces, in spite of the armies and the armaments, this dream *will* come true! That is the power of the spirit.

A PRAYER TO THE LORD

Help me, O Lord, unto the last
To speak the truth and do the right,
To heed the lessons of the past
And keep the future well in sight.

I have no answer why and how
I find myself upon this scene,
With earth below and sky above,
And what does our existence mean?

Neither the wisdom of the wise
Nor all the books I can recall
Could help me know or e'en surmise
What power is behind us all.

Help me, O Lord, to think aright,
And make my life a flame of love

To shed its luster, pure and bright,
In acts of service done above

The thought of self, of fame or gain,
Out of sheer love for humankind,
For soothing grief or healing pain,
Or bringing comfort to the mind.

Few are the years allowed to us
To rise above our me and mine,
To think of self a little less
And a bit more of Thee and Thine.

A world in which each one of us
Exists but for oneself alone,
Must end in sorrow and distress,
Selfish and callous to the bone.

The aim should be to make our life
A fount of happiness for all,
To keep aloof from lowly strife
And rise in action straight and tall.

It is not wise to act in haste
When we know little of our self,
We may then barter gems for paste
And sell our soul for sorry pelf.

Help me, O Lord, to spend my days
In thought and action, true to Thee,
And let me, like sun's orient rays,
On every side Thy glory see.

Then only my bound soul can rise
Beyond its chains of mortal flesh,
And win again the sovereign prize
Of life eternal, young and fresh.

CHAPTER TWELVE

This essay was written as a spontaneous response to a letter from a friend, in which a copy of an advertisement for Alan Watts's autobiography was enclosed. Though the ad provided only the barest clues, it was enough to give Gopi Krishna an insight into the well-known author's sometimes troubled life. In 1975, the piece was published by E. P. Dutton, New York, as part of a collection of essays, titled *The Awakening of Kundalini*.

THE CASE OF ALAN WATTS

It is not difficult to see that Alan Watts was one of those intellectuals in whom the evolutionary metamorphosis is almost complete, though they know nothing about their internal physiological conditions responsible for the same. This partial awareness leads to spontaneous flashes of mystical experience and intense yearning for transcendence. In such cases, the sexual-*cum*-evolutionary mechanism acts both ways, creating sometimes an all-consuming thirst for the beatific vision and, at the same time, an insatiable hunger for sexual experience.

The condition denotes, from the evolutionary point of view, a physiologically mature system ripe for the experience, and a highly active Kundalini pressing both on the brain and the reproductive system. But the activity of Kundalini, when the system is not properly attuned, can be abortive and, in some cases, even morbid. In the former case, the heightened consciousness is stained with complexes, anxiety, depression, fear, and other neurotic and paranoid conditions, which alternate with elevated blissful periods, visionary experiences, or creative moods. In the latter, it manifests itself in the various hideous forms of psychosis, in the horrible depression, frenzied excitement, and wild delusions of the insane.

The same life energy (prana) that, when pure, leads to glorious visionary experiences of the harmonized mystic, when slightly tainted, can cause gloomy moods of tension, fear, depression, or anxiety and, when irremediably contaminated, creates the shrieking horrors of madness.

What Mr. Watts ascribed to himself in his autobiography, *In My Own Way*—his "wayward spirit," "addiction to nicotine and alcohol," "occasional shudders of anxiety," "interest in women," "lack of enthusiasm for physical exercise"—can apply to many highly intelligent and evolved people who have either reached or are on the threshold of mystical consciousness. Their condition does not remain uniformly blissful, happy, or creative because of various environmental, psychic, or organic faults.

This commonly met traumatic condition of the modern, highly intelligent, or creative mind is the result of gross neglect of evolutionary needs and should form the most urgent field of study of science. But since modern savants are either ignorant of or apathetic toward the spiritual or, in other words, the evolutionary requirements of human beings, the world will continue to suffer till a breakthrough is achieved. The evolutionary effort is directed to the building of a still wider dimension of consciousness on the lines experienced by mystics in the higher states of ecstasy. It needs a greater exercise of willpower and more of self-discipline to keep a mind, working at higher levels of cognition, in constant check when up against temptation or faced with the never-ending acute problems of life.

The emotional content, becoming more powerful at each step of the ascent, needs a corresponding increase in the power of self-control also. It is the disproportionate state of development between the two that is often at the root of the neurotic, discordant, restless, fear- or anxiety-ridden, overambitious, unhappy, excitement-seeking, unsatisfied condition of the intellectual mind. Mental tension in all civilized countries is mounting because the life we lead and the social environment we create is anti-evolutionary. This is the explanation for the totally unexpected and startling revolution that has occurred in the thinking of the youth about the validity of the present social organization, which has, from the evolutionary angle, outlived its utility. It now poses a real menace to human security and progress. A decrease in the moral stamina of a people is the first symptom of degeneration. A state of constant effort and vigilance is necessary to avoid deterioration of the moral sense built through centuries of civilized existence.

It is not society nor civilization that has been the cause of ethical growth. They helped in its development. The cause is the evolutionary impulse in the race. Psychologists err grievously when they ascribe control or repression of wild, natural instincts to civilization. The two are interdependent and both have their origin in Kundalini, the evolutionary force still active in human beings. Enhanced moral stamina, with a strong will and a greater degree of self-control, together constitute a *sine qua non* of a blissful, enrapturing mystical consciousness, operative even in dreams. Without them we often have what we find in the case of Mr. Watts: a variable mental state; prone to visionary mystical experience on the one side and anxiety states on the other; relentless teasing of Cupid; addiction to nicotine, alcohol, and other drugs to ease inner tensions or palliate uneasy or even agonizing states of mind much more acute at higher dimensions of consciousness.

If the evolutionary demand is not heeded and the present political, social, and educational systems are not reoriented to meet this need, the intellectual of the future will be a sorry creature, gifted with mystical consciousness but so much at the mercy of abnormal mental states, awful visionary experiences, fear, tension, depression, loss of sleep, ennui, distaste for work and healthy physical exertion, with overmastering sex, that instead of being a source of peace, his life will become an unsupportable burden from the age of puberty to the end. This is happening now, and the symptoms can be read in the case of millions who, once lost to a sober and regulated life, take to wandering, drugs, promiscuity, and other pastimes without understanding the reason for their own rebellious frame of mind. They are an enigma to themselves and to psychologists.

The paramount importance of all revealed scriptures has been that they drew attention to the imperative need of self-discipline and certain norms of conduct and noble mental traits, without which evolution can only lead to disaster. The theophanic conceptions were used as a peg to hang their teachings on. How in the olden days could the multitudes be persuaded to accept a morally oriented life without assigning a supernatural reason or the need for the propitiation of divinity? Actually, the need sprang from the changes brought about in the mind and body by the inexorable pressure of evolutionary processes.

With the accelerated activity of the evolutionary mechanism, there occurs a tremendous enhancement in the production of life energy or sex energy. When the organism is in perfect condition, the sublimated energy streams into the brain, raising the consciousness to inexpressible heights of oceanic knowledge and rapture. But when the system is impure and the pranic radiation becomes even slightly contaminated, then nature tries to adjust the situation in two ways: The radiation either still finds entry into the brain in the contaminated form, leading to anxiety, fear, tension, depression, craving for some kind of excitement or mind-altering drugs or the like. This is the "dark night of the mystic," the depressive, sterile mood of the genius, or "a fit of the blues" of the intelligent mind. Psychologists have no explanation for this unpredictable change in moods and unhappy states of mind. The other way is by enormously increased pressure at the other end of the evolutionary mechanism—that is the sexual region—resulting in irrepressible amativeness. In such cases release becomes unavoidable to overcome the maddening pressure on the brain. The dominant position very often occupied by sex in the minds of creative intellectuals and their utter capitulation before it can be readily understood from this.

What Mr. Watts expressed is the basic reality on which the ancient tantras take their stand—namely, the passions and appetites planted deep in human nature. The disciplines prescribed are aimed at combating these inherent tendencies. Even so, they cannot be and should not be suppressed altogether. Moderation is the key.

It might have interested Mr. Watts to know that the unknown author of the famous hymn to Kundalini, *Panchastavi*, has almost expressed himself in the same way when he sings in a state of perennial ecstasy: "Free from all sense of dependence, neither seeking anything from anybody nor deceiving anybody nor servile to anybody, I clothe myself in fine garments, partake of delicious foods, and consort with a woman of my choice, because You, O Goddess, are blooming in my heart."

The singer raises no question why the mystical experience has been thrust upon him, for according to the tantric tradition, neither extreme asceticism nor immoderate indulgence is an answer to the spiritual problem of man. The use of wine and the association of women in tantric worship and ritual has therefore a plain reason behind it, provided the limit of moderation is not violated. Alcohol as a stimulant in depressive and fear-ridden moods and the association of a member of the fair sex—one's wife or a companion—have often been a necessary element in tantric disciplines and worship. The injunction is repeated over and over again that both are to be partaken of sparingly as an offering to the divine energy or Shakti. There are elaborate rituals to regulate the use of either.

For combating the depressive or anxiety states often attending heightened consciousness, there are specific Yoga practices and disciplines that have to be mastered from the very start. The prescribed icon of the goddess or other deity, to be kept before the mind in the practice of meditation, is imagined with one of the hands upraised, making the gesture of dispelling fear, which with repeated practice can tend to create a mental barrier against fear-ridden and depressive moods. Also the cultivation of a healthy sense of detachment (Vairagya) toward the body and the world or surrender to the divine will, prescribed in most Yoga disciplines, often serves as means to the same end.

The actual position is that the needs of the flesh and the vagaries of mind are recognized, and due provision exists in these ancient, tried systems to guard against pitfalls and make available the possibility of mystical consciousness to those leading a normal life. The severely puritanic and monastic life is as inimical to the spiritual progress of mankind as a sensuous and libidinous one. Those who raise their finger at one who acknowledges the frailty and weakness of flesh in his excursion into the mystical province, or in the quest of the supreme light, make fools of themselves before the unfathomable mysteries of nature, therefore, and try to limit the whole gigantic scheme of human evolution to the size of their own puny intellect.

A humanity with inhibited appetites and repressed desires can neither propagate nor survive. There can then exist no possibility of evolution for a totally inhibited and emasculated race. In spite of the teachings of sundry prophets and saints, the multitudes continued to live their normal lives, trusting in the grace of God and sometimes even the intercession of their spiritual heroes. This was nature working to preserve the race, because the other extreme would have been worse and even suicidal. Man must learn to strive for perfection to live a most fruitful and noble life. But he must desist from uprooting, distorting, or completely and drastically suppressing any basic urge planted by nature, for in that lies danger to himself and the race.

Mr. Watts is to be honored and admired, like Rousseau, for his candid admissions. His frank confession should help many aspiring souls to overcome fear and depression at the thought that in their daily behavior they fall far short of the ideals they have in view and therefore will have to pay for their lapses with a barren outcome of their search for transcendence.

"O son of Kunti," says Krishna in the *Bhagavad Gita*, "the excited senses of even a wise man, though he be striving, impetuously carry away his mind." The real aim of spiritual disciplines is to strive for self-mastery, not total negation of basic appetites and desires, and to leave the rest in the hands of divinity.

There are so many factors that go into the development of mystical consciousness, including heredity and the social environment, that it will take centuries for scholars to unearth the laws and to prescribe infallible methods for the attainment of healthy and ever-blissful states of transcendental consciousness. The instability and sharp variation in mental moods experienced by Mr. Watts can be due to a number of factors, like lack of practice in self-discipline, ignorance of some of the basic facts of Yoga and the evolutionary mechanism, adverse biological factors, use of drugs, and a defective system of education and social organization. From my point of view, his autobiography should be of incalculable value to the future investigators in the sphere of mysticism, when the biological implications of the spiritual thirst in man are empirically established and understood. I have voiced my opinion about the probable factors responsible for the divided personality of Mr. Watts without the least idea of disparagement, but only to help in understanding other aspirants on the path.

According to his own views, "essentially Satori is a sudden experience, and it is often described as a 'turning over' of the mind, just as a pair of scales will suddenly turn when a sufficient amount of material has been poured into one pan to overbalance the weight in the other." This possibility is readily admitted in almost all systems of spiritual disciplines and often ascribed to "grace." But what should doubtless excite the curiosity of a thinker knowing of the available data on body-mind relationship is that this sudden insight occurs only in an extremely limited number of cases, generally in highly intelligent men and women, and that in the vast majority of cases, even after rigorous and prolonged application of sundry spiritual disciplines, this instant or even gradual realization—that is, mystical experience—never occurs even in dreams.

What lies behind this apparently insolvable mystery? Is the grace gratuitous or the harvest of accumulated Karma? A highly gifted artist, a man of genius, a woman of exceeding beauty and grace, a great inventor, or a great military commander are all said to be gifted or blessed. Those who believe in Karma ascribe their talent or beauty or skill or intelligence to Karmic causes. But in either case, at this stage of knowledge, can we deny that whether a fortuitous gift, divine grace, or the fruit of Karma, in every case there is a close link between the talent or beauty exhibited and the organic structure of the individual, even though we may not be in a position to specify all the details at present?

By what flaw in our thinking do we then isolate mystical experience—the rarest of all extraordinary mental traits—from the other exceptional categories and persist in holding that only religious striving or grace is accountable for it? If it were so, and the organic frame did not come into the picture, why should the breath, body, and mind be the center of action in all systems of religious discipline? What is then the need to control passions and desire, and why, from the earliest times, has the purity of the body and the mind always been prescribed, if Buddha nature can exist, happily and with safety, in the words of Alan Watts, "in a dog"?

"A potter who wants to make earthware," says a well-known

Chinese master, Chih I (also called Chih Che), "should first prepare proper clay that should be neither too hard nor too soft, so that it can be cast in a mold; and a lute player should first tune the strings, if he is to create melody. Likewise in the control of mind, five things should be regulated." These five things are food, sleep, body, breath, and the mind. The same injunction is repeated again and again in the *Bhagavad Gita*. The regulation of these five things is also necessary for health—mental or physical. If this regulation is not done and the mind is not controlled, meditation can lead to deceitful, awesome visionary experiences, to serious mental disturbance, or even to insanity, according to Master Chih I.

"He whose cares about the phenomenal state have been appeased, who, though possessed of a body consisting of parts, is yet devoid of parts and whose mind is free from anxiety, is accepted as a man liberated in life (Jiwan-Mukta)," says Shankaracharya in *Vivekachudamani* (430). The extreme necessity of attuning the mind and body to the higher level of consciousness has been clearly recognized in all ancient disciplines. The same attunement is necessary in the case of those who have spontaneous mystical experiences as the harvest of evolutionary matureness brought about by genetic causes.

Many Western thinkers, overconfident of their knowledge of psychology, by placing mystical experience in the category of visionary adventure without any relation to the organism, have been instrumental in causing rank confusion over this vital issue. They fail to see that spiritual experience represents the culmination of a regular process of biological evolution and that ignorant disregard of the laws governing this process is at the root of the precarious balance, or eccentricity, not only of the top intellectual and man of genius but the modern mystic also. Actually, the position should be otherwise, to wit: The mystic, the intellectual, and the genius should be more harmonious, calm, and balanced, as it is often they who shine as the guiding lights of humanity.

The target of the psychophysiological evolutionary mechanism, active in every member of the race, is a perennial state of mystical consciousness, free of ups and downs, devoid of complexes, tensions, anxieties, neuroses, and fears, with a firm grip on the mind and body, on emotions, passions, and intractable lusts. Even a casual glance at any authoritative ancient work on Yoga or any religious scripture would show that this is the aim before every spiritual teaching.

This state of surpassing, transhuman rapture, intended by nature to be a permanent feature of future human consciousness, can trail off into depression and fear or lead to neurosis and even insanity because of our ignorance about this vital aspect of human growth. A few more confessions such as Alan Watts's and a probe directed to the avowals of thousands of people who have had unmistakable experiences of the Kundalini force are perhaps necessary to put open-minded and enterprising men and women of science on the trail of what is the greatest mystery of creation still lying unsolved and even unattended before us.

CHAPTER THIRTEEN

"The study of Kundalini is like embarking on a voyage across the vastness of an ocean that is shoreless on the other side," Gopi Krishna wrote in the as yet unpublished Part III of his autobiography. "The strange phenomena I had witnessed in myself for several years now after the awakening dispelled every doubt I had about the existence of invisible, superintelligent forces behind the life of man. . . . The invisible storehouse of this superintelligence must be an ocean exceeding the boundaries of the material universe."

Metaphysical books can be churned out in whatever quantity the public demands, but firsthand accounts of Kundalini in action are extremely rare and will continue to be in very short supply for decades to come. This chapter was excerpted from the priceless autobiographical material left by the author when he died. As he himself wrote, it is "more for the future than for the present generations of mankind."

WRITING FOR THE FUTURE GENERATIONS

When we accept the evolution of the brain we must accept the evolution of the soul also. The idea that under the direct influence of the cosmic life energy the human brain is still in a state of organic evolution is a fact so important that, compared to it, all other discoveries of modern science pale into insignificance.

Continued evolution of the human organism, in its turn, points unmistakably toward a conclusion that is often discredited by the orthodox evolutionists of our day. What it clearly implies is that there must exist a predetermined target or, in other words, an already-drawn blueprint of consciousness toward which it is evolving.

At this stage of intelligence it would be the height of folly to assume that this evolution would be governed by accidental mutations of the genes taking eccentric directions about which we can have no knowledge at present. This study and the systematic way in which the human mind has advanced in intelligence, knowledge, and skill provide a clear rebuttal to this stand. There can be no dispute about the position that this evolution is proceeding in a certain specified direction about which we have no awareness at present.

What I argue appears strange because this is the first time in history when such an idea has been presented to account for certain phenomena of the human mind for which no satisfactory explanation has been provided so far.

The importance attached and homage paid to political leaders, financial magnates, conquerers, and great artists will then occupy a secondary place compared to the adoration and reverence commanded by the surpassing products of education and spiritual discipline combined—the Christs and Buddhas of ages to come. Once established, this possibility of a fabulous bloom of the mental faculties latent in every human organism is sure to create a revolution in human life. What proportion this revolution would assume in the ages to come we cannot even imagine.

I am writing more for the future than for the present generations of mankind. Today the overhanging threat to the survival of the race is the result of mental rust that we are not able to clean—the rust of evil custom and habit, of conservatism, chauvinism, dogma, pride, prejudice, and bias.

All our social customs are the outcome of this sort of mental rust. The brain is not able to rid itself of the poison and renovate its thinking. The reason why decadent nations take pride in glorifying the achievements of their ancestors without feeling humiliated at the degeneration that has occurred is because, like the senile, they are not able to observe the change that has taken place.

Intellectual and moral evolution involves a constant process of purification and regeneration of the nervous system and brain. These processes are not discernible to scientists because they have as yet no knowledge of the pranic energy that maintains and vivifies the organism.

The intelligent electricity—the basis of all life in the universe—is yet an unknown entity to science because it is not perceptible to any of the senses known to us. It is not possible for human imagination to form a picture of the storm of activity raging in every living organism from the lowest to the highest and the intelligence displayed in the regulation of this activity.

The play of electric currents darting through the network of wires in a telephone system serving a huge metropolis like London is a children's toy compared to it. We never know when we arise in the morning that pranic activity through billions of neurons in our system—more intricate than all the electrical lighting systems in the world—has occurred to clean and repair our brains and to awaken us in the morning as fresh as ever.

It is not possible for our science to understand or evaluate the phenomenon of life without an understanding of prana. The reason why scientists of the nineteenth century were carried away by the ideas of Darwin is because they failed to assess the profundity of life. It is only when subtle intelligent energies of the cosmos become the targets of scientific observation that the complexity of the phenomenon of life and the bewildering nature of the cosmos will be realized.

The Indian adepts use the term "maya" to describe creation, and the magic of it will always remain beyond the reach of intellect.

The only peculiarity I noticed in myself was the inner luminosity and the silvery luster around every object that came within the field of my vision. I was fascinated and amazed at the transformation but was at a loss to assign a reason for it. I had no knowledge of any precedents to make me believe that this was the pattern of consciousness experienced by mystics, more particularly those who had successfully conducted Kundalini to the Sahasara. I was almost assailed by doubt, since except for the feature of luminosity, I had not experienced any noteworthy change in my mental capacity.

There are many people who experience lights in their head as a result of meditation, or spontaneously for no apparent reason whatsoever, and are often amazed at the occurrence. Color, lights, and the brightness of objects are marked features of certain drug experiences, as for instance in LSD and peyote. But what I experienced was somewhat different.

I did not experience this alluring radiance, both outside and within myself, as something external to me or something objective but as something that was a part of myself, something that colored my whole personality. In other words, it was not the objective world that had become brighter or that appeared brighter to my eyes, but it was, in actual fact, the indwelling "I" that had become luminous. It was the observer in my mind or soul, who was ensheathed in a halo of light.

It was and still is an incredible experience. At all times during the day and night, my inner self appears like a luminous void stretched far beyond the periphery of the corporeal frame. I am a pool of consciousness always aglow with light. Preternatural light is a prominent feature of mystical experience. The visions of celestial beings, of divinity or God, are always bathed in a superearthly light.

What did it imply? Was I experiencing the mystical light as a normal feature of my consciousness, or was there any other reason for my peculiar condition? I could not solve this riddle to my satisfaction until the experience in the city of Jammu that, for the first time, revealed the emergence of talents that had never been visible before.

The main purpose of my writings is to bring this exceptional condition of my consciousness to the notice of the learned. It definitely is not an abnormality, since in all other respects my mind and my body function in a strictly normal way. The change did not occur all at once. For years after the awakening, I could only observe a chalky whiteness on every object at which I looked. It seemed as if my vision had become affected in some way. I always felt my head filled with luster, and my thought images stood against a luminous background. But there was no brightness of the external objects and no alluring veneer of light, which now holds me spellbound when I look at a grand spectacle of nature on a clear day.

Even the sky overcast with clouds, with the flashes of lightning and the roar of clouds assumes an aspect of such sublimity and grandeur that my mind almost reels at the impact. I feel as if the darkened sky, the flashing lightning, and the roaring thunder are not external or away from me but that all the awe-inspiring events are taking place in my own soul.

It is a transformation so extraordinary that I feel at a loss to make it intelligible to my fellow human beings. When I say that "My inner self is now wrapped in a sheath of light," I wonder if it would be possible for others to grasp what I mean. What I came to realize afterward is that from the very day of the awakening, my consciousness started to expand. My trials and suffering stem from the fact that I had no awareness of what had happened, what forces were now active in my body, and what the target of this activity was.

The process of evolution is active in the body of almost every human being. At its natural pace, the individual has no indication of it throughout his life. His body functions in the normal way, in health and disease, able to sustain stresses and pressures, hardships and privations, overexertion, lack of sleep, and insufficient diet with the strong reserves built in it.

There are large numbers of men and women in whom the process of this evolution becomes accelerated. The tendency to accelerated evolution is carried by the genes and runs in families, transmitted from the parents to children. A hundred constitutional peculiarities affect the evolutionary process, as they affect other characteristics of an individual. Where the process of accelerated evolution operates in an unhealthy body with constitutional faults or a genetically defective organ or organs, it often terminates in some kind of mental aberration or psychosis that is not amenable to treatment. It is often individuals of this category who feel themselves irresistibly drawn toward the supernatural or the divine.

The purpose of these urges is to enlist their cooperation with the inner process about which they have no inkling or knowledge. Right up to this day mankind, as a whole, has remained entirely in the dark about a momentous secret that is linked with his survival. There has never been an awareness of the fact that the species is still in a state of transition toward a new dimension of consciousness, the result of the slowly occurring organic evolution of the brain.

The irony is that in spite of the tremendous strides taken in the science of biology, by a strange trick of Fate, this hidden activity to this moment has remained shielded from the eyes of biologists. When the secret is unearthed, the shock waves of the discovery are likely to create a revolution in the whole realm of human knowledge that has no precedent in history.

The human race is slowly moving in the direction of a titanic consciousness. The process of evolution is not active in the brain alone but also operates to bring the whole organism in line with the highly expanded state of the mind. The average human frame of our day is not sturdy enough to maintain the brightly burning flame of cosmic consciousness. It needs to be remodeled to make the heightened psychic activity possible.

In numerous cases of psychosis, the malady is due to the disproportion between the body and the mind. The former is not able to maintain a brighter light of consciousness on account of the inability to supply the subtle fuel or bioenergy at the rate or of the standard demanded by the brain. Scientific investigation will show that legions of the inmates of mental clinics consist of the rejected models of evolution. These unfortunate creatures who, because of physical or mental disability, lack of self-control, or adverse hereditary factors, were cursed with a malfunctioning evolutionary process either from birth or at some later stage in life.

The paramount importance of a scientific investigation into the phenomenon of Kundalini will become obvious as soon as it is proved that there does exist an evolutionary tendency in the human brain. This will have the effect of an electric shock in all religions also. There is hardly any sphere of human thought that has been exploited by unscrupulous, clever individuals as that of religion. Deep religious feeling and the desire for spiritual experience have provided tempting baits from immemorial times for false prophets, pseudosaints, tricksters, and impostors to prey upon the gullibility of the searching crowds.

If religion were really the crop of a holy impulse, installed by heaven in the human mind as a means to achieve the union of the human soul with its Maker, that is the Lord of Creation, then there would occur no deviations from the straight path connecting the two. The priesthood in every religion that is supposed to be conversant with ecclesiastic canons and the ways of God has seldom if ever shown a greater penetration into the mystery of creation than normal human beings.

Millions of highly intelligent human beings all over the world have lost faith in religion. Often it is only the credulous who flock to church or to the sermons delivered by religious leaders or to the meetings organized by self-caused gurus, masters, and the like. A whole empire, in every part of the earth, rests on the support lent by these God-fearing men and women, and a whole industry thrives on their faith.

During the past thousands of years the concerted effort of hundreds of thousands of priests, mullahs, pandits, monks, saints, and ascetics has not succeeded in eradicating evil from the societies in which they lived. Crime, violence, perversion, exploitation of the weak and the ignorant, theft, robbery, rape, prostitution, oppression, and torture continue to be as rampant as they were before. In fact, one of the most terrible institutions of torture and death—the Inquisition—was a product of religion.

The brute in man is still very much alive. We come across his deprivations in the bloody acts of terrorism, in devastating wars, in oppression and in the exploitation of weak, downtrodden human beings. In the present state of society, these evils appear to be irremediable and have persisted for hundreds of thousands of years. Side by side with the achievements of science the continued existence of these evils is fraught with the greatest hazard for the race. But in our own present state of knowledge and resourcefulness we are helpless because we do not possess any defense against them.

On the contrary, the achievements of technology when used for evil can prove to be terribly destructive, obliterating all the benefits they had conferred when employed for good. One all-out nuclear war fought between two superpowers can wipe off every trace of civilization from the earth.

One nuclear device in the hands of a desperado or of a terrorist group can endanger the lives of millions. In the coming ages, with the further irresistible advances in technology, the safety of nations and even of the whole species will always hang by a slender thread, which a single mistake or a single imprudent act can cut asunder in the twinkling of an eye.

It is not possible to turn back the hands of the clock of time. Our current customs, conventions, laws, values, and standards are not designed for a state of society in possession of the powers that science has placed in our hands. Our present ideas of religion, philosophy, justice, and right and wrong are equally inappropriate to the demands of the present or the future. The time has come when mankind, as a whole, has to shed the now worn-out scale of current thought and to equip themselves with new ideas and values as a measure of survival in the age to come.

The human brain is molding itself imperceptibly in the direction of a superior type of consciousness able to apprehend the subtler levels of creation. Compelled by the limited range of our senses to perceive only a fraction of the universe, we are duped into the belief that what we experience throughout our lives is the whole of creation and there is nothing beyond it, hidden from us due to our inability to apprehend beyond the circumscribed periphery. The present-day trends in science to confine itself only to what is perceptible to our senses has been a grave error, of which the vicious harvest is before our eyes in the explosive condition of the world.

Historians in all ages have assayed to fathom the causes for the virtues that came into play at the time of the rise and the vices that led to the fall. But has anyone tried to enlighten the world about the ferment that occurred in the brain, both at the time of the ascent and the decline in the individuals or the nation as a whole?

When we critically reflect on this we are completely lost in the major problems of life. What kind of a soul resides in the body of a monstrosity, a criminal, or a genocidal person? How does Karma influence the gene, the structure of the brain, or the circumstances that make one a millionaire and the other a pauper, a king or a begger, a genius or a blockhead?

This is the province of science as well as of religion. Why science should ignore some of the most important issues of human existence no one has dared to answer. And why religion should be satisfied with explanations for these riddles, offered thousands of years ago, when space was flat, atoms were solid, and earth was the center of the universe, is equally unintelligible. It is only now that we have been able to demonstrate the weak force in atoms. The world of subnuclear particles and the forces that rule this world were unknown to scientists but a few decades before. They were not even suspected by the physicists of the eighteenth and even nineteenth century. Is it therefore any wonder that even subtler changes that operate in our corporeal frames and give rise to our ideas about the mind, soul, or consciousness are still a dead letter to science?

From my point of view, the most important feature of my extraordinary experience has been the gradual transformation of my inner being from what it was before the fateful day in December 1937 when I first aroused a sleeping force in me, to what it is today. When the glowing vision of an oceanic consciousness faded from my inner eye and I came to myself in my small room in Jammu, where I sat crosslegged for meditation, I felt as if I had returned to my normal state again.

I could not imagine otherwise, as I had no knowledge whatsoever of the phenomenon and treated the whole episode as an extraordinary experience that had befallen me as the result of meditation. I could not, therefore, account for the lack of appetite, the loss of sleep, the uneasiness I felt, and the difficulty I experienced in concentration or in focusing my thoughts on a subject.

After studying my condition for more than forty years, I now feel that even if I had studied all the literature on Kundalini available at the time, I could not have solved the problems of insomnia, psychic disturbances, and the organic symptoms I experienced immediately after the awakening. Right up to this day, I have not been able to find a detailed account of the arousal of Kundalini, meticulously describing its effects on the body-mind complex and the changes that occur in them until a paranormal state of consciousness is attained. From my point of view, there is no aspect of my experience so important for study and investigation as the slow metamorphosis that my cerebro-spinal system underwent to equip the brain for a new pattern of consciousness, not in evidence in the average ranks of mankind. The phenomenon raises a problem which, so far as I know, has not been discussed in any work on Yoga or mysticism or any other occult or esoteric system, ancient or modern.

This slow metamorphosis in consciousness, which occurred imperceptibly from the very moment of my first experience, provides the key to the conclusion I have arrived at, that Kundalini represents the upgrading mechanism behind the evolution of the human brain. What has led modern scientists to believe that the brain has reached the apex of its organic evolution is a riddle to me and to many other thoughtful minds.

What evidence they have for this premature conclusion, when the human encephalon is still a profound mystery, no one is ready to explain. How the primate brain evolved to human dimension during the course of millions of years raises a problem that no one has solved so far. The books written on the subject contain merely speculation, exciting narratives of the vanished species, the sublime, or platitudes.

In actual fact, the whole theory of evolution, as propounded by Darwin and his successors, is only a huge mass of observation and data extending now to over a century, without any solution to the issue. What is the basic mechanism that came into operation in the evolution of the human brain from that of the primates, and what intelligent agency coordinated the functions of the entire system to make changes in a complex organ like the human brain possible at each step of the ascent and to transmit the advances gained from generation to generation?

Looking back at the events that followed the first awakening, it seems to me to be obvious now that the intensity of concentration, exercised for many years, had slowly stimulated to activity a small area in the brain directly above the palate and below the crown of the head. The exquisite sensations I felt moving up the spine, which stopped and disappeared when my mind was diverted, were the beginning in the cerebrospinal system of a new activity that will be determined by science in the course of time.

Two distinct entities moved up the spine side by side with the intensely pleasurable sensation I experienced. One was a kind of radiation, orange in color in the beginning, which later on changed to silver, with a slightly golden color in it. The second was an organic essence that entered the brain at the same time as the radiation.

The organic essence was not so clearly marked on the first occasion as on the second, several years later. But there is not the least doubt that this subtle organic substance is behind the exquisite sensations of the arousal. We have not been able to determine yet how the intense rapture of the climax of love is experienced by an individual. What kind of biochemical reagent or electrical discharge is at the back of the delicious transport of the orgasm?

Modern research has shown that there is a certain area in the brain that, when electrically stimulated, gives rise to the same sensation that marks the sexual climax. There must occur some kind of chemical or electrical activity to cause a momentary rapture that has no parallel in the other pleasures experienced by the human mind. It is because of this extremely delightful, sense-ravishing transport of the conjugal union, and the release from pressure it grants to the mind, that the compelling power of the reproductive urge exists.

There is no awareness among the learned that this intense rapture of the erotic union can occur at places in the body other than the genitals. To make an assertion of this kind before an assembly of scientists is to evoke incredulity and even ridicule. But the whole mystical literature of the world and the thousands of extant works in Sanskrit on Kundalini, including the tantras, provide the testimony of thousands of individuals of unquestionable honesty and truth about this very phenomenon.

It is not possible to describe the intensity of the orgasmic sensation that occurs in the spinal cord and the brain on the arousal of Kundalini. Except for the almost identical nature of the transportive experience, there is no comparison between the climax of conjugal union and the rapture caused by the flow of this divine fire from the base of the spine to the head. The duration of the former is only of a few seconds, followed by a sense of relief and lassitude. The latter can last for several minutes at a time, creating an almost swooning condition of the mind at the intensity of the rapture for as long as he likes or as long as there is sufficient fuel in the body to cause it. On return back to normal, there is no sense of lassitude or satiation. On the other hand, one feels mentally more invigorated and fresh than before. This is the hitherto undivulged secret of Kundalini.

The human cerebrospinal system is capable of a new, amazing activity that is still unknown to science. The practice of meditation, carried on in the proper way regularly for a sufficient duration of time, tends to force a normally silent region in the brain to an astonishing activity. Like an electric current, it galvanizes the nervous system to an action that is never experienced in the normal state. From every fiber and tissue of the body, a subtle organic essence, extracted by nerve fibrils spread everywhere and carried to the brain through the spinal canal, gives rise to the ecstatic and visionary conditions associated with religion from the earliest times.

The human seed is not the product of the gonads alone. It is a compound of a subtle organic essence drawn from the body by the nerves and the secretion produced by the testicles of this subtle nervine essence that is, in reality, the concentrated fuel of life. The ancient notion that the male seed is actually produced in the head and from there descends into the genital organs has, therefore, some foundation of truth in it.

The idea, expressed in the Upanishads, that semen is drawn from all parts of the body, including the vital organs, is nearer the mark. In the normal individual there occurs a constant process in the nervous system that is imperceptible to us and still undetected by science. The subtle element that imparts vitality to the seed is imported by the nerves lining the reproductive system from all organs and tissues in the body, from the head, heart, lungs, liver, stomach, intestines, spleen, kidneys, genitals, and the rest. This organic element is extremely subtle, extracted and carried by the nerves in such a minute measure that it remains beyond detection by us.

As far as I have been able to determine, there are special nerves connecting the reproductive system with the different organs in the body through which the essence, after extraction by vast networks of nerves, travels to the erotic zone to commingle with that arriving from other organs and parts of the body, ultimately to form an ingredient of the human seed. The essence from the brain in some mysterious way comes down through the spinal cord to reach the same place of confluence of the other nerve channels serving the same purpose.

It is a fallacy to suppose that the first germ of human life— the impregnated ovum—starts to divide and subdivide by chance, adding brick after brick and block after block, until the marvelous structure of the human organism is complete, ushering a ready-made, tiny human being into the world. To suppose that unintelligent atoms and molecules that constitute the impregnated seed, with any amount of chemistry and mutual interaction, could produce a marvelous organ like the brain, the eye, the ear, the nose, and the mouth is to suppose the impossible. The tragedy is that science has no instruments as yet to detect the vibrations of the life energy or prana, which is the real source behind life.

Prana is present in atoms and their constituents. It is behind the energy fields into which matter is resolved at the end. It is the agent responsible for the ungraspable complex chemical reactions in living bodies and also in the incredibly intricate mechanisms at the back of all the complex movements of the organs and the activity of the brain.

Prana is possessed of a superhuman intelligence and memory beyond the range of our thought. It is an element of the universe infinitely subtler and more complex than the element we call matter. The study of life bewilders and staggers by its complexity and profound mystery. We are dumbfounded because the element we set out to explore is infinitely more intelligent and more profound than those who attempt to probe its mystery.

The different stages of inner growth through which I passed during the course of my transformation have led me to believe, as I have mentioned, that there is a subtle organic compound in the body that the nerves carry to and fro, after extraction from the organs and tissues, that supplies the vehicle through which the incorporeal pranic energy acts.

There is a particular reason that has led me to this conclusion. Shortly after that night of horror, during which I hovered between death on the one side and insanity on the other and was saved from an awful fate by what was almost a miracle, I noticed a rather disquieting change in my observation. It seemed as if every object on which I looked was coated with a thin layer of white. This did not affect the color or the shape of the object. Only it appeared as if a very thin coat of powdered chalk had been applied over it. The color was there with a fine coat of white added to it.

I noticed the strange alteration in the state of my vision but could not assign any reason for it. I wondered with myself, and even worried over it at times, but try as I might, I could not find any satisfactory explanation for the change.

The other fact I noticed was that there had occurred an expansion in my consciousness. This position is rather difficult to understand for the average individual. But perhaps it might be possible to convey a more clear picture of it in this way. Every one of us, when sitting in a room with his eyes closed, perceives a certain area of awareness around his head, extending even to his body when his attention flits toward it, which he calls his own self, his own inner being, or his personality. Every one of us is conscious of this area of awareness, or, let us say, our mind, but is not able to perceive or to measure this area of awareness of the other.

We assume by inference that the other, too, has the same area of his inner being qualitatively and quantitatively. But this is an error that we have no means of rectifying. The reason for this lies in the fact that we are conscious of our own inner personality only subjectively, and we have no way of making it a subject for objective observation. Hence, in the present state of our knowledge, it cannot be possible to detect the quantitative and qualitative differences in the consciousness of two different individuals apart from what is revealed to us in their respective intellectual, artistic, or aesthetic contents.

I never understood it at that time. But the actual position was that my very first experience of the awakening of Kundalini was the outcome of a widening of the cognitive center in the brain. When I returned back to my normal state of consciousness after the expansion, which I witnessed during the period of my ecstasy, I was still not the same inner being as before. The area of my awareness had widened, and this expansion had become a permanent feature of my personality.

During the whole period of the first memorable experience, the expansion witnessed was no doubt oceanic, and I had felt myself spreading in all directions, until my consciousness exceeded the limits of the cosmic image present in my mind. When the enormous proportions I had gained in my inner being began to shrink and I came slowly back to myself, I was not the same individual I had been before. But a little of the expansion still remained and continued to be there day and night, a fact I could not understand at that time.

This part of my experience is of considerable importance. The ultimate aim of meditation is to rouse to activity a dormant area in the brain. It is not the pineal gland, nor the pituitary. The awakening of Kundalini does not refer to a mere glandular change or a shift in the hormonal activity of the body. It clearly involves the operation of a new power in the body and the activation of a hitherto silent area in the brain called Brahma-Rendra, or the Cavity of Brahma (God). It is the target for which Yoga is practiced and is the real goal of all spiritual disciplines.

With the activation of Brahma-Rendra, the whole cerebral cortex becomes involved in the transformative processes that occur. Nature has planted a minibrain in the human encephalon to lead a mortal toward the solution of the mystery that surrounds him. This minibrain is the Sahasrara or the "thousand-petaled lotus," and it provides the only channel to the knowledge of the self.

The thousands of books on Yoga, both ancient and modern,

are often silent about the real secret that lies at the bottom of this discipline. Prolonged concentration, repeated day after day on a divine or sublime or noble object, activates an organic mechanism in the brain, as I have mentioned. But the story does not end here. The activation of Brahma-Rendra can create a thousand problems, and they must be tackled.

Once activated, the highly delicate and complex neuronic structure of Brahma-Rendra needs a superior fuel for its activity. The normal psychic fuel that burns in the other parts of the brain proves ineffective there. The minibrain, to be operative, must be fed by a more potent essence extracted and conserved by the nerves. I suffered from loss of sleep and appetite and fell prey to depression, inquietude, and fear, and lost power of concentration and the feeling of love for my near and dear ones because Brahma-Rendra had been activated but lacked the fuel to operate in the right way. My area of awareness had expanded, but the energy that could maintain this expanded state of awareness at an efficient level was not there.

For this reason I was not myself for months and even years. Not only had the Kundalini force operated through the pingala, or solar nerve (until the balance was restored some time later), but also my body could not supply a sufficient amount of the superior psychic fuel to the activized paranormal center in the brain. The activation of this center, the Brahma-Rendra, and the reverse activity of the reproduction system leading to the upward flow of the organic essences provided the basis for all the spiritual and paranormal phenomena witnessed in history. The experience of oceanic consciousness on the first occasion, marking the arousal, consumed the entire store of the pranic content of the reproductive system. This store had to be replenished before another similar experience could occur.

The second experience was far less impressive in comparison, but after that I could hardly concentrate in the same effective way. Mental and bodily disturbances that followed made it hard for me even to present a normal appearance. Doubts and fears gnawed at my heart.

Internally, I became a pitiable wreck, though outwardly I tried my utmost to present a sane appearance. I do not know what power sustained me in this ordeal. The minibrain now controlling my entire personality was starved of its proper nutriment, with the result that the subject of the transformation—namely, myself—appeared to be a stranger in his own house. I lacked control of my responses, feelings, and emotions. What had happened to me all of a sudden I could never realize during those days. I could not sleep because my body lacked the energy to produce a pure stream of the pranic radiation I needed to feed the activized Brahma-Rendra.

The yogis who set out to arouse Kundalini do not often succeed in raising the power to sahasrara or the last center in the brain on the first sitting. It often takes them years to do so. The energy rises chakra by chakra until it reaches the ajna chakra, in the middle of the eyebrows, which marks its first entry into the brain. Prior to that it pierces the five lower chakras, in this way gaining entry to various vital organs—the kidneys, the digestive organs, the heart, the throat, and the lungs—to improve their working to the point of efficiency where the body is able to maintain a regular flow of the superior pranic energy to feed the brain. The rigid disciplines of Hatha Yoga, aimed at cleaning the stomach and the intestines to keep the blood in a state of purity, are all designed to this end. It is not possible for a normal body to produce the subtle organic essence that forms the still unidentified part of the human seed in such abundant measure that it can supply the needs of the awakened Brahma-Rendra also. A new metabolic process is set up in the brain to achieve this purpose.

What is known as the piercing of the chakras among Hatha Yoga yogis refers to the upward flow of the reproductive organic essence from one center to the other. The orgiastic sensation, which I've described, attends the passage of the essence all through the spinal cord, increasing in volume as the nectar mounts higher and higher, reaching its maximum intensity in the brain.

After the awakening, Kundalini is led step by step toward the sahasrara. Out of hundreds who succeed in arousing the power and forcing the organic essence to rise up the spine, perhaps not even one is able, even with sustained efforts, to carry it to the Brahma-Rendra. This is the reason why the number of those who have achieved the genuine mystical experience has been so small.

In the initial stages, it is hard to hold Kundalini at a chakra for more than a few minutes at a time. After that it slides back to its dormant position at the base of the spine, when the light in the head, the sounds in the ears, and the exquisite sensation that attends its ascent also come to a stop. But once the rapture is experienced, the seeker tries his utmost to experience it again and again in the same way as a youngster, initiated into the secrets of love, is often tempted to repeat the experience as often as possible. The difference in the two lies in this, that the former does not experience the exhaustion or the weakness that affects the latter after every indulgence.

The attraction of love in one case and the lure of the supernatural or the divine provide the incentives for the experience. The organic reproductive essence, which is distinctly felt when it enters a particular chakra, moves rapidly in a sort of circular motion, which spreads out to cover the region. Observed inwardly, the chakra appears like a luminous circle in rapid motion, lighted up by a radiant current never witnessed in the body before. This phenomenon occurs time after time until the last of the five chakras is penetrated.

The whole region from the throat to the base of the spine now becomes the theater of operation of a radiant form of psychic energy that darts here and there along the nerves, like a streak of lightning in a manner extremely bewildering and mystifying to the observer. But there is absolutely no doubt that the movement of the luminous current is governed by a super intelligence, which regulates its activity according to the moment-to-moment varying needs of the organism.

The amazing spectacle presented by the shining pranic current as it moves through the nerves with lightning speed, from one organ or from one part to the other, is so awe-inspiring that the observer, hushed into silence, for the first time gains awareness of the marvelous superintelligent power of nature that maintains his body and fuels his brain to the last day he is alive on earth.

With repeated practices, carried on for years, the nervous system of the individual in whom the power is active becomes more and more accustomed to the new role it has to perform. The activity of the nerves in extracting the subtle essence from the surrounding tissues and blood becomes more and more intensified.

The reproductive organs in both women and men increase their production of the organic secretions that provide the organic essence for the upward flow from chakra to chakra into the brain. The effect of the changes that occur when the cerebrospinal system starts to function in a bewildering way on the activation of Brahma-Rendra is overwhelming. The individual feels himself completely at the mercy of an awe-inspiring, intelligent force that has the power of life and death over him.

When the nerves and the reproductive organs become more adjusted to the new function that falls to their share on the awakening, there occurs a sustained flow of the superior pranic radiation to the brain, which helps to stabilize the transformed personality. For the yogi who raises the power from chakra to chakra, the time taken in the gradual ascent, until it penetrates the brain, is often sufficient to attune the reproductive system and the bodily nerves to the new activity.

In such cases, even when Kundalini rises high enough to irradiate the Brahma-Rendra, the duration of her stay in the sahasrara does not exceed a few minutes at a time. After that, with the failure of the nervous system to supply more of the organic element, the sensations and the other symptoms—that is, the lights and the sounds—fade away or subside. This is euphemistically called by the ancient writers as the return of the Goddess Kundalini to her abode at the base of the spine.

With prolonged practice, the duration of the experience is extended, but this extension in the duration of the rapture, beyond a certain prescribed limit consonant with the resources of the body, is extremely hard to achieve. The ideal of the practice is to retain Kundalini in the sahasrara, or in other words, to maintain the flow of the organic essence into the brain on a permanent basis. This is known as the jivan-mukta or sahaja state. Cosmic consciousness becomes a perennial possession of a yogi who is able to achieve this feat. But the cases of this category are extremely rare. Kundalini is perennially active only in the case of outstanding mystics born with the gift, whose extraordinary achievements in the spiritual or religious field are a matter of history.

CHAPTER FOURTEEN

In 1975, nearly four hundred yogis, scientists, philosophers, and educators participated in an unprecedented Seminar on Yoga, Science and Man cosponsored by the government of India and several leading institutions of science and education. In his inaugural address, Dr. Karan Singh, then minister for health and family planning, called for the cooperation and collaboration of all yogis and scientists in undertaking a special project to study Kundalini. "The project revolves particularly around the books on Kundalini by Pandit Gopi Krishna, who is happily present among us today," he said. "Could it perhaps be that it is the development of Kundalini that will trigger off the new mutation in consciousness that would stimulate, irrigate, and irradiate those areas of the brain that are at present areas of darkness? Here is a truly exciting challenge to scientists the world over."

Though the project he called for was approved by the Indian government, funds were never appropriated. This chapter is a condensed version of Gopi Krishna's speech given at the seminar.

THE SCIENTIFIC INVESTIGATION

Study of the phenomenon of Kundalini provides the only channel for the exploration of prana. The channel, through which the illuminati attain to transcendence and the geniuses to extraordinary bloom of the mind, is the natural inlet through which the human intellect can come into contact with the divine forces of creation. The study of psychic phenomena or the practice of magical arts do not provide a safe avenue for this enterprise. The superphysical forces that cause psychical displays or lend potency to magic, if made amenable to human will, could place a weapon in the hands of the overambitious, the voluptuary, and the megalomanic before which even the threat posed by the nuclear arsenals would pale into insignificance. Wars can be made to erupt telepathically and multitudes made abject slaves and puppets of a few.

But nature has provided safeguards that can make it impossible for any scientific investigation to know the nature of or to control the mysterious forces involved in these occurrences at the present evolutionary stage of the race. The reason for this is simple. We know what amazing devices protect life on earth. The whole drama of organic evolution from the beginning to this moment is a miracle of divine protection continued for billions of years against staggering odds: one chance against billions, repeated interminably. Yet that one infinitely slender chance succeeded, and humanity owes her existence to that.

We also know that there are defenses that act as umbrellas round the earth—the heaviside layer, for instance, that shields terrestrial life from the lethal effects of cosmic radiation. There are defenses that keep the forces of nature—flood and tide, storm and rain, heat and cold—from attaining a fury or a rigor fatal to life. There are defenses that allow us to live unconcerned and undisturbed while the earth whirls through space at terrific speed, with flaming oceans of fire storming and raging in her interior. There are defenses in our body that protect us from the deadly attacks of malignant bacteria time after time.

There are psychological devices, as there are devices in ants and bees, that rule the social conduct of human beings and form the instinctive background of every human social order. There are devices that bring the human fold back again to the path of evolution after every departure or digression through the offices of religious teachers, revolutionaries, and reformers.

There are devices that will come into operation at the time of a seemingly annihilative nuclear war to save the race from extinction, for it is meant to fulfill a glorious destiny. In short, we are miraculously preserved and protected from every side and at every moment. But how often do we admit within ourselves that all our life is spent at the mercy of forces about which we have no awareness at all? Often we even fail to realize that there is design in every fragment and every event of the universe. But the scale of its operation is so unimaginably vast in space and time that our poor sense equipment and puny intellect fail to grasp it. Another channel of perception is therefore needed to bring the intangible controlling forces of creation within our ken.

A decrease of half a degree during the past thirty years in the global temperature of the earth has made scientists concerned about its still unpredictable effect on the climatic conditions at different places if the drop continues to occur. This shows what a delicate balance in the environment is necessary for life to survive on earth and that still unknown and unthought-of devices are operating to maintain balance.

There are similar devices that will prevent the whole global body of science from penetrating into the mystery of the super-physical forces and harnessing them, as we have harnessed the physical forces of nature, because mankind must ascend yet another step on the ladder of evolution before this can become possible. The mastery might be gained when the precondition of a further rise in the evolutionary scale is fulfilled.

The twin products of an active Kundalini—namely, the illuminated men and women and those of genius and talent—have been the two main classes of human beings responsible for every advance made by mankind so far. It has been known for long that heredity primarily accounts for the quota of intelligence and talent in human beings. This view has now been confirmed by exhaustive tests conducted on twins and other children at several places. In a recent article in the *National Observer*, Joan Rodgers writes:

> You may give a child excellent parental attention, a good home, fine schools and cultural experience, but if the youngster wasn't born smart, he will probably never be smart. It is an abhorrent idea to some but that is what several American and European scientists said in Rome at the First International Congress of Twin Studies. . . . There is an answer now, the scientists said, to the long-standing often emotional question of whether it is genetics or environmental factors that principally determine one's learning ability. They say it is nature.

In support of this conclusion, Rodgers refers to the studies conducted by Dr. Joseph M. Horn, of the University of Texas, and other scientists. "Our studies and others clearly show," says Horn, "that individual differences in intelligence among individuals in Western culture are primarily determined by genetics. We know what is involved in making statements like that, but we have no choice. The data are there. . . . When one finds a trait such as intelligence substantially determined by genetic factors, this does not mean we cannot design an environment to overcome it. But the evidence to date is that we have yet to find that environment and, what is more, we may be looking in the wrong places."

Referring to the home and school environments that have been the traditional targets of manipulation by doctors, teachers, and psychologists, looking for the best environment for child development, Horn observes: "But what we need to do now is look elsewhere to other environments to alter." The manipulation of the inner environment before birth in terms of enrichment and prevention of defects, in the view of Dr. Horn, may do far more than manipulation of the external environment.

Kundalini provides the one and only avenue for overcoming the congenital deficiencies of the brain. The paramount importance of its study can be readily gauged even from this one fact. In this lies the only hope for the mentally retarded or the deficient. In the advanced stages of our knowledge about the mechanism, it might become possible for scientists to achieve what has been impossible so far—to bring hope, cheer, and the light of intelligence to millions of mentally stunted human beings all over the world. It might also become possible to eradicate other congenital defects beyond cure at present. The evolution of the body and making it immune to death are based on this potentiality of Kundalini. It has a regenerative and recuperative effect on the system. But exhaustive research is necessary to devise safe methods for its arousal in keeping with its own laws.

The social aspect of research on Kundalini is even more important. Revolutionary changes in the current thinking on social problems and political ideologies may result. The smoldering discontentment in some of the richest countries of the West and the strong curb on the freedom of expression in the Communist lands, as a whole, provide unquestionable evidence for the fact. There is hardly any country on the earth today that, under the surface, is not a seething cauldron of unrest and disaffection.

Rings of fire and streams of blood mark at every phase the social evolution of mankind, from the dawn of history to the present day. There seldom if ever has been a peaceful transition from one social order or one political structure to another. So long as the basic reason for the need for change in the social environment of man is not understood, and mankind continues to be in the dark about this vital aspect of its evolutionary career, blood will continue to be shed.

Continued ignorance of this essential knowledge is fraught with the gravest danger for the race in the times to come. Within a few more decades all the countries with fairly large populations, and even the affluent smaller ones, will have nuclear arsenals to add to their security against the existing nuclear powers. Nuclear technology will make it possible to construct miniweapons for use by terrorist organizations and frustrated individuals. This can happen any day and lead to the plunging of the world into a nightmare of fear and anxiety at each small incident every day.

Deep-rooted instincts prescribe the social behavior of all other forms of life except man. The evolutionary dynamics of the human brain need a flexible social order amenable to revision from time to time. But conservative tendencies stand stubbornly in the way of needed change from one order to the other. The countercultures in America and the revolt of youth in other parts of the world are all indications of the fact that the time of utility of the present order is over and a change is urgently called for.

Modern psychology is unaware of this resistless impulse in the human brain. The main actor in the drama of life is entirely missing in the learned dissertations on the human mind. The alarming increase in psychic disorders is the outcome of obstructed evolution on account of unhygienic social conditions. But statistical data and study of abnormal mental behavior cannot help to bring this hidden actor to light. Another kind of study is needed to reach to the bottom of this mystery. The greatest potential for a complete revolution in the sphere of modern thought lies hidden in psychology.

Why prophets, philosophers, and political revolutionaries failed to bring about an era of lasting peace is because the divine estate destined for man and the divine mechanism designed to lead to it were never empirically demonstrated. Knowledge of the human body and the methods that could make this demonstration possible were never so advanced as they are now. But all the same, the demonstration constitutes a colossal enterprise. Once started, it is likely to become an unending quest.

Research on Kundalini is research on the very roots of life.

The fossil data in support of the theory of evolution have been under investigation for more than a century. Still, the clinching evidence has not been found, and there is a difference of opinion about some of the most vital issues of the doctrine. The theory of gravity is another example. The constitution of the atom is another. Psychic phenomena provide another category where a clash of views has been in evidence for about a century now. It would therefore be too much to expect that research on Kundalini or, in other words, on the cosmological forces of life, can produce decisive results in a day. It will prove a long and arduous quest.

But the stakes are high. Validation of the phenomena of religion and mystical ecstasy, evidence for the immortal nature of the soul, the purpose of life and the destiny of man, the force behind psychic phenomena, voluntary cultivation of genius, avoidance of destructive wars and bloody revolutions, insight into the causes of insanity, and illuminating answers to other problems of life will constitute the golden harvest yielded by this investigation bit by bit in the course of time.

Of all these categories, the most important and, at the same time, the most phenomenal is the transformative prowess of Kundalini. This sphere of its activity is so remote from our current conceptions that no exposition about it can convey the unthought-of possibilities inherent in it unless a case of this type comes actually under observation. A young Maharashtrian girl in Nagpur, India, it is reported, has been completely transformed into a Bengali-speaking shy housewife of more than 125 years ago. The girl, Sharada, as she calls herself, used to emerge for a short while and later gave way to the Maharashtrian girl. Later the spells lasted longer, and the present condition has continued for a month. The girl, who is highly educated, did not know Bengali before this transformation. According to her parents, the change began about a year ago, and the girl started to speak Bengali, a language hitherto unknown to her.

Transformation of personality, when it goes down to the very roots of an individual, betokens a transformation of the pranic spectrum. The change can occur sporadically for short or long spells of time, or on a permanent basis. The phenomenon is well known to psychologists, but no satisfactory explanation has been found so far. I have myself witnessed every phase in the transformation of my own personality. There are many mediums and sensitives who evince the same trait on a sporadic basis. During the spells of their transformation they display extraordinary faculties of mind or show evidence of talents, ways of talk and behavior, or artistic gifts that are absent in their normal life. The phenomenon has been often repeated in history.

Specific areas of the still unused potential of the brain are used to build up the other personality. The architect is Kundalini. Psychologists are content to treat such individuals as cases of double or multiple personality and let it rest at that. A complete metamorphosis in which two entirely different individuals emerge from the same brain is a phenomenon so astounding and so far in conflict with the current concepts about the mind and the organ of its expression—that is, the brain—that it is surprising so little attention has been paid to its investigation. This shows how narrow are the frontiers of modern psychology. There is no universally accepted explanation for any extraordinary or abnormal state of mind, including insanity. Yet psychologists, as a class, labor under the impression that they are academically competent to pass their judgments about the mental condition of the rest of the world in terms of their own nomenclature, which still lacks confirmation.

The process that occurs naturally in rare cases to build up a multiple personality can be set in motion voluntarily with the arousal of Kundalini. In this lie its amazing possibilities. There are well-known and well-attested cases of individuals who, in a trance or semitrance state, bloom into great healers, clairvoyants, expounders of religious truths, prophesiers, oracles, and the like. With voluntary cultivation there is no end to the possibilities of the metamorphosis. With better knowledge of the mechanism and the discovery of safer methods to activate it, the products of Kundalini can bloom into prodigies in every sphere of human knowledge, into geniuses of the highest order, into prophets, seers, healers, and clairvoyants of such surpassing nature, which is beyond anything we can imagine at present. They will be the leaders in every field of knowledge and activity in the future world.

The study can be divided into five broad parallel departments. The first of these would consist of a thorough study of the oral and written tradition. There are thousands of books on Kundalini and Yoga extant in India. The ancient esoteric treatises, including the tantras, contain valuable hints about it. The Vedas, the Upanishads, and the Puranas provide another fertile source. A study by a team of scholars can provide valuable material to initiate an empirical investigation of the phenomena. Then there is a huge mass of literature formed by the self-revelations and other utterances of the medieval saints of India. It can also provide precious clues here and there and substantiate the information contained in the scriptural texts. The writings of the Western mystics, Sufis, Taoists, and Tibetan yogis should provide a valuable mine of information. Religious lore of all the faiths and the books on magic, alchemy, or the occult, existing from ancient times, can also supply valuable material bearing on the subject. Well-known documents on Kundalini can begin the study, which can then be extended gradually to cover all the sources available for this research.

The study of the oral tradition is equally important. The hint I, myself, received about the danger of an awakening occurring through the pingala or the solar nerve was based on oral tradition. These facts are not generally mentioned in the books. The hints are transmitted orally by the preceptor to the disciple and acted upon in times of need.

For instance, in the event of an awakening leading to the generation of heat in the system, the remedy prescribed is to lay on a coat of wet clay over the body or to immerse it in a pool of water up to the neck. For the heat experienced at the crown of the head or the space between the eyebrows, the rubbing of sandalpaste is recommended. In fact, the mark applied by Hindus to the forehead is done as a sign of homage to the ajna-chakra. It is only when Kundalini enters this center that higher faculties of the mind make their appearance. The application of a mark to the forehead, which is such a common feature of worship or even adornment in India and sometimes appears as a product of superstition to foreigners, carries a highly esoteric significance and an awareness of the physiological implications of this power.

The second province of research would cover those cases in which Kundalini is congenitally active. There are five categories of individuals belonging to this class—the born mystic, the man or woman of genius, the prodigies, the mediums, and the psychotics. Out of all these categories, the last named are most easily accessible to research. Next to the cases of those in whom Kundalini becomes active as the result of certain disciplines or spontaneously later in life, psychotics provide a most fertile field for this investigation. The old view of the psychoanalytical school that insanity is a subjective phenomenon arising out of repression or other similiar causes, especially in childhood, is becoming increasingly obsolete. The latest studies show that schizophrenia, manic-depression, and other serious forms of insanity have roots deep in the organic soil of the body.

But often the roots penetrate to a depth in the finer levels of the organism that are yet beyond the reach of microscopic study. And it has now been clearly established that some forms of psychoses show definite tracks in the brain. The horrifying visions and distracting sounds that lunatics see and hear, it is now recognized, are not all mere figments of their imagination but can be maddeningly real, with their roots in the excited and altered condition of certain areas in the brain.

Even in the normal condition, our nerves are the generators and carriers of bioenergy or prana in its individual organic aspect. Modern biology and psychology have no knowledge of this activity of the nervous system, because the medium involved is subtle beyond measure with the instruments now in use. A beginning has been made with Kirlian photography, but further advancement is needed to bring this elusive substance within the orbit of research. On the activation of Kundalini, there occurs a high increase in the production of bioenergy and also an enhancement in its potency. The ecstatic visions of the mystic, the creations of genius, the performance of the prodigy, the phenomena of the medium, and the nightmares of the insane are all, without exception, products of this enhanced flow of a more potent form of bioenergy into the brain.

In the case of the born mystic, genius, medium, and the prodigy, the brain cells are already attuned to the flow of bioenergy of a higher potency. But in the case of those in whom the power is aroused as the result of certain disciplines, a certain period of time is needed to accustom the brain to the altered condition of this force. This is the most critical period in the discipline of Yoga and other spiritual exercises. Even in the case of individuals born with this peculiarity, crises continue to occur throughout life. The susceptibility to mental derangement in the case of some of the most outstanding specimens of the latter, like Newton, is also due to this fact. Research into Kundalini must make it possible to avert these crises in the lives of the most creative section of the race. The crises in the lives of great mystics and saints—their tormenting desire for spiritual experience to the point of mania—also owe their origin to the effect of this psychic radiation on the brain.

The mystic can attain such a state of absorption in this visionary experience that he can become entirely oblivious to the world and his surroundings. The very words "trance" or "ecstasy" denote this state of intense engrossment. This is also one of the characteristics of samadhi. The individual is lost to the world around him. To a lesser extent, this is also the case with creative genius. Intense absorption in the subject of study or the artistic production has been a marked feature of the creative mind. The anecdotes relating to the absorbed states of Newton are, to a greater or lesser extent, applicable to other great geniuses also. In the case of mediums, too, the mental condition undergoes a transformation during the productive periods. There is often entrancement or there are signs of intense one-pointed mental effort during the performance.

In a different form, the same symptom of withdrawal from the world marks the mental condition of the insane. The psychotic lives alienated from the world, completely engrossed in an inner experience that determines his external behavior also. But in this case, the visionary or auditory experience is not alluring or absorbing. It is a phantasmagoria of disordered imagination, of erratic and absurd thought and act, fear, anxiety, and horror. It is toxic, poisonous, and virulent, causing excitement or depression, frenzy or stupor, intense melancholy or insane laughter, and all the other characteristics peculiar to madness. The old personality disappears from the scene and a distorted one emerges, lost to the norms of behavior and sense. The disoriented pranic spectrum now reflects a disfigured being completely or in part out of tune with the world.

The studies carried out on mystics, now and in the past, and the revelations of mystics themselves involve halos of light, harmonies of sound, transporting visions, extraordinary insights, new depths of knowledge, glimpses of other planes of existence, or spiritual exaltation during the spell for which the ecstasy lasts.

There also occurs an increase of creative activity, eloquence, and literary or artistic talent according to the mental aptitude of the subject. With the flow of the polluted pranic radiation into the brain, the lights become blinding glares, the sounds distracting noises and shrieks, the visions nightmares, deep insights become crazy whims, the glimpses of a new existence become the phantom world of insanity, and spiritual exaltation assumes the form of grandiose delusions of rank and power. The increase in creative activity is translated into frenzied behavior, eloquence into raving, and increased literary or artistic ability, into insane compositions and bizarre art.

I am positive about the fact that a morbid activation of Kundalini can lead to psychoses in a variety of forms. I myself passed through phases akin to them during the period of my transition from one state of consciousness to the other. It took years for the state to be stabilized. I have witnessed the same shifts toward a borderline mental condition on the activation of Kundalini in several other cases also. The extreme hazard involved in a forced voluntary arousal of Kundalini, which has long been known in India, stems from this possibility. The abortive cases turn into schizophrenics and manic-depressives, in some instances displaying remarkable psychic gifts. Research on Kundalini is research on bioenergy and can lead to the causes responsible for vitiation of the psychic currents and their cure. Modern psychology clearly accepts the close association of sexuality with mental disorder, but the actual mechanism is never signified.

In order to understand the genesis of this form of insanity it is necessary to look a little more carefully into the mechanism of Kundalini. As has been explained in my books, the activation of the mechanism marks the start of two new and different activities in the body. The whole vast network of nerves begins to manufacture a more potent form of psychic energy (prana) and pour it into the brain through the spinal duct. The most distinguished feature of this altered form of bioenergy is that it appears as a luminous cloud in the brain. The energy in the average man and woman does not have this property. For this reason the visionary experiences of mystics are almost always bathed in light. This is the first important point to which any investigation into the phenomenon must pay attention. This is also the reason why Kundalini is always likened to the sun, moon, lightning, or fire. Flashes of light or other forms of luminosity experienced by many people during the course of meditation and sometimes even otherwise are often due to a sudden, brief upsurge of the higher prana into the brain.

The other activity starts in the genital region. On the awakening, the reproductive juices in the form of radiation are sucked up in a mysterious way and poured into the spinal canal. How this suction is applied will surely be brought to light one day by research. This juicy stream, rising through the spine, represents the "nectar" or "ambrosia" repeatedly mentioned in the treatises on Kundalini. It is the "soma" of the Vedas, the "rasa" of the alchemists, and the "samarasa" of the medieval saints of India. The whole mystic literature of India is full of references to it. Its entry into the spinal cord, and later on into the brain, is marked by exquisitely pleasurable sensations even exceeding the orgasm. This stream of organic essence is ramified into smaller streams during the course of its ascent into the cranium, and these slender streams irrigate the visceral organs through the nerve plexuses or the chakras. The stream can be distinctly felt moving into the various organs—stomach, liver, intestines, heart, lungs, throat, and the like. A new channel for toning up the organs to meet the additional needs, resulting from an increase in the area of awareness, now comes into operation. In this way the body and the brain are prepared for a more elevated manifestation of consciousness. The flow of more potent prana and this stream of fluidic secretions into the nerve centers and the brain is what is implied by the phrase "penetration of Kundalini" as stated in the ancient books on the subject.

In the case of a morbid awakening, the two movements do not start together, or there is imperfect coordination between them. The genital secretions, for various reasons, do not stream up and circulate in the system to adjust the organs and the brain to the flow of the high-potency prana now operative in the system. Overindulgence or an unhealthy state of the reproductive organs can also lead to this condition. In such an eventuality, the consequences can be terrible. Since the mechanisms for preparing the tissues of the body for a greater output of psychic energy of a more concentrated kind fail to act altogether or in the right manner, the radiation pouring into the head lacks that degree of purity and excellence necessary for the healthy functioning of the brain in the altered condition. An impure, toxic current now flows through it, creating a chaotic condition in the whole province of thought. The irritation caused in the brain cells by the contaminated pranic radiation is soon translated into the anarchy in thought and behavior of the afflicted individual.

It is no wonder that under the torment of this venomous current now flooding the brain the lunatic raves, shrieks, gesticulates, runs about wildly, laughs, foams at the mouth, resorts to violence, or lapses into frenzy in a manner characteristic of the mentally deranged. He has no perception of the radiation. What he experiences is a derangement in personality, thought, and act. The disoriented stream of prana gives rise to a disoriented human being. The suffering of the patient can be terrible. He may sink into a stupor; be entirely unable to collect his thoughts; lose all relish for food as the reflexes are deadened; experience agonizing loss of sleep; feel himself burning from head to toe; or experience other subjective, intensely painful, and tormenting conditions.

At the present moment, psychic energy is beyond the probe of science, and there is no method to determine its purity or otherwise. Scientists faced with the actuality of mental disorder, yet unable to know anything about the subtle force responsible for it, continue to put forward ingenious explanations that take no cognizance of the mysterious agent behind. Insanity is a product of an impure state of pranic radiation, whether caused by the awakening of Kundalini or otherwise due to the malfunctioning of the organism in its subtle levels involved in the production of prana. The somatic aspect of insanity is now becoming increasingly apparent to psychologists, but the basic facts are still unidentified.

There can be other variations. The pranic currents might flow through the ida and pingala, causing awful, excited, or depressive conditions. The forms of insanity caused by a malignant Kundalini, and their varied patterns in different individuals, is a subject so vast and so intricate that it would constitute a whole department of knowledge when the mechanism is empirically demonstrated.

Why it has not been possible for scientists to locate the real cause of mental and psychic maladies is because scientists have no knowledge of bioenergy and no methods or devices to detect it. Kundalini provides the one natural channel for the exploration of this still unidentified force of creation. This exploration can be both subjective and objective, provided the mechanism is rightly manipulated. A great deal of research would be needed to define the parameters of the objective evidence. But with study and patience this can be done, leading to the emergence of a new science in due course of time. The benefits accruing for the cure of mental diseases from this investigation cannot be exaggerated. In the not-too-distant future, it might become possible to control mental disorders through the discovery of prana, just as it has become possible now to control epidemics and infectious ailments through the discovery of the microbial origin of disease. Wilhelm Reich was right when he said that mental disorder is anchored in the somatic structure of the organism. This somatic anchorage is prana.

The pressures and tensions of modern life, especially in the more advanced, industrialized nations, seriously affect the delicate balance of prana, putting a heavy strain on the organic mechanism that ensures its sensitive equilibrium. The result is that there are sometimes more patients suffering from mental disorders, seeking admission to clinics, than patients suffering from all other diseases taken together. This is an alarming situation pregnant with even worse possibilities in the future, for the tensions and pressures are still on the increase. Apart from the confirmed cases of mental disorder, there are millions of people in all parts of the world lacking in the power of adjustment to their surroundings. This results in untold suffering to their partners, families, and all those with whom they are in contact every day. For a control of these conditions also, the only natural mechanism is Kundalini.

Genetic engineering, if it is ever undertaken, would ultimately lead to the same conclusions. It is the disorientation of the pranic spectrum that is responsible for all obsessions, fixations, perversions, and distortions of the mind. The channel to handle prana is Kundalini. Since an alarmingly large proportion of the race is in the grip of a mental disorder, a twist or a kink of some kind, or lacks in the proper degree of self-control and self-adjustment, the dimensions of research that can provide a panacea for all the ills of the mind and the nervous system can be better imagined than described.

The third province of research can be provided by born mystics, geniuses, mediums, and prodigies in whom Kundalini is more or less active from birth. The data obtained from the observations of the mental cases, resulting from a morbid awakening, can be put to use in drawing up a blueprint for the study of the born cases. Certain parameters of identity will always be there. The main targets of investigation should be the cerebrospinal fluid and the reproductive apparatus. In the case of the mediums, a tendency to orgasm has already been noticed in some cases. The erotic trend in mystical ecstasy is fully recognized. The sex life of geniuses or men and women of extraordinary talent must also provide indications of this type. The learned, as a class, are often unwilling to move out of the cloistered area of thought to which they are accustomed. But few of them show a readiness to march into unknown territory. The ordeals undergone by those who broke through the fallacy of a geocentric universe are well known. The empirical validation of Kundalini is sure to cause a revolution far exceeding in magnitude the one caused by Copernicus. But a tough battle will be necessary before scholastic prejudice can be overcome.

The modern concept of life is based on the assumption that a peculiar constitution and composition of atoms and molecules is at the bottom of the phenomenon. There is no conception of still unknown and immaterial forces in the universe. Although the very texture of thought and consciousness constitutes a standing challenge to this erroneous conception, any attempt made to break through this self-imposed barrier would always prove a tough undertaking. The difficulties inherent in an investigation of Kundalini must, therefore, be kept in mind from the first. The attempt is to break through the self-erected frontiers of modern science. A century of experimentation on psi phenomena by competent investigators, including eminent scientists, has not yet been able to cross this border. But properly conducted research on Kundalini, in my opinion, is sure to perform this formidable task in less than one fifth of this interval.

Once the underlying principles are known, the study of the individuals with an awakened Kundalini should be easy to conduct and organize. There must be definite biological differences in the blood, the cerebrospinal fluid, and the composition of brain matter in its subtle layers. The recent startling discoveries of new particles in the composition of the atom should make us cautious in allotting a limit to the composition of the organic cell. Its subtler layers are still beyond our probe. Our present-day concepts are built on assumptions that any fresh discovery can prove to be wrong. There is a whole world of subtle energies lying hidden in every living organism. These energies, in their turn, subsist on subtle biological fuels that the organism produces and stores in every tissue and cell. This fuel is used by the cosmic life energy, or prana shakti, to manufacture the individual prana or bioenergy. Neurons play an active part in this manufacture.

The accomplished yogis of India have been able to write with such assurance about the pranic currents in the body because in the heightened states of consciousness, prana becomes easily perceptible. A scientific study of this subtle medium, with instruments devised for the purpose, can be of incalculable value to mankind. A painstaking study of persons with an active Kundalini must at last furnish clues by which it would be possible to know the difference between the microbiology of a normal individual and a genius or a mystic, or any other specimen of this category. There can be no denial of the fact that there must exist some difference between the brain of an Einstein and that of a man of ordinary intelligence. But in spite of repeated efforts made to this end, this difference has not been found so far. The reason for this failure is that the extremely fine tissues involved have not come within the range of observation to this day.

The fourth province for study can be furnished by those in whom the activation of Kundalini occurs later in life without in any way affecting the sanity of their mind. Those who have symptoms of this kind often pass through periods of suspense or suffering because of their ignorance of the factor responsible for them. I have been receiving letters from people all over the world whom a study of some of my books made cognizant of the mysterious agency responsible for the strange and sometimes bizarre experiences they were undergoing or the unusual symptoms they noticed in themselves. This activation can occur spontaneously, but more often meditation, yogic practices, or some other spiritual disciplines are the cause. The experiences can sometimes be elevating and sometimes be distressful. They appear so varied that it often becomes difficult to trace them to the same cause.

For a study of the cases falling under this category, a widely publicized call for case histories can prove a good beginning. There is every likelihood that responses will come from all over the world. They will provide statistical data that, I feel sure, would be enough for an unbiased scientific mind to see the wide area of prevalence of the phenomenon. Out of the respondents some might be even prepared to volunteer themselves for further investigation. This can lead to the discovery of new avenues for the research. The vast variety of symptoms would also make the investigating scientists better informed about the multilateral effects of the force on different kinds of constitutions.

The study can also provide hints for the investigation of insanity caused by a morbidly active Kundalini. Since the accounts of the psychotics themselves would always lack clarity and precision, the borderline cases falling under this category can prove more dependable for a study of their symptoms also.

The fifth and the most important area of research would be provided by those cases who voluntarily offer themselves for the bold exploit of rousing the power. Among the ardent seekers after illumination there must be some who would readily lend themselves for an undertaking of this nature. This needs the establishment of a well-managed institution where the disciplines can be given. A hundred well-selected candidates will provide the minimum needed to show results, because the phenomenon is so rare. The institution should be in a temperate region and should be well provided with all the amenities of life. It should provide an environment in which the nobler instincts find the highest expression. There must be competent scientists and dedicated Yoga specialists in the governing body of this institution. An open-minded scientific approach, without the least tinge of dogmas, should be made to all problems of the research.

The activation of Kundalini even in one case out of this whole lot can be an illuminating experience. The body and the mind suddenly start to function differently. There is an increase in the metabolic processes, pulse, etc., to adjust the system to more increased production and expenditure of the new form of psychic energy. The psychic fuel feeding the brain of a mystic during his ecstasies or a genius during his productive periods is not the same energy that nourishes the brain of an average individual. This is the basic feature that investigation of Kundalini is meant to establish. In the case of a powerful awakening, there occurs a riot in the energy system of the body that is perceptible both by external observation and also subjectively by the individual himself. It is because of this highly accelerated flow of psychic energy in all parts of the body that the phenomenon has been designated as the awakening of shakti (energy) by the ancient authorities. A virtual tornado of psychic forces appears to have been let loose in the system.

Besides my own, I have come across three other cases of this type. The symptoms are unmistakable and are a part of the oral tradition. A great deal of information about the bodily reactions on the awakening can be gathered from Yoga ashrams and others conversant with the existing literature and tradition relating to the subject. The period during which the system works at an increased tempo, under the stress of the newly released energy, can extend from months to years. In the successful cases, there occurs a metamorphosis of consciousness, and the initiate's mental faculties might attain a bloom that he or she never had before. Even if this supreme consummation does not come to pass, as the result of some bodily flaw, the physiological processes set afoot by the arousal are of sufficient magnitude to throw a flood of light on the phenomenon.

This brief survey is, perhaps, enough to convey an idea of the stupendous nature of this research. There is no other area of study in the vast domain of science so pregnant with undreamed-of possibilities as this. Kundalini is the divine mechanism for the transformation of the whole race, from an aimless crowd of jostling, fighting people, unaware of themselves, into a harmonious assembly of illuminated beings who have experienced the sovereign glory of the soul. There is no other knowledge that can bring peace and happiness to strife-torn mankind. Kundalini provides the only way to settle the long-standing conflict between reason and faith, science and religion. There is no other channel except this to validate the truth of the major faiths and make known the glorious possibilities inherent in the priceless yogic tradition.

It is only through patience and humility that success is possible in this undertaking. Investigation into physical phenomena is aimed to get knowledge of the dead forces of nature, but investigation into Kundalini is to win access to the intelligent forces of creation. This investigation, therefore, imposes a great responsibility on those who would undertake it. The destined hour for the empirical study of this unique phenomenon and the disclosure of the so far secret knowledge relating to it, I feel certain, has arrived. But who will win the crown of success in the effort remains yet to be seen. In the words of the Vedas, let us pray for divine guidance, for the unity of hearts and unanimity of thought in this momentous task, for Kundalini provides the only solution to the most burning problems of the day.

CHAPTER FIFTEEN

This chapter was written for a book honoring Professor C. F. Von Weizsacker, director of the Max Planck Institute for Life Sciences, on his seventieth birthday. A number of distinguished scientists, some of whom were colleagues and former students, were invited to contribute to the book, which was published in Munich in 1982. "I am presenting Von Weizsacker in the light of my own image of the scientists of the future," he writes, "as he comes nearest to the picture I have in mind of one who presents a happy blend of the scientist, the philosopher, and the mystic in his personality. I have very happy memories of our meetings."

PROFESSOR VON WEIZSACKER AS A THINKER OF THE FUTURE

I met Professor Carl Friedrich Von Weizsacker at the suggestion of some friends. He commanded a respect in his country that, to me, seemed unequaled at that time. In a way it reminded me of the homage that Mahatma Gandhi commanded in India. This was my first visit to Europe, and the country in which I first landed was Germany.

I had never been out of India till that day and was not a little surprised at the grandeur and the affluence I saw around in contrast to the poverty of my own native country. The mechanical novelties, like self-opening doors at the airports and moving staircases, were all new to me. The internal heating system was no less of a revelation.

In Kashmir, only a few can afford the dubious luxury of obtaining warmth from large-sized, smoking iron stoves in which wood, sawdust, or charcoal is burned, and the vast majority content themselves with a smoldering kangri tucked under the "pharan" or heavy blanket—only a poor protection against the icy blasts in midwinter. The cleanliness and orderliness of the homes, the business centers, and the roads in the West are equally striking for me.

Mutual friends arranged the meeting. I had only come to know of some of the events and incidents that had made Professor Von Weizsacker well known and honored in his country. His name was a household word in 1968, and people talked about him with respect. I was reminded of it when, on a later visit to Germany, at a time when a scare had been caused by the hijacking of a plane, a police officer detained me at the airport with the object of a further examination. I mentioned to him that I was known to Von Weizsacker and showed him a copy of *The Biological Basis of Religion and Genius* with his introduction in the book, which I had with me. It had a magical effect on the officer. He was all respect at once, and conducted me for some distance toward the luggage compartment.

My first impression was of the simplicity of Professor Von Weizsacker's habits. In contrast to the rich furnishings of the houses I had visited earlier, he resided in a simple apartment. The stairway was covered with plain jute mat, and the room in which he sat was lined with books. There was no sign of ostentation or luxury anywhere. When I looked at him, his face appeared familiar, like friends I had in Kashmir, only fairer in complexion. After a short prelude we fell to talking about the purpose of my visit. Unlike most of the interviews with other scholars and scientists in Germany, his questions touched the very core of the subject on which I wished to talk to him. It was obvious that he had sound knowledge of Indian mystical tradition and knew what I was talking about.

At the parting, he gave me his hand in friendship, which has lasted to this day. I have met but few people who honored their word given at the first meeting to a stranger, as he has done through all these years. His introduction to my little work *The Biological Basis of Religion and Genius* has been a landmark in my career as a writer.

It was this introduction that made many Western readers, more so the learned class, accept my works as something deserving attention. Otherwise, considered from the prevailing Western point of view, the subject on which I write was then comparatively unknown and, for a rational mind, savored more of superstition and fantasy than the factual account of a potentiality in the human body that is still unknown to science.

Before Von Weizsacker wrote the introduction, Spiegelberg's preface and Hillman's commentary had broken the ice and affixed the seal of credibility to my first work, *Kundalini: The Evolutionary Energy in Man*. But even so, we could not find a publisher for the English edition of this book in Europe for a pretty long time in spite of strenuous efforts made by a friend, F. J. Hopman, to that end. Meeting failure in Europe, Hopman from his scanty savings and a friend of his in Delhi, Ramadhar, finally contributed from their pockets to bring out its first edition in India.

I have mentioned this little detail to show what a wall of prejudice stood in the way of the acceptance of my ideas as being worthy of attention in the climate of Europe. The intuitive acceptance of a new factor as a possible explanation for a certain class of phenomena, courage to acknowledge it, and the regard for truth shown by Von Weizsacker in writing an introduction to a work of such a bizarre nature from the strictly scientific point of view can be easily adjudged from this fact.

The Kundalini concept has since become pretty well known, at least among the circles interested in the spiritual and the occult, all over the earth, and scores of books, including some from the pen of scientists, have appeared in the market. The importance of the contribution made by Von Weizsacker to draw attention to a new hypothesis offered to explain certain abnormal and paranormal phenomena of mind, only the future can reveal.

Von Weizsacker's introduction to the second book was decisive in bringing my ideas into focus among the learned interested in Yoga and mysticism. The first English edition of the work was published by Gene Kieffer, an ardent supporter of my ideas, at his cost in New York. The German edition appeared later. The book was selected for the Religious Perspective Series of Harper & Row, Publishers, in the United States, primarily because of the introduction, I believe.

I have had several occasions to sit together and talk with Professor Von Weizsacker on the subject of Kundalini and mystical experience. He combines a fine sensibility with the exact mind of a scientist. His deep study of philosophy and

PROFESSOR VON WEIZSAKER AS A THINKER OF THE FUTURE 249

oriental traditions has mellowed in him the unbending inflexibility of an empiricist whose outlook on nature is bound entirely by the results of his experiments.

In order to evaluate the importance of Von Weizsacker's central idea of "the unity of the universe," a whole volume would be necessary. His contribution to scientific, social, and political themes has been substantial, but in his philosophical ideas about the unity of nature, Von Weizsacker's thought is definitely ahead of our time.

In order to perceive the underlying unity of the cosmic phenomena, there must be a tendency in the observing mind itself to trace the connecting links and to bring about the integration of the divergent and varied events and objects of nature. In other words, the attempt at unification must proceed from the "observer" irrespective of the nature of the phenomena observed by him. It is not possible to arrive at a unitive view of the universe purely by objective study and analysis.

Even assuming that only one single, so far unidentified, energy is responsible for all the phenomena, both organic and inorganic, it would still not be possible to experience or witness this unity or to answer the enigma of how this primary energy assumed such an infinite variety of forms as we come across in the universe. For obvious reasons, it is not possible, from an empirical point of view, to overcome the Cartesian dualism of the subject and the object or "mind" and "matter." For the strict empiricist, the "observer" and the "observed" phenomena can never assume the condition of oneness, for, in that case, the study and the experiment would cease.

The very foundation of modern science rests on a dualistic conception of the universe. Although matter in all its forms is now held to be the product of an ocean of vibrating energy, and it is even admitted that the observer and the observed phenomena cannot be separated from each other, the conceptual gulf between mind and matter still continues to exist, for it lies in the very nature of our existence as conscious beings. In the face of this unbridgeable gulf between "knower" and the "known," which is the first datum of our observation, the search for unity in the universe indicates a tendency in the mind that is contrary to the observed position.

No amount of study of the external world or philosophical

speculation can tend to efface the demarcating line that exists between the subjective consciousness and the objects perceived by it.

The perception of unity in creation, including that between subject and the object or mind and matter must, therefore, proceed from a latent instinctive urge in the mind itself. A compulsive desire to experience this "oneness" is a pronounced feature of the "mystical" temperament. The passion to experience this unity is so overpowering in one born with a strong admixture of this urge that it overshadows all other desires and ambitions of ordinary mortals not constituted that way. The extreme degree of self-denial, suppression of natural instincts, self-mortification, torture, solitude, and starvation to which the mystics not unoften subjected themselves become easily explainable in the light of this fact.

The love of God is strangely reminiscent of erotic desire. There is an element of madness in both. The desire to sacrifice and suffer for the sake of the beloved, to keep his or her image ever before the eyes, to forgo comfort and pleasure, and to carry out any command to win the favor of the adored one are common to both.

In the case of the passionate lover, it appears as if the ego aches to efface itself and merge its identity with the intensely desired object of its love. In the case of the mystic it is the unnameable reality behind creation that forms the object of desire, the elusive, tantalizing source of all. It might be a god or a goddess, a holy personage or a divine being, a picture or an idol, the longing of the passionate devotee is the same. Whatsoever the object of adoration, the deep yearning of the mystic is never fulfilled until, in the rapturous climax of "ecstasy," the veil is torn aside.

Until the blissful moment of mystical rapport, "unity" has to be taken on trust. The multiplicity of objects and the massive, external nature of the universe continue to obsess the mind. They might be one in their ultimate essence, but so far as appearance is concerned, their reality or diversity cannot be denied. Since that essence never forms an object of our observation, this assumption of "oneness" can never be an object of experience. In the same way, even when we concede that a homogeneous sea of energy is the ultimate source of all physical phenomena and, maybe, even of life itself, we fail to carry conviction, as we cannot perceive the homogeneity nor experience the identity of our own perceptual faculty with the objects perceived.

How then does this idea of unity take shape in our mind when we are confronted by diversity on every side? Relevant to the subject is also this question: How did the animistic idea, which invested the objects around—trees, stones, hills, rivers, ponds, and forests—with life, occur to the savage mind? Why at all does this thought of "unity" or "oneness" haunt the human psyche, learned or simple? Why has the idea haunted the minds of some of the greatest scientists, philosophers, and poets of all ages and climes?

This idea of oneness is not the product of vast learning or extensive empirical study of the world. With the same data of observation before them and with the same oceanic study of literature, many thinkers, philosophers, and scientists do not subscribe to the unitive view. For the behaviorist and materialist, "unity" or "plurality" does not count, for their ultimate reality is unfeeling, dead matter that, from the cosmological point of view, makes it immaterial whether it is one or more. What purpose would it serve to probe the mystery of creation further when it is established that only oblivion awaits our efforts at the end?

The search for unity in the midst of diversity surrounding the human species, which has been a pronounced tendency of the highly intelligent human mind from immemorial times, presents an enigma that it is necessary to solve in order to grasp the purpose of this impulse. The fact that in the experiences of mystics of all ages and climes one of the most pronounced traits common to all is a sense of oneness with creation and an all-pervading creative intelligence, which they called by different names, should provide us with a clue to the ultimate target to which the urge is designed to lead. It is to experience the ineffable state where consciousness, overcoming the limitations imposed by the senses and the intellect, perceives its identity with the cosmos and the cosmic intelligence—the Creatrix of the universe. From this it is easy to infer that there is a specific mystical element in our constitution that is designed to unveil the hidden reality behind creation. This impulse has formed the seedbed of every metaphysical system, occult philosophy, religion, creed, or cult.

The idea of God as the father and source of all, the concept of Brahman, the thought of oneness of souls and the monotheistic or pantheistic ideals, even the homogeneity of matter, all owe their origin to this irrepressible mystical tendency in human beings—the persistent idea at the back of the mind that there is a common factor behind all this variety of phenomena, a common source from which all is flowing out. This mystical sense is as much a part of our mind as reason, and its existence can be traced to the very dawn of the rational faculty itself.

From the day he was born as a rational being, man was never devoid of a numinous impulse or a mystical feeling that tried to trace his essential unity with the objects and phenomena around him. The expression of this instinct might have varied enormously in form, but in essence it has always been present in him. The desire to fathom the mystery of his own being was as much a part of the savage brain as it is of the cultured mind of our day.

Science, too, is the outcome of the same spirit of inquiry in human beings. The theater of operation of this thirst is the hidden, the unknown, the inexplicable, the mysterious, the supersensible, and the numinous. When it is directed toward the objective study of the phenomena of nature and the world it is science, when toward the ultimates and principles or the wisdom gained from human experience it is philosophy, and when toward the supersensible province of the soul it is religion. The basic instinctive impulse is the same.

In the assessment of our study of nature, we often lose sight of the peculiar relationship existing between the observing mind and the phenomena observed by it. The phenomena are varied, but the observer is one. The identity of the observer as a single entity remains unaltered from birth to death. Where this identity is altered or scattered, it invariably denotes disorder of the mind. The sense of identity, whether in a human being, a beast, or a bird is always of oneness. We never have two or more recipients of the incoming stimuli or percipients in any creature. Even in the case of multiple personalities, in any individual, each personality exhibited has its own identity and is never a part or segment of another. If there were a multiplicity of observers in any single creature, its survival would become impossible due to the varied nature of the responses from the different cognitive entities.

Unity is thus at the very foundation of cognition and hence of the knowledge of the universe. The observer is always one and, on that account, is able to bring coherence and consistency in the unaccountably divergent phenomena witnessed by him. If the identity of the observer were to be fragmented or diversified, rank confusion would ensue, which would make a systematic or regular study of the cosmos impossible. It is this unitary state of consciousness that makes science, philosophy, or art possible. Otherwise, the phenomena and the events would become disconnected and lose all meaning or sense for the fragmented mind.

We are so deeply occupied by the study of the physical world—its forces and its laws—that we omit to give due place to this important role of unification and integration performed by our consciousness. Again, the very aim of scientific or philosophic enquiry is to simplify the intricate and to fathom the mysterious. We are keen to unearth the laws of nature or reach to the bottom of the mysteries surrounding the still obscure phenomena, to find answers to riddles that baffle us. A physical law discovered invariably covers a large variety of phenomena occurring under different guises which without the knowledge of the law appear disconnected and different from each other. Explained in terms of laws, this whole stupendous creation, with its staggering multiplicity, durations, and distances, can be reduced to the operation of a limited number of nature's ordinances, some of which are still unknown to us.

The same is true of the biological world. The extremely complicated and intricate system of the human body and the bewildering complexity of the brain might, in the course of time, become easily explainable in terms of laws of which we are ignorant at present. Hence the role of science, too, is to explain the complex in terms of the simple, the many in terms of the few, and to reduce the staggering diversity of the objective universe to a limited number of laws and forces that, with further investigation in the days to come, might coalesce into one central law and pivotal force that would explain everything.

It is, therefore, obvious that the mystical impulse and

empirical science tend in the same direction. The highly significant conclusion that emerges out of it is that the single, undivided observer in every human being projects its own image on creation and strives to find the same unity at the core of all the infinitely varied phenomena of the universe as it perceives in itself. In other words, the sense of oneness in the subjective mind tends to serve as the unifying principle in all the objects and events observed by it. Or, more explicitly, the observing consciousness, which is the one, single mirror reflecting the entire universe, in a manner incomprehensible to us, looks around instinctively for a similar source behind the plurality of phenomena—namely, the single force or the central law from which everything springs in the same way as all our experience and knowledge spring from one single entity, the mind.

In the observation of phenomena, modern science leaves the "soul" out of consideration altogether, restricting its study to one part of creation—that is, to the objective part only. This has tended to relegate consciousness to a state of unimportance, with the result that the value of mystical inquiry has been lost. Only a moment's reflection is sufficient to show the error involved in such an approach to nature. We know very well that knowledge in its primary forms, both sciences and arts, originated from priestcraft, or, in other words, from the religious impulse in the human heart. The first abstract thinking of the savage mind, apart from its cogitation on the crude satisfaction of its basic needs, was clearly of a religious kind. Did this happen purely by accident, or does it signify a phenomenon so profound that modern psychology has still to learn a significant lesson from it?

During recent years, a definite trend to integrate the latest scientific theories about the physical world with the ontological concepts of religion is plainly noticeable. This marks a clear departure from the rigid attitude of eighteenth- and nineteenth-century men of science. One of the reasons for this change lies in the revolution that has occurred in the classical notions about the nature and constitution of matter itself. The profound theories of Max Planck, Einstein, and Heisenberg have brought a new vision of the universe before the race. With the extension of its frontiers, the physical world is slowly sliding toward an indeterminate, nebulous form, closer to the visions of mystics than to the formulations of the physicists of the previous two centuries.

With greater extension in the boundaries of physics, aided by further study of psychic phenomena, which seem to negate the known physical laws, modern science may come face to face with that incredible and ineffable force called shakti in the Indian tradition—the basal creative energy, the wellspring of the subjective mind and the objective universe both. At this point, formulation and articulation would cease, the tongue become still, and the intellect freeze, for the ocean of energy now encountered is entirely beyond the perceptual and conceptual powers of the human mind.

The brain must undergo a change and a new faculty develop for the preliminary exploration of this amazing world. This is the purpose of human life, the final object of all mental and intellectual quest, the distant target of the instinctive urge in man to know himself—to reach this ocean of primordial, superintelligent energy, the architect of the universe, with the emergence of a new organ of perception, the mystical faculty, which is slowly developing in the race.

Scientists with a mystical bent of mind show a broader and more healthy attitude toward the problem of existence in contrast to the closed-minded attitude of those who are not thus blessed. It is the eminent scientists of this class, combining the highest intellectual acumen with a budding mystical faculty, who can find solutions to the problems presented by the latest revolutionary discoveries relating to the physical world. They may not be conscious that they have a mystical temperament or that their thought is colored by the interaction of a higher sense, still unknown to science, and are on the very border of an unbounded universe of the soul, but by and large they are the forerunners of the empiricists to come—a finely adjusted, harmonious blend of philosopher, scientist, and mystic in one. It is only this lofty class of gifted men and women that will be able to guide with safety and accuracy the destiny of the technologically and intellectually highly advanced human race in the ages to come.

The prevalence of dogma and hubris among the learned is a sign of ignorance about the fact that knowledge is infinite and depends on the capacity of the "knower" to manifest it. Advancement of knowledge implies a drop-by-drop emergence of an ocean that lies hidden in the "knower," the repository of all the knowledge that exists. It does not matter whether one who discovers his oceanic self is highly learned or unlettered, it does not matter whether he is a scientist or a poet. With the discovery of the "self," his quest comes to an end.

When the source of all knowledge stands revealed, the gnawing hunger to know more and more of the visible world or the occult planes and the burning thirst to solve one's own mystery, which in some is so acute from an early age, ceases to torment anymore. It seems incredible, but from the accounts of the mystics it is clear that the mind may come to a state of calm after but one experience of the inner self. "Only the first letter of the alphabet, alif, is needed to designate Thee," says Bhulla Shah, the famous mystic of Punjab. "Having gained that beyond which there is nothing greater to be attained," says the *Bhagavad Gita;* "The light that illumines the universe," say the Upanishads.

It is for this reason that the knowledge imparted by the Upanishads is known as Vedanta or "the end of knowledge." The wonder of mystical experience lies in this, that all the knowledge gathered in a lifetime by constant study and reflection assumes the semblance of a glowworm compared to the amazing sun that stands revealed. The spectacle is so stupendous and so fascinating that the heart aches to plunge into this ocean of knowledge and eternal life, discarding the puny ego once and for all. The absence of desire for name and fame, disregard for pleasure and even toward death itself evinced by great mystics of the earth is easily explainable in the light of this fact. The experience is so staggering and so stupendous that everything of the earth, even life itself, appears trivial in comparison. Why should one live in a prison when the door to restraintless freedom is found?

The experience can be the same for the intellectual giants of our day as it has been for the simpler minds of the past. The only difference will be the greater intellectual elation experienced by the former at the incredible wonder of a short-lived, amazing state of awareness in which the entire creation, of which a million bulky volumes of intellectual study cannot even cover a small fragment, is swallowed by a nondimensional point from which all knowledge and experience emerges, as all light emerges from the glorious sun.

The marvelous products of technology do not appreciably

affect or enhance the potentiality in human beings to experience this wondrous state of union with the absolute. The sages who meditated in distant hermitages on the Indo-Gangetic Plain of India nearly three thousand years ago possessed the same potentiality and made better use of it than we are doing now. The discoveries and inventions of science are, however, extremely helpful in preparing every member of the race for this unique experience by providing him with leisure and other amenities of life. But if, instead of being treated as means to an end, technology is treated as an end in itself, as is the case now, a revolution must occur to put the race back on the right course, planned by nature to lead her to the supreme experience for which she is born. Science, shorn of spirituality, can only produce a stunted race surrounded by mechanical wonders of every kind but dead to the everlasting, glorious kingdom of the soul.

No doubt based on the experience of millennia, in ancient India worldly knowledge alone was considered insufficient as a guide for human behavior. The terms "Rishi" or "Muni" were reserved for those possessing a fine combination of secular knowledge, wisdom, and spiritual insight. This is what Plato, too, has in mind in his image of the philosopher-king. Janaka of the Indian tradition is a prototype of this class of rulers.

Scholarship alone was never considered as a prized achievement for a balanced life in India. Oceans of knowledge, whether of science or art, cannot compensate for the lack of the saving wisdom that only experience of the supernal and the mundane can grant, nor can all the marvels of technology help to instill perfection in the inner man. "That yogi alone is said to have attained perfection whose self is satiated with knowledge of the inner and the outer worlds, who is steady like a rock, in thorough control of his senses, and to whom a stone, a lump of earth, and a piece of gold are the same." (*Bhagavad Gita* 6:8)

In the time of Plato, the philosopher-king might have been a dream. But now, with the aid of science and knowledge of the cultivatable potential in the human brain, superordinary individuals of this category can become a reality. The harsh necessity of keeping the race from destroying herself with the products of ceaselessly advancing technology will oblige nations to search for men and women of this stature once the incompetency of the existing class of leaders and guides is exposed in the debacles to come.

I am presenting Von Weizsacker in the light of my own image of the scientists of the future, as he comes nearest to the picture I have in mind of one who presents a happy blend of the scientist, the philosopher, and the mystic in his personality. I have very happy memories of our meetings. He always made me feel at ease so far as my own limited knowledge of science and Western philosophy is concerned, and he never allowed it to be seen that he had studied and knew more than I. Whenever I spoke in his presence to a small circle of friends, he would, in his own talk, amplify what I had said, express more fully what I could only imperfectly articulate, add what I had left unsaid, and explain the basic points of my message in a manner more suited to the Western ear.

Once, while discussing in our apartment in New Delhi the possibility of a nuclear war, I saw signs of extreme anguish on his face, and he said in a halting voice, "The thought of a nuclear holocaust haunts me like a nightmare and, even during the night, I am sometimes plunged into a state of extreme distress at the thought of what would happen to the world if a war with nuclear weapons is fought." The anguish was so great that tears trembled on his eyelids. At that moment I could see the light of a mystic gleaming from his eyes. He sensed his close identity with the multitudes of the earth and felt their pain, sorrow, and suffering as acutely as if he himself were experiencing the agony.

This sense of participation in the joy and pain of fellow beings and even that of animals and birds becomes more pronounced in elevated minds. In mystics, it attains its maximum intensity. Ramakrishna felt the impact of a sharp blow landed on the back of another, within his hearing, so acutely that a mark appeared on his own back. "The yogi who is united in identity with the all-pervading infinite consciousness and looks on all with an equal eye, sees the self present in all beings and all beings existing in the self." (*Bhagavad Gita* 6:12)

On another occasion, during Von Weizsacker's stay in Kashmir, I arranged a meeting of a number of friends in his honor on the premises of our Research Institute at Nishat, Srinagar. When we were all seated under the shadow of trees, contemplating the beauty of Dal Lake stretched in front, a lively discussion started. Some of the friends assembled were well versed in Indian philosophy. His answers to their subtle questions relating to Indian thought were so appropriate that many of them remember the absorbing nature of the discussions to this day. Some of them even remarked afterward that it seemed he was one of them and not a stranger from the West seated in their midst.

In spite of his own heavy preoccupations, Professor Von Weizsacker consented to be the head of a newly formed organization in Starnberg under the name "Eastern Wisdom and Western Science," purely as a gesture of kindness toward me. He wished to do all he could in providing the support and the resources needed for the research I had in mind and for the cooperation of competent scientists in the undertaking.

The late Mr. C. F. Basedow, a keen protagonist of a spiritually oriented science, was made the general secretary of the group, and a number of eminent scientists, drawn by the example of Professor Von Weizsacker, were enlisted as its members. In Starnberg we held several meetings during which I was allowed every opportunity to interest the other members of the group in the subject of Kundalini. The founding of this body provided an incentive for the formation of similar groups in other places, both in India and abroad.

I visited Professor Von Weizsacker several times at his own residence in Starnberg, and every time I found the same simplicity and austere mode of life I had come across in my first visit to him, in 1968. Once, when the other members of the family were not at home, he himself served me tea in a plain earthenware kettle and cups—a mark of kindness and humility that is a characteristic of great minds. During recent years we met a few times at Zurich, in the house of Madame Kobelt, another devoted supporter of my ideas and an admirer of Von Weizsacker. I still carry the aroma of our meetings, both at Starnberg and Zurich, for they provided me every time with an intellectual feast of which the relish still lingers in my mind.

The influence for good, in his efforts for lasting peace in the world, that Professor Von Weizsacker exerted on the political life of his country has been considerable and will be assessed at its true value only when the present crisis is over. Often our memory is short and our behavior fickle. What is relished today becomes distasteful tomorrow and what is popular this week becomes unpopular the next. Scholars and politicians who take their stand on the passing fancy of the crowds to win a transient popularity are assessed at their true value by their compeers, as soon as the popular tide subsides. It is only great minds that stand up boldly against the temptation of short-lived public applause and base their stance on principles rather than on the variable approbation of the multitudes.

I wish to make it clear that in the portrait I am drawing of Professor Von Weizsacker, there is no idea to show him in an extraordinary light or a single inch taller than the stature he possesses, out of my regard for him or as a tribute to his kindness to me. I am only making a statement of facts. The reason why I regard him highly is because he conforms to my model of a highly evolved mind trembling on the verge of true spiritual illumination. I had the same feeling when I spoke to Heisenberg in his room in the Max Planck Institute or when I saw Mahatma Gandhi bowing to the crowd from a carriage that carried him in a procession at Lahore.

There are certain characteristics a more evolved mind must possess if its upbringing has been healthy and its heredity sound. These traits of character, I assume, must have been common to a greater or lesser degree to the great minds and top intellects known to history. They must be common to the foremost creative minds of our day. If they are lacking, it denotes a departure from the model, with malformation for one reason or another. The high incidence of mental disorder in genius shows how delicately balanced a superior brain can be. It is the unassuming, unpretentious humble types, with nobility of character, a fertile brain, and a brilliant wit, whose passion is "service" and ambition "conquest of the lower self" that should be ranked as the true aristocrats of the race.

The overclever politician, the flamboyant magnate, the glamorous actor, and the pompous scholar represent now an obsolete model of the past. The demand of the nuclear age is for a spiritually evolved, simple, austere, self-surrendering, and humane intellect as guide in all spheres of human activity and thought. The day of the acquisitive, aggressive, artful, and ambitious types is almost done. The sooner this is realized the better it is for the safety of the race. "Nonviolence, truthfulness, sweetness of tongue, absence of anger, tranquillity, refraining from malicious gossip, kindness to all creatures, nonattachment to the objects of senses, mildness, sense of shame in doing things contrary to scriptural ordinances, abstaining from idle pursuits, sublimity, forgiveness, absence of malice and feeling of self-importance, these are the marks, O descendant of Bharata, of one endowed with divine qualities." (*Bhagavad Gita* 16:2 and 16:3)

In the prescientific eras, the articulated experiences of great mystics and of the founders of major faiths caused time after time such revolutions in the life and thinking of human beings that empiricism and all the flood of thought it generated have not been able to match in spite of all its discoveries and triumphs. At the same time, there can be no denying the fact that science has transformed the outer life of man. It has achieved what even the greatest prophets and visionaries could not accomplish—unimagined amenities of life; control of disease, drought, and famine; and conquest over time and distance. And it has won other great triumphs, which have made human life a bed of roses compared to the rigors of the past.

The search for utopias and ideals of existence is an integral part of the human mind. The progress made by mankind from the brute life of a primitive savage to the present state of luxury and comfort is the harvest of this urge. When there occurs a state of stagnation in any society, and when it continues to adhere fanatically to timeworn habits, customs, and ways of life that time has come to discard, it denotes an absence of the fire that must kindle to lift it up from the old position toward a new pattern of life more in harmony with its inner growth.

The present hopelessly tangled position of the world is a loud warning from nature that reform is needed at once. The efforts made by stereotyped politicians, thinkers, and scholars imbued with ideas that have become outmoded now, with the advance made in science, instead of improving, are making the situation worse. A unified humanity, which provides the only answer to the overhanging threat of a nuclear holocaust, never figures in the visions or the formulas for disarmament of national leaders for the simple reason that with their eyes glued only to the accustomed rut, they lack the imagination to grasp that no other alternative whatsoever is available to guarantee the safety of the race in the even more crucial times to come. They never realize that it is sheer insanity to keep the multitudes perennially exposed to instantaneous death at any moment, which is inevitable when divided nations, fully armed with nuclear weapons, continue to play "thrust and parry" with each other.

The enlightened prophets, reformers, and revolutionaries constitute nature's instruments for bringing changes to adjust religious institutions, social orders, and political systems to the ever-changing demands of man's psychosocial evolution and the new ideals formed by his advancing intellect. In view of the highly increased tempo of our age, the need for the appearance of these spiritual guides, reformers, and revolutionaries must be satisfied with less delay than was the case in the past.

But strange to say, during the past two centuries, no spiritual giant of the stature of a Buddha or a Christ appeared either in the East or the West to bring about a desperately needed revolution in the old religious beliefs of mankind, unable now to stand against the flood of skeptical thought generated by the disclosures and discoveries of science. The learned are not yet cognizant of the fact that the birth of luminaries, geniuses, reformers, and revolutionaries is not a matter of accident but proceeds from the same mysterious sense in the racial mind that maintains the balance in sexes and the proportion of the normal and abnormal in the generations born, time after time. The profundities of life are still an unexplored ocean for science.

In absence of acceptable spiritual ideals, the changes wrought by the revolutionaries and reformers who flourished during recent times, with but a few exceptions, as in the case of Gandhi, were lopsided or partial, in which the spiritual element remained out of sight. The outcome of this vacuity has been that no church, no social order, and no political system has been able to keep pace with the long strides taken by science, with the result that the most advanced nations on the earth are still in the grip of customs and habits, notions and beliefs that are incompatible with the needs of the time. The change in thinking that, in the words of Einstein, is needed for the survival of the race, with the control gained over the terrible power of the atom, has not occurred, for the talent needed for this great task is not there.

It is only a radical change in the thought and behavior,

habits and customs, as also in the social and political orders that can carry the race safely through the hazards of the nuclear age. But where are the spiritual and intellectual giants who would bring about this healthy change? They are scarce, because the race has become barren and infertile so far as spiritual and reformative genius is concerned—the harvest of excessive emphasis on the carnal alone.

It is for this reason that dark clouds of a destructive war are gathering on the horizon. It is for this reason that sensitive minds all over the earth feel a foreboding sense of disaster that is gathering strength every day. It is the fall from spiritual ideals accepted and honored for the past thousands of years that is at the root of the crisis that may end with a forcible introduction of revolutionary changes in the thinking and structure of the human society, which the leading lights of the race had to bring about of their own accord with pacific methods, in time.

For this reason, it is only the scientists and thinkers who accord due recognition to the spiritual element in human nature, in awareness of the fact that secular knowledge alone is not enough to provide safe guidance for mankind, who can lend that balanced form to human thought that is essential to make uniform the present lopsided progress of the race. We need, now and in the future, scientists and thinkers of the class and caliber of Emerson, Toynbee, Einstein, Max Planck, Tolstoy, Gandhi, Tagore, Jung, Bergson, Jeans, Eddington, Schroedinger, Heisenberg, and Von Weizsacker, who look beyond the limited horizon of today, to inaugurate the new era in which spirit and matter receive the same amount of attention and spiritual regeneration is considered as important as intellectual advancement for individuals and nations alike.

It is this state of balanced progress that can invest the leading personalities of nations with the intellectual acumen and the moral caliber to handle safely the forces for good and evil that science is endlessly placing in their hands. As the position stands now, dimsighted politicians are placed at the head of mighty states that have the potential to destroy the world, and pygmies are put in control of gigantic power systems that need titans to handle them.

This disproportionate combination is at the root of the alarming condition of the world today. As long as this position continues and moral evolution does not keep pace with the rapid advance made by science, mankind will continue to live on the edge of a precipice, always in fear of its life in spite of all the material prosperity attained. The world is in turmoil because our choice of the individuals who should hold the front positions is wrong. It is not knowledge nor machines nor missiles, but only balanced, healthy "brains" that can build a heaven on earth.

CHAPTER SIXTEEN

Almost immediately after completing his autobiography in 1967, Gopi Krishna began writing his second book, *The Secret of Yoga*, in which he supports his views on Kundalini with citations from ancient authoritative books on the subject. "It is easy to see that nothing can be more favorable to a worldwide spiritual renaissance than an empirical demonstration of the existence of this divine power reservoir in man," he wrote at the time he sent the manuscript for publication in 1970. Two years later, the book was published by Harper & Row, New York. This chapter is taken from it.

SUPERNATURAL POWERS AND PHYSIOLOGY

It is a matter of common observation that we live in two worlds, one gross and the other subtle. The visible universe and our bodies are made of this gross stuff, but our thoughts and consciousness are formed of an intelligible substance about which we yet know next to nothing. This subtle world of thoughts, fancies, and dreams is as basic a fact of our experience as the physical universe and is decidedly nearer and more intimate to us than the latter.

But it is so inextricably linked up with every cell and fiber of our flesh that it appears to be a product of and inseparable from the body. It is true that if consciousness and thought are self-existing substances and not merely the products of cellular activity of their own, they should have an independent existence and also spheres of activity of their own. Viewed from our experience, however, this holds true only in the abstract, because we never perceive consciousness or thought operative without the vehicle of flesh.

It is precisely here that Kundalini plays a decisive role. As if alive to human aspirations at a certain stage of intellectual development, farsighted nature has planted a divine mechanism in the human body that by effecting an alteration in the vital energy feeding the brain can bring the amazing universe of consciousness within the range of awareness of an awakened man or woman.

The general idea prevailing about Kundalini is of a mysterious and fabulous power lying dormant in man that, when roused to activity, can confer amazing psychic gifts and transhuman states of consciousness. The belief is current that those in whom the energy vivifies the seventh center in the brain are transmogrified and attain unlimited dominance over the forces of nature. This belief is fostered by the high claims made in the ancient literature on Kundalini Yoga about the infinite possibilities for the elevation and deification of those who propitiate this divine power.

There is no end to the supernatural powers promised in the ancient writings to those who succeed in awakening Kundalini. The yogi, it is averred, gains unlimited powers of domination over men, fascination over women, and of sovereignty over the forces of nature. In learning, he becomes like "the guru of the celestials" and in wealth like "the god of riches." His profundity is that of the ocean and his strength that of the wind. He shines with the blinding brilliance of the sun, yet pleases with the soft glamor of the moon. In beauty he becomes like the Deva of love and reaches the hearts of women. Men bow with respect at the mere mention of his name. "He is worshiped even by kings and becomes of gazelle-eyed, lovely women the most ardently desired object of love," says *Panchastavi,* a thousand-year-old poetic work on the subject.

Only a few extracts from a host of other passages contained in innumerable ancient treatises on Kundalini have been presented here. The possibility offered by various tantric texts to gain longevity, health, and miraculous powers seems to have been exploited to the full by the early exponents of the system to attract the attention of the multitudes and to gain followers for the doctrine. The promise of these extraordinary achievements was not extended to men only but to the fair sex also.

The whole science of Kundalini is based on the manipulation of prana-vayu, the nerve junctions called chakras, and the brain. Vayu in Sanskrit means air, and the word is used with prana to denote its subtle nature. Prana and vayu are sometimes interchangeably used by the ancient authors to designate nerve energy or vital breath. Although prana is a self-existent substance, deathless and all-pervading, its manifestation in the bodies of terrestrial creatures is rigidly regulated by biological laws.

In fact, the whole animal kingdom is the product of the activity of prana and the atoms of matter combined. Prana is not something radically different from matter. Both are derivatives from the same basic substance, primordial energy.

Though it is easy to see that the achievements mentioned in the manuals on Kundalini are often highly exaggerated—a common tendency among ancient authors—Yoga can, when successful, lead to higher states of consciousness. This transformation occurs not by any unnatural methods, causing arrest of thought or respiration, as is sometimes supposed; rather, it is by a hitherto unthought-of remodeling of the brain.

The spinal cord, with the reproductive equipment at one end and the ventricular cavity in the brain at the other, is the largest repository of life force or prana in the body. This life force is a biochemical substance of a most complex formation, extremely subtle and volatile, having its roots probably in the subatomic levels of matter. Belief in the efficacy of Yoga as a time-honored method of self-realization *ipso facto* means belief in prana also, for the whole science of Kundalini Yoga is built on the possibility of employing prana as an instrument for effecting a metamorphosis of the brain and raising it to higher levels of perception.

In every form of Yoga, with meditative technique or discipline of the breath, the first object intended to be influenced is prana. The fact that modern physiology has no knowledge of this medium is of no consequence, for up to very recent times it had no knowledge of vitamins either. If science has not yet been able to fashion instruments delicate enough to detect this extremely subtle essence, it does not mean that it does not exist.

Yogis have differed among themselves about the utility of the various methods employed to gain transcendental knowledge or about the nature of the ultimate reality, but there is no dispute among them about the reality of prana. Prana is the sole agent responsible for success in any enterprise undertaken to gain higher states of consciousness.

The manner in which the cerebrospinal system, with the reproductive organs at the lower end, functions as the evolutionary mechanism is one of the most remarkable instances of the ingenuity and economy of nature. The vast network of nerves covering the whole body, penetrating to every hair and pore of the skin, to every cell of the flesh and bones, to every fiber of the muscles, and to the tiniest fragment of every internal and external organ performs also the supreme task of initiating and carrying into effect the evolutionary impulses.

Besides discharging its highly complex normal function as the communication system of the body, the cerebrospinal system also serves as the evolutionary mechanism to raise man toward a transcendental state of consciousness. This is achieved by molding the brain into an instrument capable of states of higher cognition. The method by which this is effected is, like all other devices of nature, extremely simple when it is once thoroughly understood. But as long as it is not understood, like other still-hidden secrets of existence, it appears so baffling and complicated as to be almost beyond comprehension.

Described in terms of modern physiology, the activity of the nervous system, in the evolutionary as well as the reproductive sphere, lies in extracting from the mass of tissue surrounding every nerve fiber an extremely subtle but highly potent essence. This essence may well be designated as concentrated life force. Traveling along the routes described by the innumerable nerve filaments, this concentrated life force ultimately reaches the spinal cord and the brain, both being well-protected storage plants of this highly complex and amazing substance. The essence permeates every atom of the reproductive cells.

From the upper ending of the spinal cord another fine stream of this living energy filters into the brain as fuel for the evolutionary process continuously at work in the organism. Variations in the size of this stream determine the intellectual and aesthetic development of an individual. The stream is comparatively larger in the case of men and women of genius, virtuosos, and top intellectuals. The variegated expression of genius depends on the particular region of the brain the stream irrigates and develops.

A most important role in the attainment of higher states of consciousness is played by the spinal cord, which is a longish white cylinder, oval in cross section. Its inner matter is gray and the outer matter is white. Unlike the spinal cord, the cerebellum and the cerebral hemisphere of the brain have an internal bulk of white and an outer thin gray layer on their surfaces. The cord itself is encased by the vertebrae, which form a strong, bony covering around it. In man the vertebral column consists of thirty-three vertebrae, which fit into one another in such a marvelous way as to give great flexibility to the backbone.

People who meditate generally prefer to sit in a lotus position in order to avoid curvature of the spinal cord and the central duct. This is important, because new processes occur and new forces are generated as the result of the pressure exerted on the brain and nerves by concentration of attention and rhythmic breathing, called pranayama.

Along either side of the spinal cord is a chain of ganglia called the sympathetic chain. These ganglia are connected to another chain of ganglia in front of the vertebral column, which gives rise to the sympathetic plexuses known as the prevertebral ganglia. The third set of sympathetic ganglia situated in the organism is called terminal ganglia. All these three sets of ganglia are interconnected among themselves and also with the spinal nerves.

Alongside the sympathetic there is another system of nerves known as the parasympathetic. Both the sympathetic and the parasympathetic nerves constitute the autonomous nervous system. The most important of the parasympathetic nerves is the vagus, or the wandering nerve, arising from the brain and passing on the left and right of the spinal column. The sympathetic impulses accelerate the heart action and the parasympathetic slow it down. Impulses from the parasympathetic nerves increase the motility and secretion of the digestive tract, while the sympathetic ones cause them to be reduced.

The whole area from the perineum to the navel is thickly supplied with nerves from the central as well as the sympathetic and parasympathetic nervous systems. A large proportion of these nerves lines the reproductive organs of both men and women. In brief, this is the "divine mechanism" in the human body, which, with the arousal of a specific power center located at the base of the spine, can sprint into action to effect the liberation of the soul and illuminate the mind.

This center, which plays a decisive part in the spiritual awakening of every individual who accomplishes the achievement, can be identified with the nerve junction situated between the anus and the root of the sexual organ. Of all the operations conducted by the evolutionary mechanism, the most sensitive and most important is here. The constant presence of romantic and amorous thoughts in the mind and the behavior of the sexual organs make us acutely aware of the existence of the procreative activity of this mechanism, but we have no awareness of a direct impact on our thoughts from the evolutionary side.

On the arousal of the mechanism, however, the individual is in a position to utilize the tremendously potent life force stored in this region for the all-important task of remodeling the brain and nervous system to the point of evolutionary perfection.

In the accomplished yogi, the nervous system functions in such a manner that almost all the subtle prana extracted by the nerves now irradiates the brain, resulting in the transformation of consciousness. A large part of the prana was formerly expended in procreative activity, but now the whole body, including all the vital organs, participates in this activity of the nervous system, in the case of one in whom Kundalini makes her permanent abode in the thousand-petaled lotus or seventh center in the brain.

Actually, there is no separate organ in the body that acts as the evolutionary mechanism. The function is performed by the cerebrospinal system as a whole, through the direct agency of the reproductive mechanism at the base and a still unidentified, silent center in the brain, designated by the ancient adepts as the Cavity of Brahma (Brahma-Rendra). The location of this extremely sensitive zone and the extraordinary sensations to which it gives rise have been described in precise terms by some of the great mystics of India.

Like the first whitening of the sky at the close of dawn, to herald the approach of the sun, the first sign of success in any form of religious striving comes from this region. It is the place of conjunction of the canal coming from the spinal cord and the ventricles of the brain. This cavity and those adjoining it are filled with cerebrospinal fluid. It is said to be derived from the blood and fairly akin to plasma.

For those unacquainted with anatomy, it is only possible to indicate the approximate location of the areas on the basis of the inner perception of the region or the sensations experienced there. The effects produced by an awakened Kundalini are so multilateral, from the beginning to the final stage, that once science begins a thorough investigation a host of possibilities will come into view by which the biological nature of the phenomena can be indisputably established.

A normal awakening does not arouse intense heat, as some modern writers on Yoga have stated. There is only a pleasant sensation of warmth, beginning from the lowest center, called the muladhara chakra, and spreading to the whole of the body, in the first stage of the awakening. The ascent of Kundalini up the spinal axis is like the pouring of liquid flame into the various chakras and finally into the cranium, but without heat. However, burning heat is created in the body when the prana energy released by Kundalini, instead of rising through the central nerve channel, the sushumna, streams partly or wholly through the solar nerve, or pingala, on the right side of the spinal cord.

(It is by arousing Kundalini through the solar nadi that the extraordinary feats of staying naked under ice for prolonged periods, or drying wet sheets of linen wrapped around one's bare body, can become possible.)

The phenomenon of Kundalini is fraught with so many possibilities that volumes will be required for a detailed treatment of all of them. For our purpose here, though, it is enough to say that the awakening can occur through ida or pingala instead of through the sushumna, or partly through one of the former and the sushumna. Where this occurs spontaneously in a forceful manner, the gravest danger threatens the life and sanity of the unfortunate man or woman. This morbid awakening of Kundalini is the root cause of several forms of insanity about which psychiatrists are still groping in the dark.

We can safely identify the sushumna with the spinal cord and its central canal, and ida and pingala with the sympathetic and parasympathetic chains on the left and right of it. The whole area, from the perineum to the navel, is thickly supplied with nerves from the central as well as the sympathetic and parasympathetic nervous systems. A large proportion of these nerves, as has been said, lines the reproductive organs. These chains of nerves are also joined by other nerves distributed over the right and left thigh, leg, and foot.

In an extended state of consciousness, the nerve current moving through the chain of nerves designated as pingala distinctly appears to be hot, and that moving through ida as cold. The perception of these two currents by introversion is one of the first developments that occurs on the awakening of Kundalini.

The first center, the muladhara, plays a decisive part in the awakening. This is the most sensitive and most important part in all the operations conducted by Kundalini on awakening. From the perineum to the height of the sacrum, the whole area is directly involved in the initial operations leading to the arousal.

The second chakra is called the swadhisthana and is at the root of the male organ. The remaining four chakras are in the region of the navel, the heart, the throat, and the space between the eyebrows. They are known by the names manipura, anahata, visudda, and ajana and are, in fact, nerve junctions commanding the vital organs and connecting the whole activity of Kundalini with the brain and other vital parts. The nerve chains known as ida and pingala intersect with the sushumna at all these centers.

The sahasrara, or the lotus with the thousand petals, can be identified with the cerebral cortex, the highest center of consciousness. The number of petals of this lotus has been shown as one thousand to signify its comprehensive and all-controlling character. It is the place of union of the embodied soul and cosmic consciousness.

The idea that Kundalini is a limitless source of energy capable of investing the successful initiate with entire command over the forces of nature has no basis in reality. However, the power alluded to is a potent life energy, normally in a dormant state but capable of being activated with proper efforts directed to that end. And considering the nature of the phenomenon to which it gives rise, this energy can be compared to a powerful organic electric current of which the body becomes the generator.

Just as every form of study stimulates the center of intelligence in the brain and every form of artistic activity trains the muscles of the hand, the fingers, or the throat, leading to a better coordination between the organ and the mind, so every form of religious exercise, Yoga, or occult practice tends to stir up Kundalini. In turn, by using a more potent prana and the precious substances present in the reproductive secretions, Kundalini starts an amazing process of remodeling designed to form a supersensory compartment in the brain, the ultimate object of the evolutionary impulse still active in man.

Swami Vivekananda voiced a truth when he said, "Whenever there is any manifestation of what is ordinarily called supernatural power or wisdom, there must have been a little current of Kundalini that found its way into the sushumna." In every case of genuine mystical experience and spiritual illumination, the brain is fed by the superior, highly potent prana poured into it through the spinal duct. It is obvious, therefore, that unless there is superior mental activity or the emergence of a higher consciousness to cause the phenomenon, the whole experience dwindles down to a hallucination.

It is also manifest that for a regular supernormal activity of the brain, a more potent type of energy to serve as fuel for it would be necessary. This is supplied by Kundalini. The process of transformation needed to arrange a nicely regulated supply of this energy in accordance with the metabolic resources of the body is a most complex and delicate operation that remains in progress from the time the practice becomes effective to the end.

The aspirants to higher consciousness who believe that they can force the gates of heaven open with this or that method do not realize the magnitude of the task they undertake. Whatever the method used for gaining transcendental knowledge or even occult powers, and whatever the intensity of the effort, the final arbiter of the award is Kundalini.

From the accounts of the transcendental state of consciousness left by the mystics, the purpose of every form of religious striving is to gain entry to a new, amazing state of being where one comes in possession of new faculties higher than reason and thought. The brain has in it the capacity to exhibit another kind of consciousness that can know itself, or, in other words, become conscious of consciousness. It can look beyond space and time and, what is more surprising, instead of arriving at a conclusion by reasoning, as every normal mind does, dive into an ocean of knowledge in which all that is knowable is known and all the problems awaiting solution stand solved.

From this ocean droplets of fresh knowledge trickle down into the normal consciousness according to the degree of attunement of the brain. It is these droplets of rare knowledge, not possible by empirical methods in the life-span of man, that coming down through the ages have always been honored as revelation.

Every individual who gained ingress to this state of being invariably found it extremely difficult—nay, impossible—to describe the experience in terms understandable to his contemporaries. Even the most eloquent became tongue-tied and took recourse to parable, paradox, and metaphor to express the inexpressible state. Inexpressibility has been a persistent feature of true mystical experience from immemorial times.

In the case of mystics and seers in the past, the transition from human to transhuman consciousness was sometimes sudden on account of the fact that, forced by intense meditation, burning desire, and austerity, the higher center began to function abruptly, causing as it were an explosion in consciousness. It invariably left the man or woman shaken and breathless with the vision of an astounding and entirely unexpected transformation within himself. It is no wonder that the supramental living reality that now unfolded itself in the mind was regarded as the supreme ruler, Creator, or author of the universe.

The development of mystical insight that grants to the overawed intellect a glimpse of the surpassing nature of the inner self should not be considered either a luxury or a hobby or a fancy in respect of those who pursue the goal, but as an unavoidable necessity for the survival of a sane and sober humanity.

This is because the most pressing need of our age is to widen the inner horizons of consciousness. This widening is necessary to counterbalance the staggering effect on the intellect caused by the present-day enormously increased knowledge of the universe. Brought about by modern science, this knowledge relegates the earth, even our solar system, what to say of man, to a state of utter insignificance in a gigantic whole.

The assurances of philosophers and scientists about the possibility of future boons in material progress are not sufficient to counterweigh the inner depreciation caused by the multiplication of the outer world. This sense of smallness and inconsequence may not be so pronounced in the case of those who hold dominating positions in any sphere of human activity—science, philosophy, art, industry, finance, politics, sports, and the like—but its effect on the more intelligent and more sensitive among the masses is often devastating. The explosive situation of the world today is the direct outcome of this outer and inner imbalance.

All we are and all we know are circumscribed by the capacity of the knower in us. The world appears gigantic and monstrous because we identify ourselves completely with the body and measure the vastness of the universe by its size. But through divine dispensation—for some purpose that only the future can disclose—this frail, puny creature, with a limited span of life, a body so delicate that even one blow in a vulnerable spot is sufficient to cause death, and a mind and memory so restricted that it cannot grasp more than an infinitesimal fraction of the cosmos, by the favor of destiny can soar to a state of existence where the ruthless, colossal world becomes a fleeting shadow and he the effulgent sun.

Death and fear then lose their hold, for what can harm the ocean of everlasting life beyond the farthest reach of any material influence? It is in this sense of gaining entry to a state of consciousness characterized by immortality and infinitude that it is said in the ancient works on Kundalini that the accomplished adept can create, preserve, and destroy the world at will. The underlying idea is that in the transcendental state, which he or she attains with full lucidity, the world image that first dominated his unreal, sensebound consciousness recedes into insignificance.

Transcendence is as far removed from the hallucinatory states of mind brought about by drugs, autohypnosis, autointoxication, and changes in body chemistry as the consciousness of absolute power and incomparable dignity in an anointed king, ruling over a vast empire, is removed from the delusive state of a psychotic who, disorderly and unkempt, raves at the top of his voice about his kingdom and his court.

The ancient authors made no secret of the divine attributes and miraculous powers that automatically develop in one who attains perfection. They repeatedly mention the growth of wisdom, the development of intellect, the literary talent—both in prose and verse—as well as the flow of eloquence. From immemorial times, revelation and inspiration have always been associated with spiritual unfoldment. The saints and sages of antiquity often claimed they were inspired. Revelation has been the distinguishing mark of all great prophets and illumined seers. If mystical experience of the genuine kind represents a real unfoldment of the spirit, or a vision of God, it must be attended by a bloom in the mental fabric of the individual also.

If this does not occur, and the mystic merely revels in his own enrapturing visions without possessing the ability to communicate his experiences in order to share them with the world, the whole achievement is reduced to the level of a fantasy or a daydream. However pleasant it may be for the daydreamer, it has no meaning or importance for others.

From whatever angle we examine it, the conclusion is irresistible that intellectual efflorescence is and should be an inseparable companion to spiritual bloom. The close connection between these two highest expressions of the mind has, in its turn, a profound significance in relation to the present dangerous situation of the world. Intellectual advancement must accompany spiritual growth. If the former occurs without a corresponding spiritual development, it is a sign that the growth is lopsided and therefore abnormal.

As spiritual perfection connotes the manifestation of a higher human personality that has crossed beyond the limit where common mortals come to a halt, it necessarily implies an all-round development in the mental capacity of the perfected.

The radical transformation wrought in the whole of mankind by a few score men and women of genius through the historical period is sufficient guarantee that even a few transformed adepts can prove a most valuable asset for mankind.

Mystical experience should not be viewed in isolation for any group of people nor from the point of view of any particular religion but rather as a phenomenon of a universal character.

There is every chance that once the possibility of transcendence is empirically demonstrated and the law is established, the knowledge of psychology, therapeutics, and physiology would prove of inestimable value in improving the efficiency of the disciplines and minimizing the risks.

Once the biological intricacies connected with the awakening of Kundalini are known by science, this divine enterprise will provide the most contested and most sought-after trophy for the luminaries of our time.

We live in an age of surprises, but there has been no period in the whole of history so full of surprises and, at the same time, so filled with man-caused calamities as the current century. No surprise has been so great, however, as will be occasioned when the law is empirically demonstrated. And no calamity has been so dreadful as might befall the race, at the present stage of technology, if the law is still ignored.

The development of the brain and the intellect is an unavoidable fruit of evolution, but without spiritual discipline and unfoldment the fruit cannot only be unwholesome but fatally poisonous as well. The moment transcendence occurs, the aspirant not only blossoms into a genius of a high order, but other windows in the mind open also, and to his unbounded surprise and joy, he finds himself in possession of channels of communication that, acting independently of the senses, can bring to him knowledge of events at a distance, as well as visions of the past and the future. His utterances may become prophetic and he may acquire the healing touch.

The one important lesson, especially relevant to this age, is that the colossal universe we live in is but a compartment in a mammoth edifice of which the other compartments are not perceptible to our senses at all. The other numerous compartments might be as vast or even vaster than the one discernible to us. And they all might be interpenetrating or overlapping each other without the inhabitants of one being aware of the proximity of the other.

Just as some pictures show the face of one person from one side and that of another from the other, and of a third when viewed from the front, in the same way the universe, perceptible to our senses, might be multifaced, presenting as it were a different form to each separate level of consciousness.

In the culminating state of Yoga, called turiya, we merely shift from one plane of consciousness to another. When this happens, the world normally visible to us loses its grip on the mind. Though real in one dimension of consciousness, the world becomes a shadow or vanishes altogether in the other. The classification of human consciousness into three states (of waking, dream, and dreamless slumber) made by the ancient seers is to bring into relief the fourth state, turiya. This state includes the three other states and yet is above and beyond them; in other words, turiya represents another dimension of consciousness in which the material world loses its objectivity for the yogi, who is now in direct contact with other planes of being.

Entry into turiya is entry into a dimension above the normal human level. This does not make the world, perceptible at the human level, unreal or illusory in the least. To say so would be to deny the reality of turiya also, for it is only when viewed from the human angle that the significance of turiya can be understood. If there were no human level of consciousness, there would be no turiya or samadhi either.

In the present state of scientific knowledge, when transcendence is still an unverified and disputed phenomenon and the territory is still as foreign to the normal mind as the landscape of an unseen planet, the most sensible thing for both the scientist and the mystic to do is exchange ideas in order to identify the basic factors underlying all genuine spiritual experience. Then they can devise methods to establish the validity of the phenomenon beyond doubt and dispute.

But such an investigation has to be undertaken in all humility, because in approaching the supersensible, scientists for the first time come in conscious contact with intelligent forces that are not amenable to mortal control. What those engaged in this investigation have to keep before their mind at all times is the undisputable fact that their very existence depends entirely on the benign disposition of these intelligent forces.

When benignly disposed, Kundalini can transform a commonplace, humble man or woman into a seer, a prophet, an intellectual giant, or a world teacher, with extraordinary talents and supernormal gifts. But approached arrogantly or with impure motives, the same energy, malignantly disposed, can change the most clever person into a gibbering maniac, in such a dreadful state of self-torture that death would be a mercy in comparison.

Kundalini, by its very nature as the evolutionary instinct and power mechanism in man, implanted with a divine purpose, covers all the varied facets of human life. In the present frightening situation of the world, there is no other branch of study so illuminating as this: to determine the direction of human evolution and the meaning and purpose of life.

It has to be borne in mind that the evolutionary impulse is carrying mankind toward a more glorious, more sublime, and more happy life. The superman and superwoman of the future will live, thrive, and beget almost as we do, with this difference: All their actions and desires, obeying an indomitable will, would naturally be well considered, balanced, and chaste. And they will have built a peaceful Eden free from every trace of violence, war, want, and disease. They will have created a far more harmonious and egalitarian social order to permit every individual to live undisturbed in the blissful paradise within.

Kundalini is the divine power both in the individual and the collective sense. It is the controller of evolution that is raising man from the position of a speck of protoplasm and slowly molding him into a man-god amid all the uproar and unrest that characterizes our age, to endow him with inner possessions and crown him with a glory that are beyond our loftiest dreams.

CHAPTER SEVENTEEN

The question of whether there is life after death was asked of Gopi Krishna many times, and on at least three occasions he attempted to provide a definitive answer in writing. This is the way he began a fifteen-page essay in 1973: "The question that now arises is whether it is at all possible to find a convincing answer to the mighty riddle of death. My reply to this question is 'yes.'" A few years later, he wrote twenty-two pages to answer the question "What happens when a person dies?" "Contrary to the common belief, the conscious principle behind the play of embodied life suffers no change whatsoever and is not affected in any way by mortality."

Then in March 1980, as a direct response to a number of telephone calls he had received from a young attorney in California who was deeply disturbed by the fear of death, he wrote the essay which is published here for the first time. Titled "Life Is Everlasting," it was addressed to "Dear Friend."

LIFE IS EVERLASTING
The Mirror That Reflects the Cosmos

The problem of whether there is survival after physical death is not as easy to tackle as some writers have attempted to do. At the same time, a summary dismissal of the idea of the continuance of consciousness after the destruction of the brain, as is suggested by some able scholars, does not point to a rational approach to the problem, either, in the light of the expanded knowledge of our day.

It is the height of unwisdom to believe that the universe we perceive with our five senses and the intellect represents all the knowable area of creation that surrounds us. This does not hold true even in the case of physical energies and forces.

We cannot observe the energy waves emitted by a radio or television broadcasting station with any of our senses. But they manifest themselves through any apparatus designed to translate them into sounds or bright, moving images and forms. Except for the apparatus, it would be impossible for those living in a remote area not in touch with the modern world to detect the motion of the waves or even suspect their existence by their sensual equipment or reason. For them, they would not exist at all, as they did not exist for even the wisest minds of the past.

We are lost in speculation about the possibility of survival of mind or consciousness after the dissolution of the brain because mind, too, is a form of energy belonging to another plane of creation. It is so different from all we know about matter and so remote from our ideas about being that it is impossible for us to detect it apart from the organic instrument through which it manifests itself or to have even a clear concept about it in the same way as we conceive of matter or its energies.

Our indwelling soul, the only mirror that reflects the cosmos and lends substance to it, is itself unfathomable and undepictable. It is made of a stuff that has no counterpart in the physical universe.

It is needless to point out to an intelligent observer that by no means at our disposal can we look into the mind of another human being. We are never aware of the immense world of thought in every human head. We see the individual, his body, his head, even his brain, on opening the skull, the cortical matter and the neurons to their subtlest levels, perceptible to our magnifying instruments, but not a trace of mind or consciousness. And yet it is there.

We know we have a brain, with all its extremely complex and intricate formation, as others have. But can we ever perceive how our thoughts emanate from the neurons and what storms of activity occur in the cerebral cortex when we think intensively on a subject or concentrate on a problem?

The reason why some modern thinkers and scientists have been led to a mechanistic interpretation of existence is because the knowledge of the brain is still very incomplete and because the energy of life is of such a stunning nature that we cannot frame a picture of it at all.

When we think of ourselves—that is, of our innermost being, our "I"—we are focusing our mind on itself in a vain attempt to solve our own mystery. But we always return baffled, because we try to fathom a deep that has no dimension, no mass, no form, and no property by which we distinguish one thing from another on the material plane.

The riddle of life is unanswerable because the drop that

personates as our consciousness, with five senses and the intellect, is never able to comprehend the ocean to which it belongs. The wall of the ego isolates it from the other drops and the measureless mass of water in the ocean. It is only when communication is reestablished between the drop, segregated by the brain, and the undifferentiated mass of water in the ocean that the glory and majesty of consciousness, as life, become known to the individual. Since the mind of man, with its egoistic individuality, prescribes the last limit in the scale to which life has been able to ascend on our planet, we have no idea whatsoever of what lies beyond the boundary to which our own mind has reached at the present level of our evolution.

In some cases—for instance, in the case of mystics—the frontier is crossed and a new panorama of consciousness opens to the vision of the gifted individual. The top intellects of our day are now close to this frontier and need but a moderate amount of effort to cross it. The tragedy is that in spite of the appearance, time after time, of extraordinary individuals blessed with this vision, the learned are still in the dark about a potentiality existing in our mortal frames.

For the so-called rational thinkers, the limit to which life can rise is that prescribed by the normal human mind, a fallacy at the root of the present explosive condition of the world.

The existence of amino acids in meteorites that hit the earth millions of years ago provides clear evidence that terrestrial life is not an isolated phenomenon but must have counterparts in other regions of space. There is growing appreciation among scientists that life in the forms existing on the earth might have reached even a higher grade of civilization on millions of other planets.

In making these assessments, the scientists again keep before their eyes the model of human consciousness and the human brain as the last limit to which biological evolution can proceed. There seems to be no apperception that other types of brains, far superior to the human model and manifesting far superior types of consciousness, might be a feature of life on other planets, or that there can exist other inconceivable or entirely foreign forms of life of which we have no counterparts on earth.

We are no longer geocentric in respect to our position in the universe. We should cease to be geocentric in respect to our ideas about life and consciousness, too. What an irony that it is now the elite among the scientists who make earth the center of life, just as their counterparts in olden days made it of the universe. In either case, insufficiency of knowledge has been and is the cause of error.

The incomputably varied and graduated scale of life on earth, beginning from a primary cell and ending in the extremely complicated organism of man, should be sufficient to make any dispassionate observer concede the fact that even more evolved varieties of life and consciousness are possible and might exist, even now, in the universe.

Since during the past two or three centuries, mankind did not produce a towering spiritual genius of the stature of a Christ, Buddha, Vyasa, Socrates, or Shankaracharya, nor a great scientist or philosopher favored with an illuminated state of consciousness, the intellects not blessed with the vision continued to exercise their talents and to spend their energies on the issue of whether the mind has an independent existence of its own or is but the product of the brain that manifests it. The issue has therefore remained unresolved to this day, waiting for the touch of a future spiritual giant to decide it beyond doubt and dispute.

On Survival of the Soul

My statement that we encounter mind only in the forms in which it is expressed by the organic instrument of the brain is based on the reality we see around us. We are never able to observe the mind of a living creature as we observe other objects in the universe. Nor are we able to establish communication with a disembodied mind, as for instance that of a deceased friend or relative, except through a living mind that, again, depends on a biological organ—the brain—for its expression. Our brain and mind are inseparable as long as our earthly existence lasts.

Our very personality, with all its memory, mode of behavior, ideas and fancies, aptitudes and tastes, is the outcome of this intimate relationship between brain and mind. We have to remember that the brain is only the apparatus, like a television set, to translate the incredible energy waves of life coming from the broadcasting station of the cosmic mind into moving images and sounds. Without the waves, the instrument would show no animation, think no thoughts, and emit no sounds.

At the same time, without the instrument, the waves, though active all around, would not be perceptible to any of our five senses, nor would they manifest themselves in any form cognizable by our mind. When a body is struck down by death, the animating spark of life continues to live on in its pristine glory and form. Only the broken apparatus now no longer shows the signs of animation.

Although pure, incorporate intelligence pervades the entire extent of the universe and even extends beyond, surrounding us everywhere and every moment during our earthly life, we are never able to perceive it apart from its embodied expression due to the opacity of our senses. We never perceive the real stuff in its incorporeal frame, but only assume its presence through external signs or inference.

This intangible, elusive, and incomprehensible nature of life carries within itself irrefutable evidence to show that in it we are face to face with a stuff that does not belong to any of the categories cognizable by our mind. Hence, before passing any judgment about it, we must try to enlarge the capacity of our own mind first.

What form consciousness assumes in the unembodied state after severance of its connection with the brain, it is not possible for an embodied mind to know. This is the point where some of the beliefs expressed in the religious scriptures or spiritual traditions fail to satisfy the doubts that arise in a critical mind. Can we assume that our incarnate personality survives our bodily death with all its traits and peculiarities, faults and foibles, or merits and virtues that distinguished it from others during life?

Let us expand on this issue a little to see how far such an assumption can stand the fire of a critical mind. Considering the case of an infant that passes away at the age of a few months, can we assume that its personality would continue to survive in the form of a baby even after death?

What about a centenarian, bowed down with age, torn with afflictions, completely senile at the time of departure from this world? Would the same decrepit personality persist forever after the dissolution of the shriveled body it inhabited at the end? What about an imbecile, someone with mongolism, and other retarded or stunted persons? Will they continue to live in the same subhuman forms in the beyond?

What about the schizophrenic, the manic-depressive, the neurotic, the criminal, the drug addict, or the alcoholic? Will their abnormal dispositions continue to color their personality in the other world also? If the answers to these questions be in the negative, can we portray what part of our personality persists after death and what part disintegrates with the dissolution of the body?

If the answer be that it is not possible to decide this issue with any degree of accuracy, that means we are still not in a position, on the human level, to solve the problem of survival in the same way as we solve the mundane problems of life.

Those who believe in the survival of the soul not unoften project a picture of their personality in the full glory and vigor of prime as their perpetual state of being in the afterlife. But even if this is accepted as a possibility, it can only apply to people who pass away in their prime, in full possession of their faculties. It cannot apply to the other categories already described. What is to be the lot of those who pass away at a ripe age, often in a state of mental enfeeblement and senility?

If it be argued that the soul never experiences the nescience of infanthood or the senility of age but dwells in a state of eternal prime, this question then arises: What happens to it during the course of its embodiment to eclipse its glory and to overshadow its prime? Why then does it manifest itself as a crowing infant, a prattling child, a senseless idiot, a hardened criminal, a murderer, robber, lunatic, or a tottering wreck bereft of judgment and understanding, at the fag end of life?

What other answer can there be to this problem except that the soul manifests itself in conformity to the growing and declining capacity of the brain? Also to its formation or malformation, as the case might be. If this growth, decline, or malformation of the brain is held to be the result of Karma, it still means that even Karmic traits manifest themselves through the organic frame through which life expresses itself on this planet. It means, in other words, that the soul builds up its earthly mold in concordance with the role it is predestined to act on the earth by its Karmic inheritance of the past.

Mankind on the Verge of Disaster

The current ambivalence about the real nature of consciousness is a sign of lopsided evolution of the human mind. The reason is not hard to find. The overemphasis of scientists during the eighteenth and nineteenth centuries on purely physical phenomena, and the agnostic or skeptical attitude of many gifted intellectuals in this fertile period resulted in relegating the mind and consciousness to the background. Material progress usurped all their attention, creating a vacuum on the spiritual side that has not been filled. It is only now that the study of consciousness is receiving some attention. But the glaring disparity between the physical and spiritual sides of the human personality still continues to exist.

I wonder whether any scholar today even suspects that humanity is heading toward a disaster because her most gifted minds, during the past two hundred years, failed to assess which of the two constituents of our personality merited the greater part of our attention. The one is matter, which caters to the needs of our perishable flesh, or mind, the source of our being, the magic stuff through which alone we know ourselves and the universe around.

Nature is inexorable in adhering to her time schedules and programs. The sun and the moon rise and set precisely at the appointed moment. The seasons come and go at the time prescribed for them. The entire universe obeys the sway of time in its organic and inorganic kingdoms both. A healthy child grows, crawls, stands upright, toddles, lisps, walks, and talks at the appointed intervals during the first few years of its life. Childhood, adolescence, youth, prime, ripe age, and senescence follow each other in succession as surely and regularly as dawn, sunrise, forenoon, noon, afternoon, sunset, evening, and night follow the diurnal movement of the earth.

What serious error in thinking has led us to the mistaken supposition that the evolution of our consciousness as a species is not bound by time and that it is solely our efforts that have brought us to the present height of our intellect? What would happen if we were to encourage a growing infant in its attempts to toddle, at first unsteadily and then firmly, and, at the same time, discourage it in its preliminary efforts to learn to speak? A serious disability would result, which would be hard to overcome afterward.

This is exactly what has happened to the evolution of consciousness, especially among the more advanced nations. The often vehement attacks launched against the religious concepts of the soul, immortality, God, and the hereafter by some of the ablest brains of recent times, and the atmosphere of skepticism prevailing in universities by discouraging interest in the spiritual and the paranormal, have been unwittingly instrumental in causing a serious disproportion in the evolution of the mind.

The summary dismissal of religious ideas, entertained from the remotest antiquity, almost as an instinctual heritage, without thorough study and investigation, has been one of the most irrational episodes in the cultural history of the race.

Why the so-called rationalist and positivist campaigns should have begun so vociferously while the secrets of the brain are still unknown and the nature of consciousness an unsolved riddle is a mystery. What subconscious compulsion has been at work in driving scholars to reduce their existence to a mere effervescence in mud and slime, it is hard to explain. The compulsion is still at work in many academic circles, and those affected spare no pains to convince the world that they are no more than fermented earth accidentally stirred to awareness by a strange alchemy for a while, to fall back as soil again when the ferment is over.

This unholy haste in passing judgment on an issue of paramount importance, by dampening the enthusiasm for the soul-uplifting experiences of religion, has seriously interfered with spiritual evolution at a critical phase in history. The materialistic bias in the Communist ideology and the persistence of irrational dogma and belief in the religious-minded at the present stage of knowledge are direct outcomes of the mental chaos about the real nature of spiritual experience created by the negative attitude of science.

The two most advanced nations of earth, both giants in the sphere of technology and intellectual acumen, are facing each other in a possible duel to the death because the spiritual stature of the leading minds on either side is not in keeping with the level of their intellect. This disproportion is at the root of the present crisis because inexorable nature must have her way in correcting the imbalance for the future sanity and safety of the race. It is paradoxical: The leading minds, veritable giants in intellect on one side, behave like children on the other, attaching greater value to baubles of power, wealth, office, or public applause than to the principles of truth, justice, and harmony. Mankind is on the verge of a disaster because the minds at the top lack the spiritual insight to make the right use of their intellect.

The Universe Dwells in Us

The answer to the problem of survival is beyond the present capacity of science. It will take humanity ages to solve the riddle of life and death. The exploration of this unfathomable mystery (at present) will provide the most powerful incentive to progress in the knowledge of mind and consciousness in the epochs to come.

The fear of death is the spur that will goad civilized humanity toward finding a solution to the riddle of existence when the din and noise arising from technical advancement is over. Man is not born to exhaust all his intellectual and material resources on the building of Pyramids or the Great Wall of China, as they did in the ancient world, or on devising the most destructive weapons of war, or spending colossal sums on the exploration of distant planets while millions die of malnutrition, but in finding a solution to the problem of his own existence.

We seldom reflect on the incredible nature of our own

awareness. The exaggerated importance accorded to empirical study of the material side of nature has tended to belittle the value of consciousness. We seldom take pains to correct the common error that it is not we who dwell in a universe of gigantic proportions but that the universe dwells in us.

Whatever we know about the cosmos, whatever we see, hear, touch, smell, or taste comes within our field of perception by a property in our mind about which we have hardly any knowledge.

Whatever the reality at the back of the objective universe, we know about it only through the images presented to us by our senses as interpreted by the mind. The interstellar distances, the stupendous expanse of space, the faraway galaxies and nebulae, the suns, moons, and planets, the black holes, red giants, or white dwarfs—whatever we see or know of the universe from subnuclear energy fields to colossal orbs of light, with all the multiplicity of color, speed, shape, and size—are a creation of our own mind.

Can we conceive of the world as it would appear when there is no mind to observe it? We cannot. If we say that only undefinable energy systems or some kind of a void or some nameless reality would remain, we are again using our mind to provide the answer or to draw the picture of the unknowable "something" that would be left.

In other words, we can know nothing about the universe nor can we draw any conclusion nor inference, nor build any religion or philosophy or science of physics, chemistry, astronomy, medicine, and so on, except through the instrumentality of our mind. Our consciousness is the fountainhead of all our study, observation, discovery, research, and exploration, of all our ideas and concepts. All our sense of good and bad, all our beliefs and disbeliefs, all we think or imagine, desire or dream of—in short, all that makes human life and the universe in which we live from day to day—we owe to consciousness.

This, then, is the miracle of the seemingly frail, invisible, intangible, elusive, imponderable stuff we call our mind. We seldom exhibit wonder at this extraordinary element of creation because we are never taught to look at it that way. We are amazed at the picture of the universe as unfolded by astronomy, and bewildered by the variety and intricacy of microscopic life.

But do we exhibit any surprise at the mysterious mirror that makes this study possible? Do we ever wonder at this unfathomable "something"—our own consciousness, in which all the universe, all its elements and forces, all its vistas and landscapes, and all the knowledge we possess is contained?

Do we ever care to find out the real nature of this magic-knower, which receives an unnumbered amount of impressions from outside and reflects them as the universe in which we dwell and have our being? Even the idea that these impressions come from outside is again a construct of our mind. We are not astounded at this mystery because we do not have the awareness that it is a "drop" from a boundless ocean of intelligence, which is the founthead of all the wonders in the universe. This is the unimaginable wonder of the soul.

We are not directly cognizant of this marvelous nature of our soul because, in the normal state, we are never permitted even a glimpse of the glory and the sublime nature of consciousness. A mighty king wrapped in slumber, dreaming of himself as a homeless pauper, grieving over his destitute state, remains unaware of his own majesty in the dream. The moment he awakes to it, the dream is over.

In the same way, our consciousness, filtering through the brain, creates the personality that acts on the stage of life, storms and shouts, struts and dances, weeps and wails, smiles and laughs as a puny human being, struggling and toiling among millions like himself. But when perceived, divested of its earthly vestments, in illumined states of consciousness, the same frail, puny being, assuming cosmic proportions, dazzles with its glory and leaves one speechless with wonder and awe at the incomparable majesty revealed.

The Magnitude of the Riddle

Those who propose a mechanistic interpretation of life or who attempt to explain the processes occurring in the brain to account for consciousness act verily like a dreamer who tries to explain the various occurrences witnessed in the dream while still wrapped in slumber. In plain language, they try to solve the problem of the mind by explaining the mechanism of the brain or, in other words, of an organ that is itself the product of the selfsame mind. The clash and conflict of views about the brain, the soul, and the hereafter are nothing but ferment in the mind itself. All these ideas and the logic to prove or disprove them have no existence apart from consciousness. The speculation and the polemics caused by it will cease to be once intelligence disappears from earth.

Those who devote all the resources of their intellect to prove that mind begins and ends with the brain only build castles in the air. For who is there to testify to the correctness or otherwise of what they argue except mind again?

For the materialist, mind is no more than a product of the biochemical activity of the brain. But no one of this school of thought has been able to define this product, isolate it, analyze its composition, or describe its nature. For him, too, mind is a mystery. Those who deny independent existence to the mind are seldom aware of the paradoxical position they create for themselves. Their attempt to prove that the mind is an evanescent product is doomed to failure for the simple reason that the attempt is premature, because, so far, there has been no advance in the research on consciousness.

Even after two centuries of a materialistic attitude toward the phenomena of life, science has not been able to erase the instinctive belief in a deathless soul and the hereafter in the heart of human beings. And now the mass mind is sharply reacting to this sickly creed. The revival of a deep-rooted urge for spiritual experience, in spite of the frigid atmosphere in the universities, provides proof to show how nature is retaliating.

The return to fundamentalism of millions of intelligent men and women, accepting the heartwarming though naïve scriptural explanations of creation, is preferable to the elaborate, albeit arid, theories of science and is a slap on the face of the agnostic intellect.

If mind has no rightful place of its own in the cosmos and is just a by-product of biochemical cerebral activity, where then lies the sense in abiding by its verdicts and holding them to be true and final in our assessment of the universe? If the fount of our knowledge is itself a transient derivative, depending for its existence on a certain combination of lifeless and mindless atoms or molecules of matter, how can we invest it with the authority to pass final judgment on the problem of what is real and what is unreal in this creation?

In making our assessment, it should not be forgotten that the mind alone is the initiator of the debate. It adduces the arguments, their refutation by the opponent, and the evidence furnished by either side. It is the judge who passes the verdict and is the verdict passed.

Mind is also the skeptic who rejects everlasting life, and the believer who accepts it. Compared to the infinitude of the soul, all this is like drawing lines on water that vanish the moment they are drawn. All our ideas and concepts, our opinions and beliefs, our theories and doctrines, as well as our hopes and fears arise from the mind and subside into it. If mind is not everlasting, can we point to any other substance that is? If we say matter, it again brings in the mind, for where is matter without the mind?

To this day we have not even grasped the magnitude of the riddle of consciousness. It is a mystery so profound that human intelligence will not be able to solve it in the coming tens of thousands of years. In the mystical vision, the mind is seen as a shoreless ocean out of which the universe arises, like a thick layer of foam upon the surface of a measureless deep. We are lost in bewilderment as we consider the tangible world around us as real, which it is not. Both the universe and our observing minds are the creations of an omnipotent intelligence, as impossible for us to imagine as it would be for a single ant to imagine the combined wealth of all the minds of the human race.

We have blundered in attaching excessive importance to the physical wants of man as compared to his spiritual needs. Our aim has been to surround mankind with every comfort, every facility, and every luxury we could think of or devise, leaving the soul out of count. And this effort continues to this hour. The plan of nature, on the contrary, is to evolve the brain in order to embellish the mind, and to confer a supersensory channel of perception on the race. Since the two aims collide, disaster threatens the existing order to open the way for nature's benevolent plan to materialize.

A World of Mystery

For the materialist, the tiniest pool of energy, constituting an atom, is everlasting and indestructible. But the tiny pool of consciousness that has conceived of the atom, determined its constituents, and lent lasting life to it, that forms his own individuality, is for him perishable and evanescent. The very terms "everlasting" and "real" are but formulations of the mind. How could it coin these terms unless it knew what they signify? And how could this knowledge arise unless there is something in it that partakes of both?

In general, the agnostic or materialist writers of recent times have omitted any discussion of the paranormal faculties of the mind. They either ignore this important branch of study altogether or dismiss the phenomena as the result of faulty observation, in the case of laboratory experiments, or to imposture and fraud. That many eminent men of science, after meticulous observation of the phenomena, have borne witness to their authenticity does not weigh with them at all.

That a large proportion of scientists, now said to be over 50 percent, believe in the possibility of psychic occurrences has no importance for them. They continue to air their opinions, unappreciative that mind as a phenomenon has still to be studied with the methods appropriate for this research. They know that knowledge of the brain is still extremely limited. They know they have no idea what kind of energy feeds the activity of thought, or how this energy is produced and what the actual relationship is between the brain and the mind.

But this lack of essential knowledge does not deter them from expressing dogmatic views, in the same way as the absence of appropriate instruments did not prevent the star-gazers of the past from inventing fantastic stories about the firmament that excite our laughter at present. If even a fraction of the voluminous evidence on extrasensory perception gathered during the past century is accepted as genuine, it would suffice to force a complete revision of the views held about the mind and consciousness.

The reason why many scientists convinced about the reality of psychic phenomena hesitate to take the plunge and denounce the stone wall of silence, or the stare of incredulity that meets the success of these experiments, is because the yawning chasm that opens in front, if the position is accepted, is too terrible to contemplate. In that case, all the current thinking about the cosmos, about time, space, and causality, about the mind and matter, would be shaken to its foundations, pointing behind the phenomenal world to a reality so incredible that it is entirely beyond the capacity of our minds to grasp.

Strange as it may appear, this reality comes nearer to the visionary experience of the mystic than to the picture of the cosmos drawn by materialistic science. This is what some broad-minded scientists now point out to their more conservative compeers in an attempt to loosen the stranglehold of orthodoxy. The remarkable feature of almost all categories of psychic phenomena is that they show little regard for the laws of time, space, and causality, and, in this respect, resemble the state of existence experienced in dreams. This means that in a relaxed state of awareness, withdrawn from the impact of sensory impressions, the chains of time, space, and causality melt away or become relaxed, presenting an entirely different type of experience than that belonging to the world revealed to us by the senses and the mind.

Since the dream state is as natural to us as the state of wakefulness, the inference becomes clear that the causal world around us is the result of the impact of our senses on the mind and that when this impact is absent, our awareness can look into worlds and experiences of its own, free from the rigid chains of time and space.

There is no reason why dreams should be an inseparable part of our nocturnal existence. Has any scientist been able to explain why they occur at all? They provide irrefutable evidence that consciousness persists in the dream state and even in dreamless sleep, for when awakened suddenly from deep sleep, people not unoften wake up with a brief remembrance of the last fragment of a dream they had just been witnessing.

If the mind were a product of the brain, awareness would be

switched off when the body falls in repose and the sensory contact with the world is lost. But it is neither the brain nor the body but the mind that holds the reins of the organism, controlling its movements both voluntary and autonomous from the first to the last.

In dreams, in extrasensory perception, telepathy, clairvoyance, precognition, etc., in psychokinesis, apparitions, and the rest, in mystical experience, in inspiration of artists and poets, in the performance of geniuses, and in wonder children, nature has surrounded us with a lavish display of extraordinary or uncanny attributes of the mind that no scientist has been able to explain to this day.

By separating the "observed" from the "observer," science is hopelessly trying to find only one instead of alternative explanations for the phenomenon of existence. It might be argued that it is only in the normal, wakeful state of mind that a firm and consistent observation of the world of phenomena is possible and that the dream, trance, and mystical states are so undependable, unrealistic, incoherent, and varied that it would be folly to rely on them for the study or the understanding of the world.

It might also be reasoned that our own experience and survey of the cosmos are extremely brief, that the earth existed billions of years before our arrival on the scene, sprouting unnumbered forms of life, one after the other, and will continue to do so for millions of years after we are no more. And that there exist countless other worlds, other suns and other planets, with possibly similar or other forms of life and mind, whose habits, ideas, or philosophies can be radically different from ours.

Then again, the world existed and carried on when we were uncomprehending infants and had no awareness of anything, and it carries on when we are asleep or in a swoon or under the influence of narcotics, proving that it can and does exist independently, apart from our own awareness. The fossil record from the past, the surveys made with the instruments of our time, and the artifacts or cultural legacies left by our ancestors during the past tens of thousands of years prove beyond doubt that *Homo sapiens* and other forms of life took birth, lived, and died before us, leaving no trace of the soul or sentience that dwelled in them.

All this is true, and there is no dispute about the blatant fact that the universe existed before us, exists now to staggering distances we can never hope to traverse, and will continue to exist for immeasurable spans of time after we, as human beings, cease to be. But at the same time, all this is but the play of consciousness. It is awareness that traces the past to remotest epochs; it is awareness that has left the cultural heritage from the past; and it is awareness, again, that projects itself as the future to forecast the continuance of the universe on the experience of the past.

Can any proof be provided that the past, the present, or the future can exist without the mind? It is the mind in our forebears, in us, and in our descendants that lends existence to the universe, is doing it now, and will continue to do so in the future. Science is irresistibly coming to the conclusion that the observed phenomena of the physical world cannot be separated from the observer.

Since insentient matter has no awareness of itself, we have to look for another reality that can function as the "observer" and the "observed" both. As matter is incapable of performing this dual role, we are left with "consciousness" only as the "reality" we are searching for. Therefore, the conclusion is clear that the universe is consciousness divided into the "knower" and the "known" or the "observer" and the "observed."

How this miracle comes about, how the one becomes the many, how the drop of our individual being becomes separated from the ocean, appearing frail, puny, and transient, is the great mystery that man is born to solve. We do not live in a world of time, space, and causality external to us but in a world of "mystery," and we are lost in bewilderment at the magic creation of "maya," the "inscrutable," as the Indian savants long ago proclaimed it to be.

Pure Consciousness as the Reality

As the basal substance of the universe, how can consciousness cease to be or die? To use a distant analogy, we can picture it as a boundless ocean resembling the void of space and dotted with globular icebergs of colossal proportions floating in it.

The water of the ocean is impervious to our senses, but the gigantic ice formations, a transformed form of the same water, are easily perceptible through our sensory organs. The fluidic mass of imperceptible water that is consciousness, pervading the entire expanse of space and beyond, is instinct with a limitless potential of creative energy, so inconceivably powerful that the entire multitude of billions of suns in the universe, with their stupendous dimensions, incandescent temperatures, and the incomputable volume of light and heat they radiate into space every moment, constitutes but a small fraction of the power. When observed through the senses, we see ice formations—that is, the universe—everywhere, but when viewed internally, in samadhi, the formations vanish and water in its native state is perceived on every side.

This is the only conceivable theory of creation we can frame consistent with the latest trends in physics and the mounting evidence provided by the study of extrasensory perception. It is also in line with the scenario presented by life; the phenomena of religion, miracles, and faith-healing; the rules of logic; and, above all, the unity witnessed in mystical experience—the incredible vision of the one in all and the all in one. This marvelous experience, repeated throughout the past, left everyone who had it dazzled with the glory seen.

In the normal state of perception, the soul, looking through the veil of the senses, perceives the universe of transformed consciousness in the form of earth and the sky, with all the hosts of stars, planets, and moons that mock our efforts to measure their immensity or to fathom their mystery. But when the soul looks at the same spectacle, directly through its own power of cognition, unhampered by the senses, the hard boundaries melt and fade, revealing pure consciousness as the sovereign reality behind the diversity of the sense-created universe.

This is the crux of the Vedanta and Shaiva philosophies as well as the Shakti doctrines of India. The concept is based on the alteration in the world picture experienced in turiya, the transcendental state attained as the crown of Yoga and other spiritual disciplines and designed to enhance the self-perceptive power of the soul.

Though I repeatedly make reference to the brain as the organic instrument for the expression of mind on earth, this does not in any way affect the position that mind is the reality behind the universe. The normal mind is incapable of piercing the veil of senses or of time and distance on account of the restrictions imposed by the very structure of the organ through which it manifests itself. Nature has already provided avenues for a vast increase in the powers of self-perception of anyone seeking ardently to gain awareness of one's own self. The mind then gains the ability to penetrate to its own normally inaccessible levels in the bid to fathom its mystery.

It is obvious that the only channel through which the mind can be studied is the mind itself, since it is not perceptible to any of our senses nor graspable by the intellect. This is what meditation or other forms of spiritual discipline are aimed to achieve. When this power of direct observation of the mind is gained, with a newly generated activity in the brain, a new world of being and a new vision of the universe open.

The world is lost in confusion and threatened by disaster because we have been led to believe that the immortality of the soul and the idea of an afterlife are pure myths with no substance in reality. In actual fact, the opposite is true. The world we perceive is the creation of our senses, while the observer, or the soul in us, is a minute particle of the eternal reality that, in disguised form, is the universe.

In holding that the cosmos is the handiwork of an oceanic intelligence with an infinite power of creation, there occurs no conflict with the current concepts of science about the nature of the physical universe. Creative intelligence, being attributeless, is imperceptible to our senses, but the power, manifested in a cognizable form as the universe, is perceived as such by our sensual equipment.

The universe has to be pictured as unbounded consciousness unconditioned by time, space, or causality, brimful with infinite energy, both of them entirely beyond our capacity to visualize. The energy systems behind the visible universe all originate from the primordial energy inherent in creative intelligence. What we see as an empty expanse of space or as an empty room or emptiness in any form is alive with consciousness imperceptible to our senses. We live and have our being in consciousness transformed into our material surroundings by its own unlimited power.

Scriptural beliefs that ascribe omnipotence, omniscience, and omnipresence to the God of the Christian, Muslim, or Hebrew faiths, impartially examined, point to the same conclusion. According to this definition, the Lord is present everywhere, knows everything, and has the power to do or create anything that exists, or we can imagine, and even that of which we have no idea at all. This means that God as the supreme reality pervades the universe, possesses the power to create all that exists in it, and knows everything that happens in this creation.

It means, in other words, that creation, too, is a manifestation of the power of God and that divine intelligence pervades it from one end to the other.

From this it follows that the intelligence in us is an extremely dilute beam of the sun of consciousness, which lights up the whole extent of this creation. Man, in an infinitely miniature form, portrays the dual aspect of the reality existing behind the universe. The soul is pure consciousness, albeit in an extremely attenuated form, and the body is transformed consciousness, like the cosmos, perceptible to our senses. In light of this, what we perceive in the cosmos is the play of consciousness as the frail human observer and the colossal universe both.

Relative to consciousness, matter is impermanent, subject to creation and dissolution at the will of the Creator. What inscrutable laws rule this activity of the almighty architect, we have no means to know. The energy systems we come across in the created world, from the force of gravity that controls the movements of the suns and planets, to the awful energy in the atom, are all but minor manifestations of the unimaginable power of consciousness.

There can well be other energies and forces in the universe of which we have no awareness. It is these still unknown forces that can well be at the back of bizarre psychic phenomena like psychokinesis, materialized ghosts and spirits, levitation, poltergeist displays, the strange sightings of flying saucers, and other uncanny visitors from space.

Arising from the same infinite source of energy, there might be other creations and other kinds of creatures that are entirely beyond the range of our sensory equipment. Humanity might well be on the way to learn the secrets of these subtle forces and energies and use them for transportation to distant galaxies and solar systems at dizzying speeds. We can only draw a hazy portrait of the future based on the occult traditions of the past. But even this faint picture points to a glorious destiny for the race—a life of freedom, happiness, and adventure that we associate only with angels and other celestial dwellers in paradise.

How then can death extinguish this tiny spark from the eternal flame that brings into existence and lights up the universe? It continues to shine resplendently in the beyond, as the sun shines on the other side of our globe after it has passed out of our sight at the close of the day. It is only the limitation of our senses that does not allow us to look beyond the obstruction, caused by the curvature of the earth.

If we did not have this disability, we would continue to see the sun shining brightly day and night. Similarly, if we did not have the disability that hides the conscious self in us from sensory perception, we would continue seeing the soul, bathed in glory, in the other world, even after its association with the body is over.

ABOUT THE EDITOR

Gene Kieffer met Gopi Krishna and became his literary agent and associate in 1970 after having read his autobiography and some of his unpublished writings. That same year, at the author's request, he established the Kundalini Research Foundation in New York as a means of creating interest in the scientific investigation of the phenomenon. His interest in the paranormal began in 1966 when he became a friend of the famous trance-medium, Arthur Ford, a founder of Spiritual Frontiers Fellowship, and was elected to its Executive Council.

He is also a long-time member of the Academy of Religion and Psychical Research and serves on the board of directors of the Temple of Understanding, an international organization dedicated to promoting dialogue among the world's religions. A student of mythology and Ancient Egypt for more than 20 years, he is on the Advisory Board of The Encyclopedia of Evolution.

Mr. Kieffer, a graduate of the School of Journalism at the University of Iowa, worked as a newspaperman for a number of years before entering the field of advertising and public relations.